Teachings of a

Gain power through knowledge

understand the nature of time, mind, and existence itself

He can pin a man to the floor without touching him. He can stand on one foot and hold off twenty-two power lifters and professional football players. Considered one of the world's foremost martial arts masters, he counsels Wall Street moguls, world-class athletes, even military hand-to-hand combat instructors.

Now Richard Behrens reveals the esoteric principles behind Torishimaru Aiki Jutsu, the only martial art in the world that allows its practitioners to control an attacker's movements and weapons without the use of physical contact. What's more, he shows how anyone can apply these principles to everyday life events.

Teachings of a Grand Master follows a question and answer format and is divided into four parts. The first focuses on Torishimaru Aiki Jutsu and its novice techniques and principles of control. The second discusses meditation and the nature of the mind. In Part 3, Behrens shares thirty-three deep spiritual insights, and in Part 4 he explains how to apply the martial arts principles to life and the world of business.

For those seeking a deeper, more definitive spiritual understanding of the world they inhabit, the answers lie within the pages of this book.

About the Author

Richard Behrens is Grand Master, Tenth Degree Black Belt
of the esoteric art of Torishimaru Aiki Jutsu and Head of the
World Torishimaru Aiki Jutsu Federation. He has met and
counseled numerous men and women around the world,
ranging from Islamic generals to hand-to-hand combat
instructors of the Israeli army, from Wall Street moguls to
recording artists and movie stars. Also an authority on Jewish
mysticism, the occult, and the nature of the mind, Behrens has
been teaching and lecturing for over thirty years, bringing his
knowledge and wisdom to the public. He has lectured at
colleges, universities, and hospitals, and has appeared on
television and radio.

To Write to the Author

If you wish to contact the author or would like more
information about this book, please write to the author in
care of Llewellyn Worldwide and we will forward your request.
Both the author and publisher appreciate hearing from you and
learning of your enjoyment of this book and how it has helped
you. Llewellyn Worldwide cannot guarantee that every letter
written to the author can be answered, but all will be
forwarded. Please write to:

Richard Behrens
%Llewellyn Worldwide
P.O. Box 64383, Dept. K060-4
St. Paul, MN 55164-0383, U.S.A.

Please enclose a self-addressed stamped envelope for reply, or $1.00 to
cover costs. If outside U.S.A., enclose international postal reply coupon.

Teachings of a

Grand Master

A Dialogue on
Martial Arts
and Spirituality

RICHARD BEHRENS

1999
Llewellyn Publications
St. Paul, Minnesota 55164-0383 U.S.A.

FIRST EDITION
First Printing, 1999

Cover art and interior illustrations by Wendy Froshay
Cover design by Michael David Matheny
Editing and book design by Rebecca Zins

Library of Congress Cataloging-in-Publication Data
Behrens, Richard. 1946–
 Teachings of a grand master: a dialogue on martial arts and
spirituality / Richard Behrens.—1st ed.
     p. cm.
 Includes index.
 ISBN 1-56718-060-4 (trade paper)
 1. Martial arts. 2. Spirituality. I. Title. II. Title: Grand master.
GV1101.B45   1999
796.8—dc21   98-48041
                                                          CIP

Llewellyn Worldwide does not participate in, endorse, or have any authority or responsibility concerning private business transactions between our authors and the public.
 All mail addressed to the author is forwarded but the publisher cannot, unless specifically instructed by the author, give out an address or phone number.

Llewellyn Publications
A Division of Llewellyn Worldwide, Ltd.
P.O. Box 64383, Dept. K060-4
St. Paul, MN 55164-0383, U.S.A.

Printed in the U.S.A.

Other Books by Richard Behrens

The Lost Scrolls of King Solomon

Forthcoming

Golf: The Winner's Way

To God,

my wife Sandra,

and all those seekers of spiritual truth

Contents

FELIX QUI POTUIT RERUM
COGNOSCERE CAUSAS

*Fortunate is he who has been able
to learn the causes of things*

This book was written for the accomplished or aspiring martial artist as well as for all of those outside of the martial arts who are looking for a deeper understanding of the possibilities that exist in the world around them.

Introduction

Naturally I had many formatting options available to me in the writing of this book. After careful consideration, I chose a question and answer format because it seemed, somehow, more natural and better suited to the purpose. To this end, the questions that appear in this work represent an accurate consensus of earnest inquiries that have been posed to me innumerable times over the years not only by the students of Torishimaru Aiki Jutsu, but also by those avid seekers of Truth lying outside the martial arena. Bearing this in mind, the questioner throughout the book should be regarded as a single voice representing the collective voices of countless people around the globe seeking a deeper, more definitive spiritual understanding of the world that they inhabit.

Over the years, I have endeavored to come to terms with the truth of my self-nature and my personal relationship to the matrix of existence and God. Through deep and protracted meditations, insights into what I sought began to flow, slowly at first, but, in time, more and more rapidly until, by God's grace, everything was bared to me. The answers to the questions presented in this book are the results of a number of those insights. They represent, however, just the tip of the iceberg of the numerous questions I have been asked and have answered during my teaching career. It would, of course, take volumes to tell it all. Still, you may be pleasantly surprised at the vast wealth of knowledge contained here—knowledge I am sure you will not find anywhere else.

I have divided this book into four sections. The first section concerns itself primarily with the art of Torishimaru Aiki Jutsu and some of its more basic esoteric principles of control. The second section is devoted to the nature of the mind, as well as meditation and its associative techniques. I call the third section "Cabbages and Kings." Here, I answer a broad spectrum of questions that people have asked—questions which they have never found answers for elsewhere. Finally, in the fourth section, I have taken a number of the principles taught in Torishimaru Aiki Jutsu and describe their relevance and application to both life and the world of business. I have also included a glossary and an index to help make your journey through the book a little easier.

In Part 1, I offer those outside of the art proper a little insight into the nature of some of our coveted secrets of control, our martial *arcanum arcanorum,* if you will. For those martial artists in other systems acquainted with the many stories that have been in circulation about Torishimaru Aiki Jutsu over the years, you will find the basis of those stories in this section. For those martial artists and lay people unfamiliar with Torishimaru Aiki Jutsu, you may understand it to be the only martial art in the world that offers to its practitioners techniques and principles with which to control the minds and bodies of attackers without the need to resort to the use of physical contact in order to bring that control about. In this first section

I explain some of the long sought-after novice control principles that, if carefully studied and applied, will offer the interested martial artist a unique opportunity to expand his martial arts repertoire to limits that he heretofore could not imagine. The practicing martial artist, whether a beginner or eminently accomplished, as well as the knowledge-seeking non-martial artist, will find the information and techniques presented here to be highly enlightening.

I have included within this first section, and elsewhere in the book, carefully structured, step-by-step instruction in a number of exercises that will help facilitate the reader's exploration into what all would agree are some very interesting, if not unusual, areas of knowledge, such as the use of certain principles to control the movements of others and beginning exercises with which to delve into the arcane provinces of mental telepathy, clairvoyance, precognition, and more. I am sure that you, the reader, will be astonished and extremely pleased with the results you will achieve when these exercises are properly executed.

In Part 2, I delve into the true nature of the mind and present to the public, for the first time in book form, my understanding of its character. I think that psychologists and psychiatrists throughout the world will find it particularly interesting. It is my express hope that it may open up a new avenue of thought concerning the nature of the mind relevant to mental disorders and their current therapies. In this section, I also explain some ancient methods of meditation that will give both the martial artist and layperson a concrete method of removing their daily stresses and greatly changing their lives for the better. I have also included concentration techniques that will support one's meditative efforts.

In Part 3, the questions that I answer become more eclectic and so deal with a wide variety of subjects—subjects not necessarily relevant to just the world of the martial artist. In this section, I cover such topics as the creation of the universe; the death process and what actually takes place at the moment of death; the soul; world peace; the true nature of the common cold; cancer; communication with animals; the nature of time, space, and infinity; and many others. In fact, as a novelty, I even explain which came first, the chicken or the egg.

In Part 4, I show how a number of the fundamental principles of Torishimaru Aiki Jutsu are relevant to both life and the business world. Here, I first present the principle, then I give a single example of how that principle is applied in a martial situation. That is followed by a section covering the employment of that principle in everyday life. Finally, this section covers the application of that principle to business.

It is my sincere hope that you, the reader, will not only learn but will greatly enjoy what is presented here. All I ask is that you approach the subject matter with an open mind and not hesitate to reread those sections of the book that may require it. Read, learn, and enjoy.

Yours in Peace!

Grand Master Richard Behrens
Tenth Degree Black Belt
The Torishimaru Aiki Jutsu Federation
June 29, 1998

Part 1

The Art
of Torishimaru
Aiki Jutsu

and

Some of Its Novice
Techniques and
Principles of Control

Q: What is Torishimaru Aiki Jutsu?

A: Torishimaru Aiki Jutsu means "the art of control in spirit and harmony." Many years ago, your question would have been relatively easy for me to answer. I would have said that it was a Japanese-oriented martial art that was comprised of punching and kicking techniques, projection or throwing techniques, immobilizations (restraining techniques), and weapons training (i.e., swords, knives, garrote, shaken, et al.). Today, however, my answer would have to be that it is all of that and more, much more. To give you an idea of how much the art has evolved, you might be interested to know that several years ago I typed out a list of techniques and principles that the novices in the art needed to master in order to complete their novice training and earn their Shodan or First Degree Black Belt. The list spanned seventeen typewritten pages without anything else on the list except the names of the techniques and principles.

You could say that as I evolved, so evolved the art. As I gained in spiritual insight, new vistas of technical possibilities opened up to me and the more altered the art became from its original form. This evolution lent elements to the art that transformed it into something extraordinarily special. It matured into a vibrant esoteric art, one that is alive and both spiritually and technically infinite.

Q: What is important to you as a teacher?

A: What is most important to me are my students. Understand that it is a teacher's responsibility to see to it that his students' spiritual and technical growths are assured. It is the difference between a farmer taking a handful of seed and carelessly tossing it out into the field with the attitude that if they grow, they grow, and if they don't, well, so what, and a farmer who takes each individual seed and plants it by hand, making sure that there is plenty of water,

3

nutrients, sunlight, and room for growth. I care about each and every student.

Moreover, a teacher of the martial arts has a special responsibility to his students beyond just teaching them how to defend themselves. It is important that students do not misunderstand the reason that I am teaching them in the first place. It has never been my intention to teach someone how to punch and kick their way through life. On the contrary, I am not teaching them how to fight so much as I am teaching them how to live. What is important to me is that they understand that with the training I give them comes great power and with that great power comes a great responsibility. What responsibility? The responsibility not to abuse this power by using it to harm or injure others unless they absolutely have no choice and are forced to defend themselves. It is important to me that my students understand and respect the sanctity of life and that they learn to be harmless and blameless in all things. To this end, you could say that I teach my students to fight so that they may never have to fight.

Q: **It is well known among a number of the practitioners of the martial arts that you created Torishimaru Aiki Jutsu, but what is it that makes Torishimaru Aiki Jutsu so unique?**

A: There are many things that make Torishimaru Aiki Jutsu unique but what makes it most unique among the martial arts are the principles and techniques we employ that allow us to exercise an extraordinary control over an attacker or attackers. Through the employment of the control techniques and principles, the practitioners of the art have the ability to neutralize an attacker's offenses prior to the issuance of their own counterattack. Through the proper employment of the techniques and principles, one may control not only the attacker's weapons (i.e., hands and feet) but his major motion (direction of his body) as well.

Many martial arts are based on speed, strength, and technique. That is, the faster and stronger you are and the more accomplished you are at the employment of your techniques, the better you are going to be as a practitioner of that particular art. The trouble is that out in the street there is always the possibility that you may come up against someone who is faster and stronger than yourself and who may even have more skill. Should this happen, you may find yourself in great jeopardy. But suppose that there were ways to take the speed, strength, and techniques away from the attacker. Do you understand? Suddenly, how fast or strong the attacker is, or even what he knows, becomes irrelevant. I know that a martial artist, especially, would understand the enormous advantage that this would offer him. Well, the techniques and principles that allow our practitioners to do just that are what make Torishimaru Aiki Jutsu so unique.

Q: **Could you be a little more specific in terms of why you created your art and maybe provide a little more detail about how your art evolved?**

A: Yes. You must understand that the instructors I had studied under in my martial arts career were really all quite excellent at what they did. They were all worthy of respect. However, I always had the feeling that there was something missing in their instruction—something that, at the time, I couldn't quite put my finger on. After a while, I realized that what was missing was the spiritual aspect of the martial arts. It was simply not there. Years later, I embarked on a spiritual quest, a sort of spiritual odyssey if you like, for I knew instinctively that many more answers than my former teachers had given me could be found within the limitless omniscient realm of the Eternal. And so I turned to the Eternal in an effort to learn the secrets that would eventually lead me to the answers that I so badly needed.

5

The further and deeper I traveled in my spiritual endeavors, the more I uncovered.

One day, it became clear to me that, if a person's mind does, in fact, control his body, there must be a way to influence a person's mind in order to control his body. This seemed logical. To this end, I thought that if reliable techniques could be developed that would allow a defender to influence the mind of his attacker, then that defender could, in effect, control not only the attacker's gross physical movement, but the movements of his punches and kicks, as well. The concept has fascinated me for many years.

Over the decades, I have been blessed with innumerable spiritual insights that have led to the development of many principles and techniques that allow me to do just that, to control an attacker's mind and body. Once I understood the nature of the human mind (that it is comprised of both the lower mind or everyday mind and the higher mind or the all-knowing mind), the shield (a field of energy surrounding and generated by all matter, known also as the aura), feminine energy or M'retz Na'she (the energy that comprises the shield or magen, often but mistakenly termed Ki, Chi, Prana, and life force), the sheath (the subtle ethereal body containing the soul), the physical body, and the special relationships that existed between them, the art evolved quite naturally. Of course, to combine the insights I received with practical fighting techniques required time, and I had to go through the laborious efforts of trial and error. Torishimaru Aiki Jutsu is the result of those efforts and understandings. I learned many wonderful things over the years and I am happy to tell you that I am still continuing to learn, assuring that both the art and its students will also continue to evolve.

Q: Why did you wait so long before making public some of the novice control techniques and principles of Torishimaru Aiki Jutsu?

A: There are several reasons why I waited until now to write this book and extend to those outside of the art some of the novice principles of control. First of all, for many years, I didn't want to give outsiders any information that would place the practitioners of my art in jeopardy out in the street. It would have been irresponsible for me to do that.

> Listen! One day, an eagle was soaring high in the sky when it suddenly felt something strike its chest. As it began to fall, it realized that it was dying. Glancing at its chest it noticed that it had been struck in the chest with an arrow. Then, looking down the shaft of the arrow, it came to the shocking truth that the arrow was plumed with its very own feathers.

What this little story means is that we often ignorantly give those who would do us harm the very means with which to destroy us. If the eagle in the story hadn't carelessly dropped some of its feathers, the fletcher would not have been able to fashion the arrow that killed it. When I teach this idea to my students in the art, I simply refer to it as "Dropping Eagle Feathers." Certainly, it would be unwise for the master of any martial system to place students in jeopardy by frivolously exposing the secrets of their defense to those who may possibly turn that information into techniques that might cause those students harm.

Secondly, the techniques and principles that I explain in this book were originally techniques and principles that were taught only to black belt students. At the time, they were closely guarded secrets. However, that was quite a few years ago. Since that time, I have developed a great many new principles and techniques so sophisticated and so esoteric that I had no choice but to place the former techniques and principles into the novice training program. For all intents and purposes, you could say that I declassified them. Besides, once the techniques and principles were placed into the novice training program, it was really only a very short step to airing them publicly.

Thirdly, I realized that there are many sincere and devoted martial artists in the world who are literally starving for an insight into the more esoteric martial possibilities that exist—insights and experiences that are, to their disappointment, currently lacking in their particular martial style. Unfortunately, most of them had no idea when they started to train in those systems that the spiritual elements of the martial arts that they were looking for originally were missing. Besides, disclosing a few novice techniques and principles is my way of offering them a very special gift, one I hope they will accept in the same respectful spirit with which I offer it. It is also my hope that they will not abuse others through the misuse of what I am presenting to them.

Finally, I wanted to offer non-martial artists an extraordinary opportunity to expand their horizons into areas that I knew they must be curious about. I wanted to let them know that the world is more than they ever imagined it to be and wanted to back up that profound statement by offering them the techniques and principles that would allow them to experience the truth of it for themselves. This is my gift to them. I have every confidence that they too will find what I have written not only interesting and useful but highly enlightening, as well.

Q: Where did the martial arts originate? Some claim that all of the martial arts began in China, and others argue that it began in Okinawa. Still others claim that it originated in Korea. What do you say?

A: I grant you that some excellent and very respectable martial arts developed in China, Japan, Korea, and Okinawa, but the fact is that the martial arts really had its humble beginnings back in the dim and misty regions of prehistory when, for the first time, one ape-like man witnessed another ape-like man strike a third ape-like man and asked to be taught how to do it. That was truly the beginning of formal instruction in the martial arts. After that, newer and more modern techniques and principles were developed, and better and more dangerous weapons of destruction were created and mastered. And so, master instructed student from then until now, and it continues to be so, and will continue to be so, from now onward into the future. This has always been the way of things and will continue to be the way of things until man has finally freed himself from the insidious desires that lead him to violence against his fellow man. When that time comes, and it is coming, the martial arts will no longer be needed and will not be practiced.

Understand that as humankind is today—even as it was during the obscure days of our prehistory—were we to place two or three untrained human beings in the same environment for a protracted length of time, we will have, sooner or later, the need for the development of a martial art. Unfortunately, this is the current way of things.

In truth, every society, every nation, every people in the world has or has had a martial art, however humble and unsophisticated it may have been, developed somewhere within its borders at one time or another during its history. Certainly, they may have borrowed techniques and principles from each other, but that is all. Where or how

9

a particular martial art began may be interesting to some, and a dubious source of pride to others, but it is—in the final analysis and to me—ultimately unimportant.

Q: **Some people say that your art is the best art they've ever seen. Do you agree?**

A: No! Obviously, the people who say this are not students of mine. I teach my students better than that. If there are people who do say that, I am not offended, naturally, but let me say that the true spirit of the martial arts has nothing to do with racing toward some inane martial superiority. Torishimaru Aiki Jutsu is Torishimaru Aiki Jutsu, that is all.

Q: **You say, as do many other martial arts masters, that you are nonviolent, and yet the art that you teach seems pretty violent to me. How do you justify this seeming paradox?**

A: Justify? To understand my answer you must first accept the fact that the martial arts are just that: martial arts, warrior arts. If a martial art exists that is truly nonviolent I've yet to hear about it. Even those arts that claim to be humane arts are, to some degree, violent. To this end, Torishimaru Aiki Jutsu, being itself a martial art, is not any different. It would be absurd for me to claim otherwise. However, I believe that you are confusing the philosophy of an art with the ostensively violent nature of the techniques inherent in that art. This is a grievous error.

I, along with many other practitioners of the martial arts, embrace nonviolence as a matter of course because I know through my years of training both the meaning of and the devastating consequences resulting from violence. I teach my students that the only viable and honorable path for a martial artist is one of nonviolence. Of course, there are some instructors and students of the martial arts who, for reasons apparent only to them, choose violence as an alternative to peace, but that is their way of life and neither mine nor the students of Torishimaru Aiki Jutsu.

Life is composed of innumerable choices and as such the results of the choices we make will either lead us to happiness or lead us to a grim and foreboding future laden with pain and suffering. The wise choose the former, the unwise opt for the latter. The wise among us choose the path of nonviolence, the unwise choose the path of violence.

Never confuse the martial action that is taking place in the dojo (school) with the philosophy of peace generated by the teachings of an art and practiced in daily life by its instructors and students.

Q: **What is the singularly most important aspect of the martial arts?**

A: Of course, I cannot speak for the other martial arts or other masters, but in Torishimaru Aiki Jutsu the most important aspect is what it does to develop and promote an individual's personal spiritual evolution, what it does to open a student's eyes in a very spiritual way. Once a student comes to the realization that the world is much more than he had ever imagined it to be, changes begin to arise in him. Gradually, he not only comes to understand that there are innumerable arcane forces in existence that he was never aware of, but he learns to both understand and work with those forces. Increasingly, he comes to understand that the development of his ability to fight, although important, should always be secondary to his spiritual growth.

Q: **What makes a good student?**

A: There are three kinds of students: the superior student, the average student, and the inferior student. The superior student has admirable qualities. He trusts his instructors implicitly and follows whatever instructions are given him without complaint or debate. He understands that his instructors were once students, too. He understands that his instructors only have his welfare in mind when they teach him. The superior student is pliable, honest, sincere, respectful, and has a zest to learn. He understands that mastery in the martial arts, or in any endeavor, does not happen overnight. He knows that it often takes a long time to achieve proficiency and, understanding that, he is more than willing to make that noble commitment. The superior student practices diligently at home and looks forward with joy to each and every class. Further, he learns from the mistakes committed by others and diligently avoids perpetrating those same mistakes himself. When he does make a mistake, he understands that it is a natural part of the learning process and does not become sullen or angry when receiving correction. The superior student is worthy of both the respect and admiration of his instructors.

The average student is one who likes the idea of learning but lacks the drive necessary to carry him all the way through the rigorous process. At times, he grows angry and questions both authority and motive. If it is raining or snowing, he may or may not show up for class. He practices at home only when the mood strikes him and that is not very often. He sees the mistakes of others but, more often than not, learns nothing from those mistakes. Only when he makes those mistakes himself does he learn.

The inferior student, oddly enough, does not even know why he is studying a martial art in the first place. Maybe it was a choice between joining a bowling league or spending his night "playing" at the martial arts. Maybe he happened to see a martial arts movie one night and was so taken by the ease with which the hero or heroine used their martial skills to defeat an enemy that he ran right out the next day and enrolled in a school, thinking that he could achieve that same level of mastery within a few weeks of training.

His attendance in class is faltering, at best. When he does manage to show up for class, the inferior student is only half there and his training is only half-hearted. He questions both the instructor's manners and motives. For instance, if the instructor is teaching him the precepts of the art, he cannot believe that the instructor himself actually practices those precepts. In fact, the inferior student is generally so utterly cynical that he cannot believe that anyone, anywhere, at any time, can or does actually practice such noble principles. Why does he believe this? Because he, himself, believes only in the myriad things in life that bind him eternally to worldliness and misery. He understands nothing of life, nothing of the world, and bases all of his opinions on the illusions he has created in his lower mind. To him, his instructor is nothing more than someone he hired to entertain him a few hours a night. This self-centered, egotistical attitude leads him to believe, falsely, that the instructor he "hired" should be eternally indebted to him for his patronage.

The inferior student attends class only when there is nothing worth his while watching on television, such as an "important" football game or a favorite movie. In class, he is unmotivated to learn, and is more interested in socializing with the other students than he is in applying himself to diligent practice. He will often tell the instructor what is expedient and not necessarily what is true. Further, he tries to sow the poisonous seeds of unrest and dissension among his fellow students by spreading lies and half-truths. He does so not merely because of his infinite ignorance, but more simply because this behavior is, unfortunately, a great part of his present nature. He learns nothing, neither from the mistakes of others nor from the preponderance of mistakes that he himself commits. He continues to make the same mistakes over and over again, relentlessly, *ad infinitum,* without making any effort at correction. Inferior students are to be avoided by serious instructors.

These, then, are the three types of students. A person should always endeavor to become a superior student, especially if he really wants to learn anything well. Regardless of what course one is taking—whether it is a martial art, a college course, or a course in ceramics—one must always strive to be a superior student. It is the noble thing to do.

Q: **In Torishimaru Aiki Jutsu there seems to be differences in the techniques that I see being applied. They seem to vary slightly from student to student. Could you explain?**

A: You must understand that all students are the same, and all students are different. It is the difference between students that a good teacher must address, especially in the martial arts. Torishimaru Aiki Jutsu, for example, is both a projecting art (an art that employs throws) and a striking art. I am five feet five inches tall. I cannot expect a student six feet eight inches tall to fight exactly the same way that I do. It would not only be unrealistic but would, in the final analysis, be greatly detrimental to that student's personal evolution. Because his body is different and has different assets and limitations, certain allowances have to be made. Being tall in a projecting art is not ordinarily very advantageous. Having a large body, in general, restricts the practitioner a great deal by limiting the nature of the projections that he would most likely find himself, in the street, legitimately being able to use. When one is six feet eight inches tall, for example, just about all of the attackers that this man will come into contact with are most likely going to be a good deal shorter than him. This difference in size will prevent him, for example, from utilizing a number of the *tenken* or inner circle projections. Yes, he can and must learn these projections, but he must concentrate,

14

ultimately, on those projections that will be the most practical and advantageous to his personal defense.

In Torishimaru Aiki Jutsu, a student must be trained to become the best fighter that he can be, and so, even though a student must learn all the techniques of the art, the individual must choose his specialty. That is, a student must choose those techniques that he is best suited to execute. This, after all, is why the average person studies a martial art in the first place, isn't it?

And so, to this end, the art of Torishimaru Aiki Jutsu really becomes very personalized and, as a result, a student not only learns faster but invariably maintains a very high degree of self-confidence throughout training.

Q: I've heard you say, "Learning is fun, training is boring!" What does that mean?

A: Just that! Learning is fun, training is boring. There is nothing hidden in it. However, learning happens to be a process that just about everyone not only enjoys but actually looks forward to. After all, learning is the reason why students make the effort to come to class in the first place. But those newly learned techniques and principles have to be earnestly practiced in order for them to be mastered, and this is where training comes in.

The training process is important in any learning endeavor but in the martial arts it is absolutely indispensable. Training is repetition. Over and over again, each of the newly learned techniques and principles have to be practiced. This means executing that technique and applying that principle not just ten times, or a hundred times, or even a thousand times, but ten thousand times in order for a martial arts practitioner to achieve some semblance of competency in employing them. This is training. Superior students understand and accept the rigors of training as a necessary evil. But to the average and

15

inferior students, the degree of repetition that the martial arts demands—though the reasons for such training are explained to them repeatedly—find its stringency extremely boring and so they avoid training as much as possible.

Just to understand the mechanics of a technique or the basis of a principle is not remotely enough; everything that is taught to you must become an active, living part of you. You have to be able to utilize a technique and employ various principles without having to give them the slightest thought. Superior students understand this very well, and so they enter into training with the right attitude. The average and the inferior student, on the other hand, understand nothing of this, and so very quickly become disenchanted and bored. The inferior student often thinks that all he has to do is be taught the technique or principle and that is enough. To him, he "knows" a technique the instant that he is shown it, and to have to practice it would be, to his way of thinking, not only boring but a complete and utter waste of his time. Because the inferior student does not understand the value of training, he drops out of class thinking that he would have been better off paying close attention to the martial elements in some dubbed, plotless martial arts movie on television.

Learning is like taking a forkful of food and putting it into your mouth. Training can be thought of as the chewing and swallowing of the food. As you know, food naturally only has value to the body when it is masticated and swallowed. The better it is chewed, the easier it is to swallow, and the easier it is to digest.

16

Q: **What are the philosophical goals of Torishimaru Aiki Jutsu?**

A: To gain peace of mind and to be harmless and blameless in all things are the overall philosophical goals of Torishimaru Aiki Jutsu. The fighting aspects of the art, after all, are ultimately unimportant in comparison. To have wonderful or even what some people consider to be amazing techniques and principles means nothing when compared to the achievement of peace of mind. To become a good fighter or even a redoubtable fighter is also nothing when compared to the vast esoteric knowledge that brings one the understanding of the nature of existence and leads to a sense of unity with that existence. Anyone who is caught up in the idea that the acquisition of superior martial prowess is the ultimate goal of my system is mistaken. To pursue the physical and ignore the Eternal would be like striving after wind in a dream. In the final analysis, the wise know that if one does not have peace of mind, nothing much is of any importance—not money, not fame, not family, not wonderful fighting techniques—nothing.

Q: What do you mean when you say that, very often, the difference between peace of mind and a life of fear, anguish, and misery is simply a question of priorities?

A: I mean that the path leading to peace of mind begins by first rearranging one's priorities. People should know, for example, that much of the stress they suffer in life is directly attributable to the order their priorities assume on their individual priority lists. In arranging their priorities, people ignorantly make the mistake of basing that arrangement on the mind-constructed concepts that have them living their lives as if they were permanent residents here. They squabble over money, status, personal principles, and material possessions. Their priorities are all mixed up. They never take the time to look into the truth of the nature of things, into the reality of their own self-nature and its relationship to the very matrix of existence. I find this very, very sad because it needlessly creates endless grief, both for themselves and those around them.

When people's priorities are based on erroneous information offered to them by their lower minds concerning the nature of the world, then it follows that there will be errors arising in the list of what those people deem to be important. When people's lower minds convince them that the world is real and that they are, in fact, permanent residents here, then there grows in people a great, overwhelming attachment for material possessions and a place of leadership and control over other people. When people become attached to not only material possessions but to erroneous ideas of existence as well, grief is almost always sure to follow.

Suppose that you were to be granted one wish, and that one wish could only be used on yourself and not for some world-saving altruistic purpose. What would that one wish be? Would you wish for a million dollars, a fancy car, an expensive home, a beautiful woman, a handsome man, or would that one wish be for peace of mind? If you use that wish to be granted peace of mind, then you would be very wise, indeed. Why? Because if you were granted peace of mind, you would have everything—there would be nothing lacking and, regardless of what you had or did not have, everything would be well with you. That is the ultimate blessing, isn't it?

Q: **There are degrees to be obtained in your black belt ranks, but why don't you have a colored-belt system for the lower ranks like many other systems do?**

A: I believe that colored-belt ranks in novice training sends those students the wrong signal. Novices are, by and large, very impressionable and to "reward" them for their learning is, I think, counterproductive. How can you, for example, teach them to be detached from the material things of the world when, at the same time, you are encouraging them to be attached to things like the color of a belt and the acquisition of rank? It would not be logical for me to teach that way. Once, however, novices enter into the black belt division, the idea of rank has long since ceased to be a factor in their training and they are free from such menial and demeaning notions. My black belt students have learned that a dog, though adorned in the most excellent of royal finery, does not have the majesty that an unadorned lion displays purely by his inherent merit.

Naturally, there are those beginning students who do seem to have the need for such a reward system. It is as if they think that, if they had to defend themselves, their colored belt would do all the work for them and keep them safe from harm. Generally, those who think this way are better off going to schools that have ranking systems better suited to their lower-mind appetites. Understand that having a colored-belt system in their novice ranks, of course, by no means makes those martial systems necessarily bad or inferior. I have seen some excellent martial arts systems, taught by some very talented and accomplished instructors, which maintain colored-belt degrees in their novice ranks. It is really just a difference in how I prefer to teach.

Q: There are no formal tests for promotion in Torishimaru Aiki Jutsu. This is probably the first art I've heard of that doesn't have that requirement. I would be very interested to learn why. Could you explain?

A: Suppose, for the moment, that you looked out of your window every morning and saw your neighbor carrying fifty pounds of trash to the curb. You see him do this every morning for several years. One day, you walk up to your neighbor and ask him if he would like to take a test. You want to see if he would be able to carry fifty pounds of trash to the curb. You do this knowing, immediately, what the result is going to be! Obviously, if you already know that your neighbor can do it, what would be the point in

19

testing him? It is non sequitur and makes no sense to waste time and effort in this way.

So it is with the students of the art. Myself and the other instructors are with the students constantly, every class. We know what each and every one of them is capable of doing. We carefully monitor their progress over a period of years and know what their weaknesses are, as well as their strengths. What is the point, then, of testing a student, when the instructor has been with him every step of the way? When a novice student reaches the stage in his training where he is functioning at a senior student or black belt level, he is simply promoted to that rank. It is not in keeping with the precepts of the art to make a big show of raising a student's rank.

Q: **You teach anatomy and physiology to your students. You even make it mandatory for your students to have a book on anatomy. Why?**

A: First let me say that the techniques that comprise Torishimaru Aiki Jutsu afford its practitioner an extremely wide range of techniques with which to handle an attack. Our techniques range from simple projections, nerve center techniques, and joint-twisting techniques that cause little or no damage to the assailant to techniques that bring about very serious damage or even death. Unfortunately, although Torishimaru Aiki Jutsu instills in its practitioners a philosophy of nonviolence, it is a philosophy that is not necessarily shared by others. The point is that the nature of our defense has very little to do with what we want to do or what our personal attitudes are toward violence—the attacker himself and the nature of his attack ultimately determine it. Bearing this in mind, you must understand that if the nature of the attack forces us to use striking techniques, then those techniques must be as devastating as practicable in order to end the aggression as quickly as possible. The longer we allow the attacker to aggress, the larger grow the possibilities that he might prevail.

The use of striking techniques is a very serious matter, one that could very well determine your survival and, as such, should not be thrown in a capricious or haphazard fashion to indiscriminate targets. It is not enough just to throw strikes that are mechanically perfect. In order to be effective, truly effective, they must be used to strike specific targets well suited to the purpose at hand. To this end, one must become extremely intimate with the structure of the human body. After all, the human body is our arena, it is where we do our work. A student must study and know every relevant facet of human anatomy and physiology if he is going to be proficient. He must have a working knowledge, for instance, of the locations of the sensitive internal organs so that he can execute the maximum amount of damage with the least amount of effort, and must understand exactly what happens to those organs when they are subjected to both blunt as well as penetrating trauma. He must comprehend, for example, that should the integrity of the spleen be compromised, there will be a massive hemorrhage of arterial blood via the splenic artery that will fill the peritoneal cavity. He must also know that the spleen, unlike the liver, cannot be surgically resected, and that, should it be torn, it must necessarily be removed.

The student looking for proficiency in the art must also learn how to damage specific areas of the opponent's body that are not so easily mended or even addressed. For example, he must learn how to create damage to the sensitive retroperitoneal cavity. He must understand just how vascular that area is, and how even the most competent of surgeons treat that area with a great deal of respect should they have to enter it even under the best of surgical conditions. Further, the student must know the size, shape, and location of all the bones of the body and how those bones break. He must learn that different bones break in different ways. He must be aware, for example, that the tibia is a clean-breaking bone, while the ribs break sharp and jagged. There is an enormous amount to learn.

By being well-grounded in the knowledge of human anatomy and physiology, a student of the art would be able to understand much more quickly the nature, location, and expected results of their strikes to an attacker's body. For one rigorously involved in the study of a martial art, I cannot understand how the study of anatomy and physiology can be avoided. To me, it would not be that different from sending a medical student to a medical school that negates the importance of anatomical and physiological studies by filling the entire medical course with nothing but techniques designed to cure disease and illness. Clearly, any doctor who does not understand the anatomical structure and physiological processes that compose the human body is placing his patients in unnecessary jeopardy. When a martial artist is not trained in those areas, he is placing himself in unnecessary jeopardy as well.

Q: I have heard you say that when you strike someone, you don't really care whether or not that person feels any pain. Isn't the infliction of pain on an attacker the whole idea?

A: Striking another person is a very serious business and not one to be taken lightly. Striking another person will damage him greatly and so, if at all possible, we should always try to avoid doing it. If, on the other hand, we are placed in a circumstance where all other options are taken away from us by an attacker and we must resort to striking him, then, it is true, we care very little about his pain. When we are forced to strike an attacker, we are not looking to create pain, we are looking to create structural damage. Clearly, whether he feels the pain or not, a broken leg is a broken leg, a torn liver is a torn liver, a ruptured spleen is a ruptured spleen, et cetera. When a man's leg is broken, whether he feels the pain or not, he can no longer walk, kick, stand, or use that leg in any way against us. When his arm is broken, he can no longer use that arm to try to inflict injury on us. Damage is always more decisive than pain.

In the movies, fight scenes seem to go on forever. It is entertainment, after all, and there is a great deal of artistic license taken. The effects of the numerous staged punches and kicks in the scene have to be contrived—that is, until it is time for that particular action scene to end. Then, suddenly, the strikes become realistically effective. In actual life, however, we are not looking for any sort of entertainment effect. We do not look to impress anyone with our fighting skills and endurance. In real life, the longer a fight goes on, the more of an opportunity we have of getting injured. You must understand that even an untrained man can deliver a strike that can injure or even kill you. So the fight must be ended very quickly, and the only way to do that is to make sure that each and every strike that you throw is a strike that will cause great damage to the attacker's body. The fight is never our idea, it will always be started by the attacker. The nature of his attack will always determine the nature of our defense. If that attacker forces us to resort to strikes, then those strikes must cause enough damage to end the fight within seconds.

In Torishimaru Aiki Jutsu, the only time we look to induce pain in an opponent is when we are utilizing nerve-center techniques or have him in an *osae dore* (joint-twisting technique) or in some other immobilization technique. Then the production of pain becomes an important factor, because it is pain that will keep the attacker under control.

Q: You use the terms "targets" and "paths." What are they?

A: Simply stated, targets are the internal structures of the body that a strike is directed to. A path is the route that the weapon takes in order to reach that specific target structure. For example, there is only one target in the head and that target is the brain. There are, however, sixty-two paths in the head area that lead to the brain. Depending on which path a particular weapon takes, it results in a different sort of damage. For instance, if the path that the weapon takes to the brain is through the frontalis or forehead area, unconsciousness can be expected. If the path to the brain is through the temporal plate area, then the minimum anticipated damage will be a skull fracture, and the maximum damage will be death. There are hundreds of paths in the body and each path is responsible for the creation of a particular type of damage. A student of the art must be well trained in this area. He must be well grounded in the knowledge of all of the body's targets and the specific paths that lead to them. This knowledge is indispensable.

Q: What is the special relationship that the mind and the body have when it comes to the development of speed and power? Can meditation help?

A: The mind and the body have a very direct relationship to each other; in fact, it is very much a marriage of sorts. In Torishimaru Aiki Jutsu, we look to develop strength and power through relaxation. That is, we believe that power increases almost geometrically as the body relaxes. When the mind is tense, the body is tense, and when the body is tense, the mind is tense. How do we know this? Through our own experience. I am sure that you have experienced this also. For example, have you ever noticed what happens to your body when you are in a tense situation? It tenses, doesn't it? You can feel that tension in your muscles. On top of that, adrenaline is pumped into your body by the adrenal glands, located just above the kidneys, which only exacerbates this condition.

When muscles tense they contract, and that contraction results in an inward pull toward the body. If you are throwing a hand strike, for instance, its execution necessarily involves a motion of the hand and arm away from your body. Well, if you want to throw a strike that is moving away from your body but, because of tension, the contracting muscles are pulling your arm toward your body, what would be the outcome? That's correct! Your hand strike would not only be very slow but would lack a great deal of power, as well.

Logic will tell you that the contracting muscles of the arm, chest, and shoulders, working against the outward motion of the arm, will effectively slow down your strike. So it follows that the more relaxed the body is, the faster the strike will be, and that increase in speed will translate into an increase in power.

Understanding that a tense mind creates a tense body, it also follows that if we can relax the mind, the body will relax, and that is where meditation comes in. Through the systematic practice of meditation the mind learns to relax, which, in turn, relaxes the body, translating into an increase in both power and speed.

Q: **How does one develop strength and power in Torishimaru Aiki Jutsu? Does weight training have anything to do with it?**

A: Torishimaru Aiki Jutsu is the art of the mind. It is not founded on any arbitrary conceptions of physical strength. Physically, a person can only become so strong, and this type of strength will inevitably diminish as one grows older. As the body ages, it becomes increasingly more difficult to sustain the physical structures responsible for the production of a person's physical strength. This fact, in itself, should be enough to cause a person seriously involved in the practice of a martial art not to place too much trust in his physical strength in order to gain a valid and lasting expertise. In fact, a person's physical strength, even if he is young and in his prime, will often waver even throughout the course of a single day. It can even change from moment to moment. Knowing this, a practitioner of the martial arts should forsake the vain pursuance of physical strength for the enduring security afforded him by good solid technique and the enormous power available to him through his spiritual endeavors. One must discard forever the physical strength mindset for the techniques and principles that will offer one a different type of strength, a strength that will not diminish or waver over time, but will, on the contrary, actually increase as time passes.

Let me give you an example of a very common physical-strength mindset. A woman is struggling, trying to open a jar with a stubborn lid. She makes only a few valiant but unsuccessful attempts to open it before handing the jar over to her husband or boyfriend. He takes the jar and, like her, also struggles with it, but there is something different taking place. Yes, he can't open the jar either but he, unlike the woman, refuses to give up trying. Why? Because of the male ego-generated physical-strength mindset. Finally, after watching him struggle over the jar for several minutes, the woman, out of a combination of impatience and annoyance, seizes the jar, takes a knife or spoon, and firmly taps around the perimeter of the lid. She then, with very little effort, unscrews the lid. Does this sound familiar to you? Of course

26

it does. What happens in situations like this is not very difficult to understand. Where the stronger man, with his physical-strength mindset, failed to open the jar, the smaller, weaker woman succeeded by utilizing proper technique. Proper technique will always defeat physical strength.

There are, of course, two types of strength, physical strength and spiritual strength. The physical type of strength is that genus of strength that everyone is familiar with and is typified by big bulging muscles. The second type of strength is the strength that comes to a person in a very spiritual way as a natural byproduct of the combination of both deep meditation and valid technique. That spiritual strength, in the martial arts, is variously called Ki, Chi, Prana, and so on. We call it Ruach. Once Ruach is developed within a student, concepts revolving around the acquisition of mere physical strength no longer hold an allure for him. He has changed and has suddenly traveled light-years beyond that sort of primitive understanding.

In Torishimaru Aiki Jutsu, as in a number of other martial arts, great stress is placed on the development of spiritual strength and I, myself, discourage students from involving themselves in weight training for a number of important reasons. First, it is not just the actual practice of weight training but even the desire to engage in it that clearly demonstrates to me that the student is caught in a physical-strength mindset. Second, large bulky muscles impede a person's physical movements. Obviously, this is undesirable in a martial art. Third, but no less important, is that tight muscles, large or small though they may be, diminish both a person's physical speed and flow of Ruach, as well. To a martial artist, all of these impediments are totally unattractive.

In order to develop Ruach, one has no choice but to meditate. This is so because Ruach is developed well beyond both the limits and the aegis of the lower mind. In fact, the presence of the lower mind, to any degree, would actually interfere with the development of Ruach. The source of true spiritual strength lies secreted and dormant, waiting to be tapped, within the highly reachable mystical climes of the higher mind. To reach this realm of spiritual strength, the

27

lower mind must be calmed to quiescence and the higher mind must be brought forward to assume dominance. In order to bring the higher mind forward and mute the loquacious and interfering lower mind, meditation is not only the answer but is an absolute and unavoidable necessity. There is simply no way around it.

Doesn't the generally accepted and professed premise underlying almost all of the martial arts read: "Our system of self-defense allows the smaller, physically weaker person to overcome the stronger, larger person"? Yes, of course it does. It was with that concept in mind that the sundry techniques of the various martial arts were created. Certainly, many of those arts have evolved into extraordinary systems of defense because the masters who created those arts, as well as the countless masters who have subsequently continued the traditions of those arts, were spiritual men of peace, ability, and unwavering insight. They understood, very well, the ultimate value of the spiritual over the physical.

As you may know, I have worked with numerous professional and amateur athletes in various sports. Among them is an excellent athlete who is a world-class competitive weight lifter. In fact, he currently holds several power lifting world's records. He has enormous physical strength, but even he knows that if his lower mind interferes with any of his weight lift attempts, the results of his efforts would be, at best, less than satisfying.

One evening, he called me and told me that in an upcoming competition he was going to attempt a new world's record. He asked me if I could give him a technique or two concerning the mind that would give him the "edge" and lead to a successful lift. This I did. He practiced and applied the techniques. As a result, he broke the world's record by an impressive margin.

During his world record lift, his lower mind remained very quiet and did not interfere. This quiescence of lower mind allowed his higher mind to dominate, to command. Since it is the higher mind that controls the Ruach, he was then able to draw on that strength. The result of his world record attempt is now found in the record books. Do you understand? It wasn't just a mere physical lift that gave him the world's record, it was a spiritual lift.

When I speak of the Ruach or spiritual strength, I am speaking of the strength that flows naturally through the body when the lower mind is quiet and the higher mind dominates. When the lower mind is quiet, the muscles of the body are relaxed and supple, and this further facilitates its flow. The rule is: the more relaxed the body is, the more Ruach will flow.

Everyone has heard, at one time or another, amazing stories about various spontaneous acts of supernormal strength coming to the fore in the lives of some very ordinary people. An example of this would be the woman who, after a terrible automobile accident, found that her son was helplessly pinned under the car. Panicking and utterly frantic, she runs to the car and, without a thought, without the slightest idea of "can" or "can't," lifts up the front end of the car and frees her son. What actually occurs in situations like this? What is it that could give a frail, frightened woman enough strength to lift an enormously heavy car? It is really not very difficult to understand. In the example that I just gave, the woman was clearly in shock. That is, her lower mind was so shocked by the enormity of the situation that it literally shut down. The shutting down of her lower mind now allowed her higher mind to reign, which, in turn, allowed her Ruach to flow. This suddenly acquired spiritual strength afforded her the enormous power to lift the heavy car and free her son. If her lower mind had not gone into shock, then there would have been no way that she would have been able to do it.

Naturally, we in the martial arts do not want to place the lower mind into shock. What we want to do, however, is to quiet the lower mind to the point where the higher mind can come to the forefront and command. This is accomplished through the discipline of meditation. To sit in meditation is a necessary event in the development of spiritual strength in a martial arts practitioner. But sitting quietly in meditation is just one method. An advanced student learns not only the sedentary methods of meditation but also how to continue his meditation throughout the course of his normal day's activities. Here, everything that he does becomes a meditation. When this happens, then, his higher mind is always in the position of control and his quiet spiritual strength is always flowing. Through this, he becomes serene in mind and powerful in spirit.

Q: Could you explain more about special relationships, like the one that exists between the lower mind and the higher mind?

A: Yes, certainly. There is a very special relationship that exists between the lower mind and the higher mind. To understand this relationship, one must understand that there is great difficulty that exists when it comes to the free exchange of information between them. Suppose, for example, that you want to create a situation whereby you want to cause an attacker to freeze, to stop dead in his tracks and stand like a marble statue, unable to move. Naturally, in this situation he would not only be unable to continue his attack but would be unable to even defend himself. Can it be done? Certainly it can. In fact, it can be accomplished in numerous ways, but for now, I will explain just one way of bringing this about.

In order to execute one particular type of freeze, one must both create and sustain a dialogue or debate between the attacker's lower mind and his higher mind. To begin to understand how this is done, I must first preface the explanation by introducing you to a basic principle. That is, a person will, if given the option, invariably defend himself not only prior to issuing an attack but even during the execution of that attack. In other words, if a punch were coming at you, you would first attempt to stop that punch in some fashion before you offer your attack. Even if you were in the actual process of executing an attack, should a strike be launched against you, you would temporarily break off your attack and enter into a defense mode in order to safeguard yourself against it. Automatically entering a defense mode is a natural response to attack. You must understand and accept this idea as axiomatic in order to fully understand the rest of my explanation.

As I said before, we have to involve the attacker's lower mind and his higher mind in a dialogue or debate with each other. How this is accomplished may at first seem a little difficult to understand, but with just a little thought you will find that it is all perfectly logical. Suppose, for example, that the attacker is standing some ten feet or so away from you. His lower mind is set in an attack mode. That is, his lower mind is ready to order his body to offend. If I were to respond by executing a movement that would appear benign to his lower mind, no dialogue would ensue between his lower mind and his higher mind because both would be in agreement as to what was taking place before them. They would agree that they are in no immediate danger and, as a result, I would have no control over his actions. However, if I were to respond by performing a movement that would appear benign to his lower mind, yet within that movement I was able to strike his shield (the field of energy surrounding the body) with a moderate column of feminine energy or

31

M'retz Na'she, an argument would then ensue between his higher mind and lower mind as to what was actually taking place.

This is how it works: Being some distance away from the attacker, his physical senses would transmit the necessary details to his lower mind and his lower mind would, as a matter of course, regard what was taking place as nothing very serious. Why? Because his senses would tell him that I was too far away from him to do him any immediate physical harm. Also, my actions themselves would appear harmless and of little consequence. However, when I simultaneously strike his shield either with my own shield or with a column of feminine energy, we have another situation taking place wherein his higher mind, responding to the attack on his shield, is absolutely convinced that he is, in fact, under attack. So, what we have now is this: His lower mind is saying, no, we are not under attack, and his higher mind is saying, yes, we are most definitely under attack. Do you understand? I have now created a situation where the attacker's higher mind and lower mind are engaged in an argument over what is actually taking place.

For the attacker's body—or for that matter, anyone's body—to move, it has to be under orders to do so. Those orders have to be issued either by the higher mind or the lower mind. Here we have created a situation where the attacker's lower mind and his higher mind cannot agree as to what is actually taking place, let alone agree what to do about it. Since orders to defend or not to defend, to offend or not to offend, must be issued by the mind, but that mind is too busy arguing with itself, no orders of any kind can be issued. There are no directives mandating his body to move forward, none to retreat, none to offend, and none to defend. As a consequence of this process, the attacker becomes incapacitated and is, effectively, frozen in place.

Q: You have made reference to something that you called the "sheath." What exactly is the sheath?

A: The sheath is the subtle body sometimes referred to, in certain circles, as the astral body. It acts in various ways and has various functions. First and foremost, it is the subtle body that clothes the soul or spirit. Secondly, it is the mold that is responsible for both the growth and eventual appearance of the physical body.

The sheath, containing the soul, is introduced to the egg at the moment of conception and from that time, as a matter of course, is filled in through the biological growth process. However, the sheath, unlike the readily degradable physical body, is indestructible by physical means and invariably survives the physical body at death. It is for this reason that, when a person is unfortunate enough to lose a limb, the sense of still having that limb continues to exist. That is, the person may still have the sense of feeling pain, pins and needles, throbbing, et cetera, there. Kirlian photography, a special photographic technique that has the ability to capture the image of the sheath on film, has shown not only that the sheath does, in fact, exist, but that the integrity of the sheath remains completely intact even when the physical body is variously disfigured.

When a person is reposing in a deep sleep, the sheath, under certain conditions, can be seen floating gracefully over the physical body. The sheath is tenuously attached to the physical body by a subtle, silver-colored cord that can also be seen under the proper conditions. This silver-colored cord might be thought of as a slender esoteric umbilical cord that not only tethers the sheath to the body but also functions as a subtle data highway that allows the transfer of necessary information between them. At death, the silver cord begins a natural process of disintegration, culminating in what is referred to as "total separation." It takes, on the

33

average, forty-nine days to one year for this to occur. Until that time, the sheath is earth-bound, forced by circumstance to remain on this plane of existence. When seen, the sheath is often referred to as a "ghost" or "spectre." When one understands the intricate relationship existing between the physical body, the sheath, and the mind, one is well on the way to understanding not only the subtleties of my system of self-defense but the subtleties of life, as well.

Q: **You mentioned the "shield." Could you explain just what the shield is?**

A: The shield or magen is commonly called the aura, but it is very much more than just a colored glow surrounding the body that advertises the magnitude of a person's emotional state. The magen is an extremely subtle field of energy that not only surrounds all things, inanimate objects included, but is actually a field of energy that is generated by those objects. The density of an object's magen is dependent upon the amount of feminine energy (life force) that person or object has at any one particular time and ranges from dramatically tenuous to extremely dense, almost plasmic.

Just as the body offers its sensory information to the lower mind, the shield offers its very special sensory information to the higher mind. Actually, the magen is really a person's first line of defense. In times of immanent danger or often even in non-dangerous times it intensifies, expands, and acts in the capacity of an early warning radar system that alerts the higher mind to the relevant events of particular situations. The higher mind, in receipt of that information, in turn attempts to relay that intelligence to the person's lower mind, but because a person's lower mind is often cluttered with numerous thoughts that impede the reception of that information, he or she simply receives the message in the form of a funny feeling, a hunch, or an

35

The shield or magen (indicated by the dotted line) is commonly called the aura; beneath the shield lies the sheath, or astral body.

ambiguous flash of intuition. When people learn how to quiet their lower minds and listen better, their efforts are sure to pay off at one time or another, and may ultimately save them a great deal of unnecessary grief. It may even save their lives.

Try This: If you would like to experience the reality of the existence of the shield or magen first hand, you can perform the following. Take both of your hands and place them, palm facing palm, in front of you approximately three to four inches apart. Slowly pump them back and forth toward and away from each other. What you should experience is a slight pressure between them. It should feel cushion-like; something very much reminiscent of what you would feel if you placed two magnets together, like pole to like pole, and pumped them back and forth. If you try this and feel this pressure, what you are actually feeling is your own magen.

Try This: To experience the reality of another person's sheath, you can perform the hand-pumping exercise described above with a partner. You will be able to feel each others' magen. You can also experience the shield that surrounds your partner by lightly pumping your hand toward and away from him approximately three to four inches from his body. The pressure that you feel on your palm is the subtle pressure created by their magen.

Q: **What is the special relationship that exists between the higher mind, lower mind, sheath, and shield (magen)?**

A: It is the special relationship that exists between the higher mind, lower mind, sheath, and shield (magen) that actually

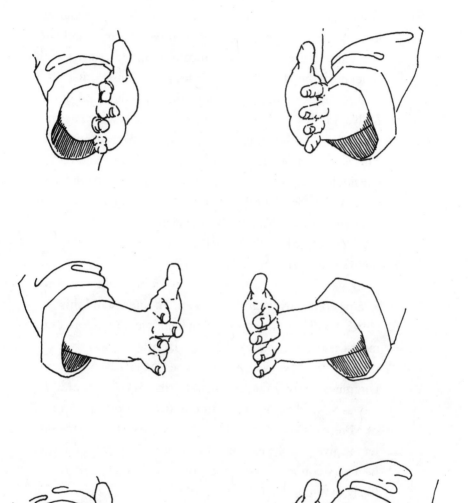

Hands pressing back and forth to feel the shield or magen.

forms the basis for many of the unique principles and techniques extant in Torishimaru Aiki Jutsu. Of course, as you may have already guessed, it is a subject that requires a lengthy explanation. Perhaps it requires one too lengthy to allow me to cover all the ramifications and intricacies at this time; nevertheless, I will try to give you a sense of it.

As I have said before, the lower mind is the mind of the body and, as such, receives, ingests, and digests whatever sundry sensory information the body has to transmit to it. This is, of course, very well known to everyone and is considered axiomatic. However, when it comes to the higher mind and its special relationships, the average person is not only unaware of the extraordinary information that it receives but, ironically, is totally unaware of the higher mind's existence at all.

I have already mentioned the magen or shield functions as a person's early warning system. To understand this better, I will present you with an example. But before I do, I must first preface my explanation by offering you this simple rule: Wherever the mind goes, M'retz Na'she or feminine energy flows. In other words, when the mind moves toward an object, it automatically projects a stream of M'retz Na'she toward that object. This having been said, let me give you the example I promised. You will find it to be a very common experience, one that you may, more likely than not, be able to identify with.

You are sitting in a restaurant, enjoying your meal, and minding your business when suddenly you feel an odd and uncomfortable pressure on the nape of your neck. Suddenly you have the uneasy feeling that someone, somewhere in the room, is staring at you. When you turn around to investigate, you notice that a young man sitting several tables behind you is, in fact, staring at you. If this has happened to you and you have experienced the uneasy feeling that I have just described, then my explanation should certainly interest you.

What is actually occurring in a situation like this is that the mind of the person who is staring at you is flowing toward you. The subtle movement of his mind toward you subsequently causes a stream of M'retz Na'she to move toward you as well. When his M'retz Na'she reaches you and presses or strikes your magen, all sorts of silent alarms are set off and a great deal of sensory information is then transmitted to and received by your higher mind. What sort of information? Attack information! That's correct, attack information. Your magen is relaying the message to the higher mind that you are being probed, assailed, attacked. The higher mind responds by attempting to get an urgent message through to the lower mind regarding the specifics of the unwarranted intrusion. The problem is that the lower mind, being so constantly cluttered with myriad thoughts, cannot hear the message clearly, and so all it can understand, all it can deduce, is the unspoken sense of the message but, unfortunately, not the letter of it. This sense of the message is what is commonly called a hunch, intuition, or a feeling, and is an experience that you've had, no doubt, at some time or another during your life. So it is the probing of your magen that begins the process that culminates in the feeling that someone is staring at you. It is not the result of telepathy, clairvoyance, or anything of the sort. It is simply the natural response of the higher mind to perturbations in the magen. Of course, if the lower mind was quiet, then the voice of the higher mind would be able to transmit extraordinarily clear and amazingly precise information concerning the probing.

I will give you another example concerning these special relationships, one that I am quite sure you can identify with. Suppose you are enjoying an evening at a local bowling alley. You are with friends and everything is fine. Then, just as you are about to bowl, a sudden loud and violent argument erupts several lanes behind you. There are

39

egregious threats, thunderous shouts, and numerous obscenities being exchanged. When the argument first breaks out, you react for a second as if you were somehow personally involved in the fracas yourself. That is, both your pulse and breathing suddenly quicken and there is a temporary stiffening of your body. It is not until you turn around and see that the conflict is actually taking place between two people some distance away from you that everything in you begins to relax, your breathing begins to normalize, and the tenseness in your body begins to dissipate. Of course, the reason prompting your relaxation is the realization that the violent argument does not involve you personally and your recognition of the fact that you are safe and that there is nothing for you to be concerned about. Have you ever experienced something like this? I'm sure that you have.

But what actually takes place to make you feel this way? What takes place to make you feel as if you, personally, were under attack? Let me explain.

Imagine, if you will, standing waist-deep in a swimming pool with a number of other people doing the same. The surface of the water is calm and everything is fine. Then, someone on the far end of the pool suddenly moves, sending out a ripple on the surface of the water that extends outward from his body. As you watch the ripple, you notice that it moves outward from his body in a circle and eventually reaches and touches everyone else in the pool. When someone explodes in anger, it is much like the ripple created in the pool—his magen expands very rapidly, spherically, out from his body and strikes everyone else's magen in the vicinity. When the angry man's magen reaches and strikes your magen, silent alarms are set off and attack information is then relayed to your higher mind. The higher mind, as a result, automatically causes you to enter into a defense mode. Simultaneously, your sense of hearing

40

transmits attack information to your lower mind. We now have a situation where both your higher mind and your lower mind are in total agreement as to what is taking place—attack. It is as if you are truly being assaulted; as if you are, yourself, the one on the receiving end of the other person's anger. Well, believe it or not, as odd as it may seem, in a very real sense you are. Not only is your magen being struck by his expanding magen, but your sense of hearing is supporting the information created by that event. Yes, you are indeed being attacked by that man, even if that attack is inadvertent on his part. Of course, when you turn around and realize that it is an event that is actually taking place between two other people and that you are safe, one by one your alarms shut off and you enter into, if not a normal mode, then at least a normal standby mode.

Although we do not utilize the *ki-ai* or karate shout in Torishimaru Aiki Jutsu, what actually causes the ki-ai to paralyze one's opponent is almost exactly as I describe above. That is, two things are actually taking place simultaneously when the ki-ai or karate shout is delivered. First, the physical senses of the body are picking up some very strong sensory material. That is, it is receiving the tremendous sound or blast of the shout, as well as receiving the vision of the attacker executing the ki-ai. This information is transmitted to the lower mind for processing. At the same time, the ki-aier's magen expands rapidly from his body and strikes the receiver's magen. The information generated by the now-struck magen is then passed on to the receiver's higher mind for processing. Clearly, the information that is passed on to both the higher mind and lower mind speaks of attack and, as a result, both minds are in agreement. Now, ordinarily, when the higher mind and lower mind are in agreement, one would be able to respond to an attack with a rapid and adequate defense. However, here we have a situation where the massive auditory signal

41

coming to the physical senses is, in a very real way, too powerful. This causes an inordinately large signal to be sent to the lower mind, causing it to suddenly tense and temporarily freeze. This, in turn, causes the muscles of the body to tense and become temporarily immobile and the body is, for the intended purpose, effectively paralyzed. Does the ki-ai work? Yes, it does. It is an extraordinarily effective technique. Even so, we employ other, more subtle, more sophisticated techniques in my art to bring about paralysis in and control over our opponents, which I will explain in detail later.

Q: **In your art you stress the importance of meditation. Why do you place so much emphasis on it?**

A: Because without meditation, all of one's actions, including defensive actions, are dictated by the lower mind. For the martial artist, this is highly undesirable. The lower mind, as such, is much too capricious and uncontrolled to be reliable, especially in a situation where your life or the life of someone else may hang in the balance. No, this is not what I would want.

If your life or physical well-being were imperiled, wouldn't you desire the very best assistance available to help you out of that situation? Of course you would. Clearly, the best assistance available is your very own higher mind.

Unfortunately, the lower mind is much too prone to making mistakes to be placed in charge of our defense. The higher mind, on the other hand, incapable of making a mistake, is obviously the better choice. If offered the option, which would you choose to take charge of your defense? Would it be the mistake-producing lower mind, or the faultless higher mind? Yes, of course, you would choose the higher mind. But, even so, there is still more to consider.

The lower mind, because of its often overpowering emotional attachments, has a tendency to either do nothing or to overreact to an event, while the higher mind invariably has the tendency to remain cool and clear under identical circumstances. Where the lower mind would ponder the situation incessantly, the higher mind would immediately know what has to be done and would do it with a calm expediency. There are no magical pills to take or potions to swallow to help place our higher minds in charge of our lives. It has to be done on the zafu, or pillow, steeped in the serene and infinite depths of meditation. This is the reason I stress the practice of meditation. In fact, it should be the reason for all martial arts to stress meditation. Meditation is the quickest and most viable way to quiet the lower mind and place the higher mind in control.

Also, it is important to me that my students experience at least something of the unity that exists in the physical universe. It is not enough for me merely to stand in front of them and explain the mysteries to them. That simply wouldn't do. You must understand that to walk a spiritual path, any spiritual path, requires more than merely acquiring the rudiments of a lower mind philosophy. To do that would be only superficial at best and, as many people learn, changes that take place only on the surface, in the final analysis, are meaningless. It is like trying to change who and what you are by merely putting on a mask and changing your name. Change must take place within the deepest and most arcane recesses of one's being. You must transform yourself slowly over time within the carefully spun protective silken cocoon of meditation. It is there that the metamorphosis will take place that will transform you from a caterpillar steeped in ignorance to a spiritual butterfly—beautiful, tranquil, alive, and free. This, also, is why I stress the importance of meditation in my art.

43

Q: Could you explain in more detail why you stress meditation?

A: Meditation in the martial arts is undoubtedly of paramount importance in order to have the proper spiritual evolution take place within the student. It is indispensable. As I have explained before, the lower mind is fraught with myriad inconsistencies wrought by the rising and falling waves of emotional and intellectual involvement. The higher mind, on the other hand, sees a particular event or situation clearly and without emotion. The higher mind is intuitive, clear thinking, and incapable of making a mistake. When I say "clear thinking" you understand, of course, that what I mean is the ability to "think without thinking." It is the sort of thinking that lies well beyond the lower mind's limited ability to both produce and understand. It is, in fact, the purest kind of thinking, the purest kind of thought.

When a person first begins his study of a martial art, he is naturally taught the fundamental principles of that art as well as its particular physical techniques. These martial principles and techniques are recorded simultaneously on both the finite lower mind tape and the infinite higher mind tape. The lower mind tape, however, is generally cluttered to a fault with random thoughts, narrative musings, and attachments. It is also the home of thought-provoking emotions. As a result of the presence of these things, the information taken into the lower mind is partial at any one time, and is maintained in a highly disorganized way. This disorganization is further exacerbated by the numerous and, at times, enormous emotional and intellectual waves created by the lower mind when responding to data supplied it by the physical senses when those senses are exposed to the often arbitrary and sometimes volatile unforeseen winds of circumstance.

Without the discipline of meditation, the lower mind, by default, will continue to reign almost godlike in a person's

44

life, creating an inner world fraught with insecurity, fear, and confusion. How could it be otherwise, when it bases the very construction of that inner domain on the incomplete and distorted view it has of the exterior world around it? This, of course, is an extremely unfortunate situation for anyone, but for the truly motivated martial artist, it is an absolute tragedy. With the lower mind reigning supreme during an attack, a great problem arises that makes it nearly impossible to retrieve the correct technique and mount an adequate defense. The problem that comes up when the lower mind is in charge of a person's defense is really one of proficiency. In order for the lower mind to respond to the attack, it has to wade through a seemingly endless morass of emotional, intellectual, and psychological land mines until reaching the area on the lower mind tape containing the perfect technique. This, in and of itself, will make the proper defensive response to attack slow and unreliable. But there is more. Should there exist, recorded on the lower mind tape, more than one technique to cover that particular attack, the lower mind then has to engage in a very ponderous judgment-making process. This, of course, is very time consuming and can be dangerous or even fatal.

If that isn't enough, there are several other lower mind processes also taking place at the same time that further exacerbate the problem. There is not only a deluge of sensory information assailing the lower mind due to the present dangerous circumstances that it must assimilate and process, but there are intelligence loops set in place that are also feeding data to it as well.

An intelligence loop is a phenomenon that occurs in the lower mind when current sensory information, as it is received, spontaneously triggers the introduction of one or more correlative data inputs coming from past traumatic events of a similar nature previously existing on the lower mind tape. These past traumatic events may be factual in nature, totally imaginary, or delusional, or somewhere in between. That is, they could be sources of thought-input coming from actual events that the lower mind had distorted in some way prior to recording those events and responses on the lower mind tape. This isn't unusual. It is the nature of the lower mind to embellish memories— sometimes to the point where they are so distorted, so convoluted, so corrupted, that they become either totally, or at the very least, partially untrue and yet are considered by that person to be unfabricated, undistorted, and absolutely factual. This is part of the insidious nature of the lower mind. And so for the martial artist to rely on the lower mind to defend his life is not something that I would recommend. When data is compounded like this, a sort of data overload is created that can, and often does, lead to a state of both physical and psychological paralysis. This is often referred to, euphemistically, as being scared stiff. That is, to become so frightened, so inundated by thought, that one cannot even move or think, let alone offer a viable life-saving defense.

Through the practice of proper meditation, the higher mind of the martial artist is brought forward and assumes a serene control over his actions. The advantage of this higher mind domination becomes evident when we realize that the higher mind does not have to wade through a ponderous sea of emotional and intellectual molasses and does not find itself in the unfortunate position of making involuntary connections, however tenuous they may be, to past traumatic experiences. Immediately, the creation of psychological loops normally responsible for one's inability to respond to danger when the lower mind dominates become totally nonexistent under the aegis of the higher mind. Further, since the higher mind has the useful innate ability to see the future, it intuitively begins the defensive process not only with the thought of assault coming from

46

the attacker, but actually plans out its defensive strategies prior to that thought. The higher mind, then, without fear or frenzy, without conflict or debate, extracts the proper technique *aequo animo*, with a calm mind, from its infinite tape, and employs that technique with proficient and almost uncanny expediency. This, my friend, is the value of meditation in the martial arts.

Q: **What form of meditation do you consider the most useful for a martial artist?**

A: There are numerous forms of meditation available and many of them are useful; however, for the martial artist, Zen meditation would undoubtedly be the meditation of choice. Zen meditation, different than many other meditational disciplines, trains you to be here and now and helps you to become centered and focused while active in the world. This is what a martial artist must be: centered, focused, and calm amidst the chaos of battle. There is an old adage that states "A good fighter is not an angry fighter, a good fighter is not a frightened fighter." Yes, this is certainly a good idea, but what does it really mean? What the adage is saying is that so long as a fighter is governed by his emotions, his proficiency will be greatly impaired.

The emotions lie within the sphere of the lower mind and, as such, will only involve themselves in the business of battle when the lower mind is in the position of dictating our defense or offense. As I have already explained, the lower mind is highly incapable of functioning to our advantage in times of great danger. It is capricious, mistake-prone, and altogether unreliable. The emotions, in fact, lie even beyond the aegis of the intellect, and so may cause a person to do silly and perhaps even dangerous things. Wherever and whenever the emotion-ridden lower mind is called on to defend us, you can be sure that disaster will be almost certain to follow.

Listen! Once there lived three great kings, each the monarch of a vast empire. The first king's name was King Emotion. He was a very powerful king, but a very vain, self-centered, self-serving, child-like king who was much too capricious to ever govern his people wisely.

The second king's name was King Intellect and, like King Emotion, he too was very powerful. Unfortunately he too, at times, was extremely self-serving, self-centered, and arrogant. He did what he could to be fair to his people and govern wisely, but alas, a majority of his regal decisions would, invariably, be based on very few facts, and the outcome would often be disastrous.

The third king was, undoubtedly, the most powerful and successful of all the kings. His name was King Wisdom and his subjects, without exception, were always happy. They loved, admired, and respected their king very much. Why? Because they were ardently loved and tenderly cared for. King Wisdom, unlike King Intellect and King Emotion, did not rule over his people, he ruled *for* them.

One day, King Emotion was very upset, more upset than usual. He had heard how well the people were faring under the reign of King Intellect and was so envious, so jealous, that he began to speak of declaring war on him and his kingdom. Hearing of this, King Intellect, under a flag of truce, went to parley with King Emotion. While King Intellect tried to reason with King Emotion, King Emotion ranted and raved and did not hear a single word. Finally, out of frustration, King Intellect grabbed King Emotion and, covering the king's mouth, kept him immobile and unable to talk. Applying painful pressure to the back of the king's neck, King Intellect was finally able to get through to him. He whispered into King Emotion's ear, "You are so emotional that you are not thinking clearly at all. Why do you set your sights so low? My kingdom is larger than yours, yes, but King Wisdom's realm is ten thousand times as large as ours combined. Why don't we make a pact? You and I will combine our forces and then attack and conquer King Wisdom's realm. Then, we can divide all of it equally between the two of us."

Still feeling the painful pressure on the back of his neck, King Emotion reluctantly agreed and they soon united both of their small armies into one huge formidable army. With the two kings riding at the head of this great army, they proceeded toward the realm of their now-mutual enemy, King Wisdom. Before long, their army was gathered in siege about the castle of King Wisdom. When one of King Wisdom's generals came to see him, seeking instructions as to what to do about the siege, the wise king simply smiled and said, "Do nothing, my friend, do nothing." Confused, the general bowed and left the king's presence, obedient to the king's will.

King Wisdom was a wise king and knew that even the combined armies of the two lesser kings could never hope to breach his castle's walls, and so he wisely decided to be patient and wait. He knew that however long it took, however long he had to wait, eventually the two lesser kings would have to give up their campaign and want to parley. And so, month after month, year after year, the combined armies laid siege to the great castle. Even so, life went on as usual within King Wisdom's realm, much to the wonder and dismay of the two lesser kings.

Finally, after seventy frustrating years passed, the two lesser kings looked at each other and came to the realization they were so old that, even if the kingdom of Wisdom could be taken by force, it would certainly be an empty and short-lived victory, at best.

Having agreed, both of the lesser kings walked slowly up to the castle gate waving a tattered white flag of truce and called out to King Wisdom for his mercy and hospitality. Hearing this, King Wisdom commanded his general to open the gates and allow his two noble visitors entrance.

At first, the two lesser kings stood in awestruck silence before King Wisdom because of his powerful presence, and then, prostrating themselves, begged once again for the king's forgiveness and mercy. Further, they asked how they could achieve such peace and wisdom before they died. To this, King Wisdom gently replied, "I welcome you, noble brothers, to my humble kingdom. How vain and ignorant you both have been. How very foolish you were to think that through the out-of-control base emotions or by way of the prideful machinations of intellect you could come into the possession of wisdom. However, when you finally laid your weapons down and entreated entry as friends, ah, that was the very beginning of wisdom and the first lesson. If you truly aspire to wisdom, you must throw your weapons away forever and give yourselves over to the learning of it."

You must understand that to achieve wisdom, true wisdom, is really a very simple matter. However, it cannot be taken by force nor can it be achieved by cravenly yielding to the emotions. Neither can it be gained through the unwieldy and often prideful machinations of the intellect. To achieve true wisdom, one must be willing to yield to it, to boldly lay one's emotions aside and quiet the tumultuous and opinionated intellect. To do this, one must meditate and be willing to yield to wise instruction. Otherwise, wisdom will forever elude you and you will go on suffering, not only in this present life, but in all your future incarnations.

True wisdom is not the wisdom of knowing what to have for breakfast or which brand of soap powder to buy. It is not the wisdom of knowing how to close that business deal or how to take advantage of others without suffering retribution because of it. True wisdom is none of those things, but is something entirely different.

There is knowledge, there is understanding, and there is wisdom. They are three different things. Once knowledge is imparted to you, you must make every effort to absorb that knowledge. Once that is done, you must realize that knowledge without understanding is utterly useless to a person, and so you must make every effort to understand that knowledge in all of its aspects. Once, however, you have achieved that understanding, then and only then will you find yourself standing at the very gates of Wisdom—but you are not yet inside. True wisdom exists only when knowledge, combined with understanding, turns kinetic. It is only when knowledge and understanding are in motion that they are of any real value, and only when that combination is used is wisdom attained.

There are those who know a great many things and think themselves wise, but are not. There are those who understand a great many things and think themselves wise, but are not. True wisdom is the combination of knowledge and understanding brought to a boil in the great cauldron of the Eternal, and ingested by those who have learned the use of that magical elixir in the healing of their own beings.

Q: I've heard the expression "oneness with the opponent." Everyone in the martial arts seems to use that expression, but no one seems to really know what it means. What does it mean? Could you explain?

51

A: Oneness with the opponent is not a very difficult concept to understand. Still, I have to agree that many practitioners of the martial arts lack an understanding of it. For all of their sakes, as well as your own, I will explain it.

In Torishimaru Aiki Jutsu, every effort is made to impart to the student, *ab ovo,* from the very beginning, the importance of the principle of oneness with the opponent for proper self-defense. To this end, oneness with the opponent is carefully explained early in a student's training so that he can employ it throughout his martial arts career. It is one of the fundamental principles of my system.

To give you a sense of it, I must present you with an example: Suppose, for example, that you have a particular technique that is used to defend against an attacker who is throwing a roundhouse punch at you and that, as a result of employing that particular technique, the attacker is quickly and easily projected to the ground. If I were to ask you what it is that you need the opponent to do in order to utilize that particular defense technique and send him crashing to the ground, what would you say? Think about it. What is it that you need the opponent to do in order to execute your technique? Yes, of course! You need him to throw that roundhouse punch. Why? Because, if he does not throw that roundhouse punch, you will not be able to use that particular technique. Do you understand? You need him to attack you with that roundhouse punch, don't you? Of course you do. Therefore, you must consider the attacker's actions not as something that you should dread but, on the contrary, something that you should welcome. In this example, the attacker's roundhouse punch is actually a necessary component of your technique and not something separate and apart from it. In fact, your opponent's roundhouse punching attack is not only part of your technique, it is an absolute and inescapable necessity! Without that particular attack, your particular technique is positively useless and unemployable. So, in understanding that the opponent's attack is required in this case, you should change your concept of him and his attack as being something external, malignant, and separate from your defense.

Understand, oneness with the opponent doesn't just apply to your defensive techniques. It applies, equally, to your offensive or attack techniques, as well. Again, you cannot offend against nothing! There must be someone or something there to receive your offensive techniques and that someone or something must be understood to be a necessary component of your technique. When you understand this, then, you are well on your way to becoming one with your opponent. When you understand this, then the idea of having an opponent at all ceases to exist. In part, that is why I say that there really is no opponent. Those who are of the mindset that has them focusing in on their opponent like a bull concentrating with all of its might when attacking a matador cannot possibly be practicing oneness with the opponent. This is sad because they miss so much that would eventually turn them into redoubtable practitioners in their respective arts.

Still, as easy as the concept of oneness with the opponent is to understand, you must not mistake brass for gold. A mere intellectual understanding of oneness with your opponent is a beginning, yes, but just a beginning, after all. This new way of considering or viewing the opponent must become more than just an idle philosophical idea. It must become an intricate part of both you and your technique. It must merge with the deepest part of you until the slightest trace of intellection concerning it is no longer present. Then, and only then, will you have achieved the elusive oneness with your opponent, and it will be with you always—not just throughout your martial arts career, but throughout your everyday life, as well.

Q: In a demonstration for television, I saw you stand on one foot and hold off twenty-two men who were lined up, one behind the other, trying to push you over. Some of these men were world-class power lifters and some were professional football players. That same evening I saw ten of the largest of the twenty-two men attempt, in unison, to pick you up off the ground . . . and they couldn't budge you. You called it "being one with the earth." How is it possible? Could you explain?

A: There are several principles at work here. First, an esoteric strength has got to be tapped into and, once done, you must be the vehicle through which it flows. Your own physical strength really has nothing whatsoever to do with it. The strength that I am talking about is the strength of the Ruach. It flows without flowing; it is still, and yet it flows like a great rushing river. To tap into it, you must first be relaxed and empty. You must allow the flow of Ruach to pass through you as if you were hollow. To do that, you must throw yourself away. Harbor the slightest thought of yourself and it cannot and will not take place. To achieve it, proper meditation is an irrefutable necessity, for through meditation you will eventually be brought into a state we call Ku, or emptiness. Ku is not a morbid state of abject nothingness, it is a highly evolved state of everythingness, where everything exists in an indefinable oneness where nothing whatsoever is lacking.

Now, assuming that you are in a state of Ku, you must allow the higher mind to unite with the river of Ruach flowing from the infinite Void of God, and allow that great river to stream through your body, from the top of your head downward through the soles of your feet, through the earth and outward again toward the infinite depths of the Eternal Void. You must become that flow, you must become that mystical river of Ruach. If you entertain any such thoughts as: *I must do this,* or, *I must do that,* or, *I am doing this,* or, *I am doing that,* then you will not be successful. Should there arise in you any thought of an opponent or opposing force then, again, you will doom yourself to failure.

You must remember that where the mind goes, the sheath goes, and where the sheath goes, the body goes. If your lower mind actively enters into what is taking place, then you will be forced to struggle with its froward machinations and all will be irretrievably lost. Why? Because it is the nature of the lower mind, invariably, to look to oppose circumstances and objects, to look to control circumstances and objects, and to manage them to its own purpose. It considers all objects, all events, all things to be separate and apart from itself, and in so doing it creates illusions of duality that have no basis in truth. Bearing this in mind, the lower mind must be made quiescent if you are to be successful at Oneness With The Earth.

Remember, you must not oppose or struggle with thoughts, objects, or anything at all, but rather abide in the pristine state of no-thingness or Ku. And in order to do that, again, the lower mind must be made mute and the higher mind brought forward. Then you will be successful.

Try this: Stand with your arms and body relaxed and your feet shoulder-width apart. Have two men—one man on each side of you, holding you with both hands by the upper part of each arm—simultaneously attempt to lift you up. The first time they try, I want you to stiffen your arms and body and consciously try to stay on the floor. If you like, you can think of something symbolic, such as, "My feet are glued to the floor and I am immovable," or "I and the earth are one and inseparable." When you are ready for them to lift you, simply nod your head. You will find that they will have no trouble at all lifting you off the ground.

55

Now, try it a little differently. Allow the two men to secure each arm as before, but this time, I want you to relax your body as much as you can. Let your body go limp and, above all, do not allow your lower mind to attempt to resist their lift. Feel as if everything inside you has turned to an ethereal liquid and that liquid has merged with the great flow of spirit deep within the Void of God. You are one with that great stream of Ruach. Visualize that great stream entering your hollow body just below your navel. Feel it flowing down through your hip area, down through your hollow legs and into the molten core at the center of the earth. You must do this by thinking without thinking. That is, it should not be an actual thought, but more of a feeling or sense of flowing. Once you have this feeling, then indicate that you are ready by nodding to the two men. This time, they should not be able to lift you off the ground. But even if they do manage to lift you, they will suddenly notice a tremendous difference in the effort needed to do so. Meditation and practice are essential in order to master this technique. But in time, with the proper meditation and practice, you will evolve to the point where you will be able to execute this technique against four, six, eight, or even ten men.

Try this: The next time someone hands you a jar that is difficult to open, secure the jar the way you normally would to open it. This time, however, I want you to relax your body as completely as you can. Your grip on the lid of the jar should be just enough to keep it from slipping in your hand. Do not grip the lid with any more strength than that. Clear all thoughts from your lower mind and just relax and do not entertain a single conscious thought relating to the opening of the jar. Have the sense that you are dissolving in the Eternal Void of God, becoming one with that great flow of Ruach. When you are ready, when you have the feeling of oneness, simply twist the lid of the jar with one quick, smooth motion. You will be amazed at your sudden increase in strength and how easily you were able to open that stubborn jar lid.

The opening of the jar, like the principle of Oneness With The Earth, is a simple example of what we call flowing—the term "flowing," of course, being a direct reference to the natural flow of Ruach, or spiritual strength.

The key to flowing and mastering the exercises above, as well as the numerous exercises of this type, lies in one's ability to quiet the lower mind and relax the body. The only way to do that is to meditate. Just in passing, let me say that the same spiritual strength that is utilized to make you one with the earth is the same spiritual strength that could and should be applied to one's hand strikes, elbow strikes, shoulder strikes, knee strikes, and kicks. In fact, it should become so natural, so second nature to you, that you are flowing constantly as a matter of course.

Q: **What is the principle of the feminine vacuum?**

A: In order to explain the principle of the feminine vacuum, I am going to have to explain, very briefly, the basic premises of both the Newtonian Gravitational Theory and the Einsteinian Gravitational Theory. I must do this because I am introducing publicly, for the first time, the principle of the feminine vacuum as the Third Law of Gravity.

Briefly, the Newtonian Gravitational Theory states that a natural attraction or gravitational pull exists between any two physical objects. The amount of attraction objects possess toward each other is based on the masses of each of the objects and the distance existing between them.

Mathematically, the magnitude of attraction between any two objects is determined by the following formula:

$$\frac{\text{mass x mass}}{(\text{distance})^2} = \text{the force of attraction}$$

As the formula indicates, Newtonian Gravitation states that the force of attraction between any two objects is determined by multiplying their individual masses and dividing that figure by the squared distance between them.

Einsteinian Gravitational Theory states, briefly, that a physical object actually warps or bends the space that it exists in, as well as the area of space that surrounds it. That is, an object bends or distorts the space that it occupies, and this warped space causes other nearby physical objects to fall into that warp.

Having briefly explained the basic ideas of Newtonian and Einsteinian Gravitation, I will now explain the principle of the feminine vacuum, a naturally occurring phenomenon that I realized existed some years ago. Simply stated, a feminine vacuum is a vacuum that is created by spatial relationships.

Take two solid objects, for example. They both have a very large mass and density in relationship to the air-filled space that exists between them. In fact, in comparison to the two physical objects, the space between them seems almost void-like. The two objects are actually less drawn toward each other, as explained by Newtonian Gravitation, than they are by the warped space that exists between them as explained by Einsteinian Gravitation. However, when it comes to the mind—since the mind, like water and electricity, always takes the path of least resistance—it is drawn toward or "falls" into the space that exists between those two objects. We know that where the mind goes, the sheath goes, and where the sheath goes, the body goes, and so, in essence, wherever the mind goes, it induces the body to go.

A good example of a naturally occurring feminine vacuum, and one that I am sure that you can identify with, concerns itself with heights. If you have ever stood on a roof, or have been up on top of a tall ladder or on the balcony of a very tall building and, while looking down, felt the uncomfortable sensation of being drawn into the abyss, then you have experienced what I call a naturally occurring feminine vacuum. In fact, the draw of the vacuum may have been so great that it actually frightened you. Why? Because, in some inexplicable way, some way that you could not at the time understand, you felt as if you were compelled to jump or throw yourself into that void. It is an almost suicidal feeling, and one that would make most people extremely anxious, to say the least.

When I first realized that the mind seeks to take the path of least resistance, I realized that a brand-new principle was shown to me, a principle that I knew held tremendous possibility. It was just a question of learning how to apply what I had uncovered and to gallantly explore that new and intriguing avenue of knowledge. The more I looked, the more I saw how common the influence of this principle was in everyone's life. In fact, its effects on all living entities cannot be avoided.

Everyone experiences the effects of the phenomenon of the feminine vacuum each and every day of their lives without consciously being aware of it. Let me give you a very common example of a feminine vacuum situation and see whether or not you can identify with it. Suppose you are walking toward a mall entrance composed of eight doors. As you approach the entrance, a door several doors down from the door before you opens. Your mind is now automatically drawn to the vacuum created by that open door and you find yourself actually walking out of your way to go through it. Understand, because there is a closed door in front of you that is resistive and stops the mind's flowing, and an open door, say, to the right of you that is open and non-resistive, it draws your mind not only to it but literally *through* it. This is an example of a naturally occurring feminine vacuum.

The next time you go to the mall, try to be aware of what you feel as you approach the entrance and this phenomenon occurs. Also, if you like, you can stand outside and watch it happen to other people. As a matter of fact, you can even practice using this principle to control the paths that other people take by standing just inside the mall's doors and, when you see one or more persons approaching a door, simply open your door and see what happens. You will find that you will draw them toward the feminine vacuum that you have just created. If you do this, you will have just controlled their movements! You will have caused them, literally, to go out of their way in order to enter your door. This you will have done, by the way, without physically touching those people. Do you understand? You will have controlled their movements without any sort of physical contact.

When I work with professional athletes, such as pro golfers, for example, I have them stand by the tee and experience the effects of the various feminine vacuums of the fairway. I teach them to allow the changing terrain of the golf course to work for them and not against them. When they understand and experience the draw that the various feminine vacuums have on their minds and bodies, their golf scores are not only greatly improved but their games are transformed into an almost enlightening experience.

I have also taught this principle, as well as other principles, to a number of professional NFL football players and NBA basketball players over the years, bringing about new and rewarding changes in their games.

I truly believe that every athlete, professional or amateur, should be trained in the understanding and use of the Feminine Vacuum principle. When understood, the principle of the Feminine Vacuum will greatly enhance their performances. In fact, it will completely transform their games beyond their current limits.

Of course, the principle of the Feminine Vacuum, as well as many other principles in the art, can be utilized with astonishing success in many areas of human endeavor. For example, it can be applied to military strategy, business, advertising, and even politics. The feminine vacuum can be used, but is not limited to, determining military strategies that would determine the best way to deploy troops in order to trap the enemy by offering the enemy little choice in the direction of their movements. It can also be used to determine the direction of aggression of an enemy prior to that enemy's movement. In business, it can be applied with enormous success in pulling in new clients, keeping old clients, and determining the best time and direction for growth. In advertising, it can be used to draw the mind of the potential customer directly to the information that the advertiser most wants the viewer to be aware of, as well as determining the best way to approach the public based on the nature of what is to be advertised. In politics, it can be utilized quite effectively in leading the minds of voters in directions that are politically beneficial. It can also be used with enormous success in what is euphemistically called *spin control.* There are so many areas and so many ways in which the principles of the art can be used that it would make a full explanation ponderously lengthy.

I have created many interesting and highly effective ways of artificially creating an enormous variety of feminine vacuums and have incorporated a great many of them into the art of Torishimaru Aiki Jutsu with tremendous success, furthering the uniqueness of the system.

61

Q: I am a little confused about the term "feminine." I think I understand, but I am not sure. Is feminine energy the same as M'retz Na'she? Could you explain?

A: I use the term "feminine" in two contexts. First, when I use the term "feminine" relative to a physical or mental action, I am referring to a yielding, recessive movement. That is, a moving away from the point of contact or confrontation. For example, if I were to move my body or weapon away from the opponent, my body or my weapon would then be said to be moving in a feminine way. If, on the other hand, my opponent is moving away from me, he would be said to be "going feminine" or moving in a feminine way.

Now, of course, the mind can also move in a feminine direction. Suppose, for example, that a man was confronting you and threatening you with violence. His posture and speech may both show a great deal of aggression and would seem to support his threat of violence; however, if he really does not want to fight, if he is really harboring a fear of fighting, then regardless of what he is saying or doing, his mind would be referred to as going or moving in a feminine direction.

In the second context, I use the term "feminine" to refer to a very special esoteric form of energy, an energy called M'retz Na'she. The two terms are interchangeable. What makes feminine energy, or M'retz Na'she, so special is that it is the energy that sustains the entire manifest universe. Nothing can exist without some degree of feminine energy to uphold it . . . nothing! It is the feminine energy or M'retz Na'she, in fact, that is responsible even for the formation of, and mystical power in, the energy called Ki or Chi. Feminine energy is the ultimate indivisible archetypal genus of energy. It is the manifestation of the power of the feminine aspect of God in all of existence. It is primal, pervasive, and pristine in all things.

Q: In 1995 you participated in a series of videotaped experiments and demonstrations at a neurologic center in Florida. Could you elaborate?

A: I was asked to participate in a number of experiments in order to establish whether or not some of the more esoteric principles that I teach can actually affect a person to the extent that it would be recordable on EEG and EKG machines. What surprised the clinic's staff most, I suppose, was the fact that I was able to affect the power flowing to the subject's heart. I did this by "injecting" M'retz Na'she into his heart at a distance of approximately ten feet. This appeared on the EKG machine's recorder as tall thin spikes corresponding to a marked increase in the amplitude of the subject's generated heart waves. The frequency of the heartbeat remained the same, but, depending on what I happened to do, there would be a prominent increase or decrease in the amplitude of the power to the heart.

When I utilized Pulsing and No-Hit Principles (which I will explain later), I was able to affect the subject's alpha wave activity. At one point, I was able to suppress his alpha wave activity for as long as fourteen seconds. That is, I stopped his brain activity and took control of him for fourteen seconds. Also, when I applied other principles, such as M'retz Na'she withdrawal principles, where I would withdraw M'retz Na'she from the subject, there would be a prominent contraction of the subject's muscles to the point that the specific target muscles would actually contract and lock. There were a number of other positive results, but they are to be spoken of another time. The whole experiment was documented on videotape and will be made public at some future date.

63

Based on the results of these experiments, the chief of neurology at the clinic indicated that he now has to rethink his view of the physical world. He now understands things exist that he once thought impossible.

Q: **What is the technique of No-Hit and what are its effects?**

A: No-Hit is a classic technique of Torishimaru Aiki Jutsu. When employed properly, it causes the attacker's physical body to respond as if it were being struck, even though no physical contact of any kind is actually being made. In other words, when the No-Hit technique is applied, the attacker's body will bend, twist, falter, writhe, jerk, and generally respond as if he was actually being worked over. In fact, when a series of No-Hits is properly applied, one can actually work a man to the ground without the need to resort to any sort of physical contact.

To execute the No-Hit technique, we must strike the opponent's shield with short bursts or pulses of M'retz Na'she (feminine energy) that are projected from the palms of our hands while we are, simultaneously, executing short non-contact striking movements.

When we strike the opponent's shield with compact pulses of M'retz Na'she, his shield responds by issuing attack information to the higher mind, which sets off the appropriate higher mind alarms. This sends his higher mind into a defense mode, the particulars of which his higher mind automatically communicates to his lower mind. This attack information immediately sends his lower mind into a state of confusion. Why? Because it does not make sense to his lower mind. The information concerning the attack does not correlate with the data that his lower mind is receiving from his lower mind senses. The higher mind is telling him that he is being struck, that contact is being made, but his lower mind is receiving information that tells him no such contact is occurring. That is, his eyes see our short striking movements but they are understood by his lower mind to be of no consequence since the distance between us is so great. The reception of such paradoxical attack information creates a dialogue or argument between his higher and lower minds as to what is actually occurring. His higher mind says, "We are being struck" and his lower mind says, "No, we're not." The longer the No-Hit technique is applied, the longer this fruitless argument continues. This causes him to get stuck in a defense mode that he cannot extricate himself from. I call this defense mode situation a defensive loop.

While an attacker is stuck in a defensive loop, he can neither offend against us nor mount an adequate defense. The defense that does occur is an awkward defense that is higher-mind based. That is, he finds himself yielding to the information coming to him from his higher mind concerning the fact that he is actually being struck and responds accordingly by attempting to pull the particular struck target off the line of attack. If we were to No-Hit his stomach area, for example, he would jerk his stomach area back defensively. If we apply No-Hit to his face area, he would pull that back. When the No-Hit technique is applied in specific combinations, it can totally incapacitate an attacker and even drive him to the ground. Of course, we need only apply the technique long enough to allow us to gain the advantage and launch our own offensive— composed, naturally, of real strikes.

To the casual observer not seeing physical contact, the subject would appear to be acting. Of course, the person on the receiving end has a different reality of the No-Hit technique. To him, everything that is occurring is real and he reacts accordingly.

When applying the No-Hit technique, great care must be taken in the execution of your movements not to make any sort of physical contact with the subject. If physical contact inadvertently occurs, his higher mind and lower mind would then come to an agreement as to what was actually occurring. With the argument ended, the defensive loop that we created in him would immediately be broken and he would be free to either offend or mount a more suitable defense. Of course, returning control of his body back to him would not be in our best interest.

Novices in Torishimaru Aiki Jutsu must not only understand the No-Hit principles and techniques but must be able to apply them smoothly and proficiently. In the student or black belt ranks, the No-Hit techniques become a great deal more subtle and sophisticated.

Q: What is "pulsing" and how does it affect the attacker?

A: "Pulsing" is a subtle but highly effective variation of the No-Hit principle. Employing the Pulsing principle, we can bring about several interesting control responses in our opponent. We can, for example, stop his attack altogether or, if we choose, merely slow down the speed of his attack. We can also utilize the pulsing principle to either stop or slow up the motion of his individual offensive weapons. We can, if we like, stop his major motion of attack, that is, the motion of his body, without affecting the motion of his strike in any way. Or, if we choose to, we can reverse it and prevent his strike from coming out without effecting his major motion. There are numerous combinations that can be created; the list is quite extensive.

Suppose that you want to use the Pulsing principle against a man who is in the process of attacking you with a haymaker or roundhouse punch. (Note: The haymaker or roundhouse punch is the most common punching attack in the street.) In order to effectively employ the Pulsing principle, one must first understand the process that an attacker goes through in order to deliver a haymaker. You must know, for example, that the haymaker is actually composed of three parts. First, there is intent or the thought of the attack, that is, the mental process that takes place within the attacker prior to the attack that often involves not only intent to strike but a conscious decision as to which weapon to throw, where to throw it, and how to throw it. Secondly, in the actual execution of the strike, there is a feminine movement or withdrawal of the arm away from the intended target and toward the attacker's rear. Finally, there is the forward motion or masculine movement of the arm toward the target. All three events must take place and cannot be avoided by the attacker in the execution of a roundhouse punch.

Whenever there is attack, there is intent. That is, an attack is a premeditative act that, regardless of the particulars of the psychological stimuli, has as its goal some sort of physical dominance. That intention also requires the aggressor to choose a particular weapon and embrace a specific target. Even if the aggressive act seems spontaneous, intent and its associative elements still exist.

In all cases of physical aggression, the attacker's lower mind will always lead the attack. That is, the very first movement to occur is that of the attacker's mind moving forward toward the chosen target. This is immediately followed by the movement of his shield toward the target, and then, finally, by his body or weapon.

In our example, as the attacker begins the physical movement of the roundhouse punch, his arm will withdraw toward his rear much like an archer drawing back a bow. We say when his arm is executing such a wind-up movement that it is "going feminine" or moving in a negative or feminine direction. Only when his wind-up motion is completed will he then begin to move his arm forward. As his arm begins to move forward, it will do so with what we call an extremely weak masculine motion. That is, it will have very little speed or strength as it begins its journey toward the target. It will gradually pick up more speed and strength as it travels, culminating in maximum speed and strength just prior to contact.

A novice pulse may be defined as a quick, but not too quick, striking motion executed with the palm of the open hand from which a bundle of M'retz Na'she is projected. If a defender were to strike the shield surrounding the attacker's fist with a strong pulse of M'retz Na'she during the brief period when the roundhouse punch is in the state of weak masculine motion (i.e., at the beginning of the strike's forward motion), the attacker's fist would be effectively stopped. Since the attacker's fist is moving with a weak masculine motion, it will not be able to overcome the power of a strong masculine pulse. The larger the bundle of M'retz Na'she one is able to project to the shield surrounding the attacker's fist, the more dynamic the results will be.

But why does Pulsing work? It works predominantly because of two factors. One, because all of an attacker's offensive actions are directed by his mind, and the mind, like water or electricity, will always take the path of least resistance. By Pulsing, the path that his weapon is about to take is effectively blocked. This causes his lower mind to retract the command to strike and a process of reassessment begins. Two, striking the attacker's shield with a pulse of M'retz Na'she triggers a defensive response in the higher mind, which subsequently issues a defense order and overrides any attack orders issued by the lower mind.

Of course, timing is of prime importance and one must remember to apply the pulse to the attacker's strike when his strike is at a weak masculine point. That is, the pulse must be applied at the moment that his strike turns or changes from a withdrawal movement to a weak masculine forward movement. The rule of thumb is: The weaker the opponent's masculine movement is, the easier it is to stop.

Naturally, as one continues to evolve in the art of Torishimaru Aiki Jutsu, application of the Pulsing principle becomes more subtle and more sophisticated and one reaches the point where it can be executed quite easily prior to a physical movement. A skilled practitioner of the art can, in fact, stop his opponent's attack at the time of the opponent's first thought of attack.

Variations of the Pulsing principle not only allow us to stop the strike completely but also allow us to permit the strike while simultaneously controlling its speed, even to the point where the strike is visually moving in slow motion.

Q: **How is it possible to stop an attack at the moment the attacker thinks of attacking? Can it really be done?**

A: Of course it can be done. In Torishimaru Aiki Jutsu it's considered a necessary skill, especially in the higher ranks. To do it, one must not only develop sensitivity in certain areas but must become intimately acquainted with the mechanics and principles involved in the process. To begin with, one must quiet the lower, ordinary mind and allow the higher, all-knowing mind to come forward. Once this is accomplished, it dramatically increases one's sensitivity to one's own shield. This increased sensitivity then allows one to experience the subtle disturbances that assail it, including but not limited to those created by the aggressive thoughts of others. You must realize that thoughts generate feminine energy and that those thoughts that have an external object as its subject project a stream of feminine energy to that object. If, for example, you were to think about a particular object like a chair in your room, your thought would project feminine energy toward that chair and augment the amount of feminine energy of its shield. Gentle non-aggressive thoughts produce a gentle steady stream of feminine energy, while violent, aggressive thoughts are often choppy and produce pulses of feminine energy. When the thought of attack first arises in the mind of the attacker, a pulse of feminine energy is projected outwardly from his person and strikes the shield of his intended victim. If one

69

has developed the necessary sensitivity to one's own shield then, when that pulse of feminine energy strikes it, one is automatically aware of the assailant's intention. At this point, a simple pulsing movement directed toward him would destroy his attack. Now, since the assailant's forward physical motion wouldn't have begun yet, the pulsing movement employed could be quite subtle, often nothing more than a gentle press with the hand. When the feminine energy that you project through the pulsing technique strikes the attacker's shield, he is sent into a defensive mode, effectively preventing his thoughts of offense from maturing into the actual physical action of attack.

Q: **You've demonstrated your ability to stop an attack without even moving. How is that done?**

A: There are a number of ways to bring this about and a great number of situations in which it can be quite effective. It can be applied, for example, to the situation that I just explained concerning the stopping of an attack with the opponent's thought of attack. But what you just said about me not moving isn't exactly true. Granted, I may not be moving physically, but I am still moving. It is my mind— specifically, my higher mind—that is moving. Remember, as I just told you, that feminine energy is directed by the mind to the object of a thought. All I do in this particular situation is to generate a powerful thought of attack and have the attacker serve as the object of that thought. The quieter my lower mind is, the more powerful becomes the thought that I can generate through the auspices of my higher mind. When the feminine energy generated by that great thought strikes the attacker's shield, he immediately enters a defensive mode and his attack is effectively stopped. It's really very simple. Of course, there are many other methods of controlling an attacker without moving, but they are quite intricate and would take too long to explain at present.

70

Q: There is a technique I have seen demonstrated in your
   school called "pinning." I found it very interesting because I
   saw a man seemingly welded to the floor and unable to
   move. What exactly is pinning and how does it work?

A: Pinning is a control technique based on the premise that
   a man cannot move in more than one direction at any
   given time. That is, if he is moving forward, he cannot
   simultaneously be moving backward or, if moving left,
   he cannot be moving to the right, et cetera. Bearing this
   understanding in mind, it should be clear that when one
   employs a technique that will have the attacker moving
   downward, all other motions are automatically negated.

   > **Try this:** The next time that you spar and the signal
   > to begin is given, instead of moving forward or
   > backward, quickly drop your body into a deep low
   > stance. When you do this, you will be creating a
   > feminine vacuum that will draw your opponent's
   > mind into it. You will notice that your opponent will,
   > because of that feminine vacuum, simultaneously
   > lower his stance. You now have his mind and body
   > moving downward. The downward movement of his
   > body now precludes the possibility of him moving in
   > any other direction and so, in essence, you are
   > pinning him to that spot. The rule is: The deeper you
   > drop, the deeper he will drop.
   > The problem now, of course, is that if you were to
   > rise, which you would have to do in order to move
   > forward, you would release him and he would be free
   > to move in the direction of his choice. To prevent his
   > release when you rise, you must keep his mind
   > moving downward. To do this, as your body rises
   > slightly to free you for your forward movement, take
   > your lead hand and lower it, pointing to the ground
   > just in front of him. This movement will take his
   > mind and continue leading it downward.

71

The lowering of your hand and pointing of your finger will now allow you to move forward without your opponent being able to move his body. Since you have caused his stance to lower, his descending body will, effectively, pin both his legs to the floor and he will not be able to offer a kicking defense as you close in for the "kill." It is important, however, that after you drop your stance, while you are lowering your lead hand to point to the ground, that you move your body forward in a downward arc. If you don't, you will release him.

This, of course, is a very basic novice pinning technique but, when mastered, it is undoubtedly devastating. In fact, once you understand the elements of pinning and effectively employ them, they will end the match in only seconds.

Understand that making the opponent's mind move downward causes his sheath to move downward, which, in turn, causes his body to move downward. The downward movement of his body causes him to pin to that spot and any aggressive forward motion that he may have had, or even intended, will be effectively neutralized. This principle is applicable to one or more attackers.

Q: There are techniques and principles in your art that can actually reduce an opponent's physical strength. Could you explain just one?

A: Yes, we have many techniques and principles that concern themselves with the reduction or, at times, depending on the requirement, even the increase in the magnitude of an attacker's physical strength. These techniques and principles range from very basic physical techniques to some extremely sophisticated and quite subtle procedures. I will describe a typical novice technique and the principle lying behind it.

Suppose that an attacker places you in a straight wrist grab, where, standing in front of you, he secures your left wrist with his right hand. The very first thing to understand is that whenever you are grabbed by a person, it is merely that person's way of controlling you in order to limit your physical movements. Second, that he will utilize only enough strength in order to bring that about, no more, no less. Bearing these two understandings in mind, the very first thing you must do when the attacker grabs your wrist is to yield to him; that is, as soon as you are grabbed, you want to immediately relax not only your arm but your entire body as well. When you relax your arm and body, the attacker will automatically reduce the strength he is using in his grab. Remember, a man will only use the minimum amount of strength required in order to exercise physical control over you.

Now, on the other hand, if you resist or struggle against the grab, you will feel the magnitude of strength in his grip increase. Your increased resistance will warn him that he may lose control over your wrist, and so he will automatically increase his strength in an attempt to nullify or compensate for your sudden increase in strength.

Try this: Have one of your friends grab your wrist. Then, offer resistance to his grab by trying to move your arm. Immediately you will feel your friend's grip tighten. The stronger your resistance becomes, the stronger his grip will become. By offering resistance to his grab, your friend will find himself needing to use more strength in order to maintain his control over your wrist. His increase in strength, of course, will not be his idea, it will be yours. By applying this technique, you will have a basic method of increasing the physical strength employed by an attacker, which often proves necessary in the execution of certain

73

self-defense techniques, such as breath projections, where we need the attacker to maintain his grip.

Try this: Let your friend grab you again, but this time, suddenly relax your hand, arm, and body. Let your arm go as limp as you can make it. What you will experience, as you suddenly relax your arm, is a corresponding decrease in the strength of your friend's grip. Here, you are reducing his strength. Since his strength is suddenly diminished, you would find it very easy to apply an escape technique at this point and free yourself.

Q: **During a demonstration, you had me grab your wrist. You tapped on my arm and I became so weak that I couldn't prevent you from escaping. It was amazing. Could you explain what you did and how it works?**

A: The principle of Tapping is really a very basic strength reduction principle and although it is taught as a novice principle, it has such a universal relevance to good self-defense that its employment is both a valid and necessary component of good technique executed at any rank. Of course, as a student ascends the ranks, the principle becomes more and more subtle, until it reaches the point where it becomes totally imperceptible to the attacker. This principle can be applied in many different ways and in many different situations, not just in defending against grabbing attacks. Still, for simplicity's sake, I will use the grab that you placed on me during that demonstration as the basis of my explanation.

What happened was this: When you grabbed my wrist, you secured it with the intention of controlling the movement of my arm. That is, by securing my wrist, you had the intention of restricting my physical movements.

This intention of control on your part was an overt act of volition. This act of volition means, naturally, that your lower mind is directly involved in the procedure. Why? Because every act of volition, every premeditated action, requires thought in order to execute it. What produced the great strength that you applied in your grip was directly related to the degree of concentration that your lower mind placed on that sight. This means that there was a direct path created between your lower mind and your hand. This path is called the mind path. In other words, there was a clear, unobstructed circuit set up between your lower mind and the action of grabbing. When I gently tapped your upper forearm, I created a signal that interfered with and effectively blocked your lower mind's ability to maintain that mind path. You could say that I instigated the creation of a new mind path, a shorter mind path, one that stopped your lower mind at the point of the tapping and prevented it from traveling the rest of the distance to your hand. And since your original strength was the product of a volitional and conscious act, your mind had been easily diverted from its inceptive intention, and your grip weakened to the point where you made it very easy for me to escape.

Understand, every movement that a person makes, whether they are grabbing your wrist, throwing a punch, or just reaching for a salt shaker, can only be accomplished when the mind orders the body to do it. Without that order, no volitional physical movement can be executed. The introduction of any tactile stimuli at any point between the target and the mind will weaken an attacker's intended action. That tactile stimuli could be a gentle tapping, a sound, a gentle puff of air across his face, a wink, almost anything, but that anything must be subtle and non-threatening. If I had yelled, for example, when you had my wrist grabbed, your grip would have tightened immediately because the noise would have startled you and would have

75

sent you into a defensive mode. And since you already had my wrist secured, you would have tightened your grab in order to exercise more control over me. This, of course, would have defeated my intention to weaken you.

There are many variations of this principle and many varied and interesting self-defense applications, all resulting in a weakening of an attacker's strength.

> **Try this:** Have a friend grab your right wrist with his left hand or, if your prefer, have him grab your left wrist with his right hand. This is what we call a straight wrist grab. To assure that you are suitably impressed with what you are about to do, have him use as much strength in his grab as possible. Then do the following:

>   1. When you are ready to act, slowly move your free hand in a non-threatening way and place it lightly on the upper portion of his forearm.
>   2. As you quietly speak to him, gently begin a very light tapping of your fingers on his arm.
>   3. While you are tapping his forearm, you will feel his grip begin to loosen. Keeping your elbow close to your hip, open your gripped hand wide and, bending your arm, bring your thumb toward your ear. You will find yourself free of his grab.

Q: I have seen you blindfolded and brought into a large room that had several people placed at random throughout it. You raised your hand and, amazingly, were able to point out the location of each individual in the room. You called it "scanning." How is this done?

A: Briefly, the rudiments of the Scanning principles are introduced in the latter part of novice training. In the black belt ranks, it matures into something rather interesting.

To comprehend the Scanning principles, you must first understand and accept the fact that everything, whether animate or inanimate, generates an energy field within which it is encased, not too dissimilar from the electric field that surrounds a wire through which an electric current is passed. This energy field is called the shield or magen. Those knowing individuals outside of our discipline refer to it as the aura. Simply stated, the principles and techniques of Scanning, when properly applied, can readily detect those magen. The ability to do so allows us the capacity to perform tasks that the average person would consider impossible.

A good rule of thumb concerning the magen is this: The more animate the subject is, the stronger and more palpable its magen. In other words, humans have stronger magen than animals; animals, in turn, have stronger magen than plants; and plants have stronger magen than those found in the mineral world.

Try this: Stand in a room with your eyes closed, and then have someone stand somewhere in front of you (the distance doesn't matter). Exhale through your nose and hold your breath. Then, with your left hand raised, palm facing outward, slowly "sweep" your palm in front of you from the left to the right, and then from the right to the left, as if your palm were a sort of radar detection device (which it is, by the way). You may now breathe normally.

What you should experience on your palm as your hand begins to cross the location where the person is standing is the sensation of heat. As your palm sweeps past him, it will become cool again.

As you scan and the sensation of heat on your palm turns cool, you know that you have passed him. Slowly bring your palm back and try to focus or zero in on the location of the heat by making your sweeping movements smaller and smaller until you feel the area of maximum heat. You'll find it bordered by two areas of coolness. When you are sure that you have found the other person, point at him with the index finger of the sweeping hand and then open your eyes. If you did it correctly, you should be pointing directly at the person. If you are, then you just successfully employed, in a very basic way, the principle of Scanning.

In Scanning, the quieter your lower mind is, the greater the sensation of heat you will feel in your palm when you scan. Therefore, a good regimen of meditation should be implemented in order to maintain the necessary quiescence of mind that would result in good Scanning abilities.

The use of the Scanning principle can also be used to locate people and objects even when separated by a wall. Certainly, this would be a useful technique for a police officer, for instance, who chases a suspect into a building and wants to locate the suspect before entering the building after him. All that officer would have to do is to stand outside of the building and scan. This would not only pinpoint the suspect's location but indicate the number and location of anyone else who may be in the building. Scanning can also be used to check your home at night before you enter it, in order to locate an intruder, or it can be used to scan your car as you approach it. The possible uses of this particular technique are, of course, innumerable and are limited only by your imagination.

Try this: Have someone position themselves somewhere in the next room. Then, facing the wall to that room, begin to scan for him as described above. The area of heat, bordered by coolness, will give you his exact location. Once you are sure, go into the room and you will find that you were correct.

Try this: Stand outside of your home and scan the entire front of your house. Employing the Scanning technique, you will be able to not only count the number of people there, but you should be able to pinpoint the exact locations of those people, as well.

This principle and other advanced principles of Scanning can, of course, be used in numerous other ways. It can, for example, be used to develop great proficiency in the use of one's psychic powers.

Try this: Take an ordinary deck of playing cards and remove an ace and five other cards. Then, shuffle the six cards and lay them in a line, side by side, face down in front of you on the floor or table. Now, before you proceed, you first must clear the lower mind. That is, you must quiet your lower mind by stopping your random thoughts. In order to do this, exhale as much air as you can from your lungs, and then hold your breath for a few seconds. You will notice that all your thoughts will stop.

Your first few inhalations and exhalations thereafter should be slow, steady, and controlled. Then, take normal inhalations followed by slow, protracted exhalations. In other words, your exhalation in this case should be longer than your normal inhalation.

A second method of clearing your lower mind can be accomplished by closing your eyes and saying "clear" mentally to yourself. It must be said firmly. It is best for a beginner to employ both techniques. That is, first with the controlled stopping breath, followed by the command "clear." With experience, the command "clear" should be sufficient to stop your thoughts.

From this point, one must have a clear understanding or vision of the object of the search, which in this particular case is the ace. So, after you have quieted your lower mind, you will identify the object of your search by firmly saying or thinking "ace." Now, without another thought, you will take your hand, palm facing downward, and pass it slowly over the line of cards. If your lower mind is quiet enough, you will experience both heat and a slight pressure as your hand passes over the ace. The heat that you are feeling is actually generated by your own higher mind, which already knows the location of the ace. Remember, the higher mind knows all things.

What takes place is this: When your higher mind reaches out for and identifies the ace, a small amount of M'retz Na'she or feminine energy is spontaneously transferred to that card. Your hand, as it passes over the ace, should be able to sense the heat generated by that excess of M'retz Na'she. When the scan is executed properly, the difference in M'retz Na'she contained within the magen of the ace becomes very noticeable, and it will stand out from the rest of the cards.

As you become more and more proficient with the technique, you can increase the number of cards that you are using until you are able to spread all of the cards out face down on a table and locate any card in the deck.

This is an example of clairvoyance in relationship to the principle of Scanning. It has, of course, many, many uses. It can, for example, be used to locate lost or hidden objects.

Try this: Have someone hide an object somewhere in the room. For the sake of this explanation, we will say it is a coin that is hidden. The first thing that you must do is to position yourself so that, when you scan, your scanning can cover the entire room. Secondly, you must clear your mind using the stopping breath technique. Then, you must clearly identify the object of your search, which in this example is the coin. You must think "coin"! The word "coin" need only be said once mentally. You will then scan the room with the palm of your open hand. As your scanning hand nears the location of the coin, you will experience on your palm the heat coming from the magen of the coin. There will, of course, be a cooling sensation on your palm as your hand passes the location of the coin. At this point, all you would have to do is to zero in on the coin's location. Then, simply walk over and retrieve it.

This same technique can also be applied to locating lost or missing objects. If you cannot find your car keys, for instance, all you would have to do is scan for them. Naturally, in this case, the trigger word would have to be "keys."

Try this: To apply the scanning principle to the phenomenon of telepathy, ask a friend to withdraw ten cards from a standard deck of playing cards. Then, ask him to look at the faces of the cards and mentally select one of them. Once done, have him shuffle the cards and lay all ten cards face down on the floor or table. Tell him to continue to concentrate on the card that he picked, making sure he understands that he is to have a clear picture of the chosen card in his mind.

81

You will then execute the stop breath technique and/or give the "clear" command to quiet your lower mind. When your lower mind is clear, begin scanning the cards until you locate the card generating heat. This card, of course, will be the card that your friend has chosen and is concentrating on.

Why did the card of his choice generate heat? It did so because, through the natural machinations of his higher mind, a psychic gate was created with that card. Through that gate a small amount of his M'retz Na'she passed and was transferred to the magen of the chosen card. The excess of M'retz Na'she contained in the magen of the card is felt in the form of heat by your hand as you scan. The other cards will, naturally, be cool by comparison and so the subject card is easy to identify.

Q: Is it possible to use the scanning principle to locate new oil and mineral deposits? How about locating things like new archeological finds, such as ancient Egyptian tombs, sunken ships, or buried treasure? Can it be done?

A: Yes, certainly. All of the items that you have asked about could be found utilizing the Scanning techniques and principles. There is really nothing difficult about the process once you have quieted your lower mind enough to give your higher mind free reign. Remember, the higher mind has access to information beyond the reach of the lower mind.

Years ago, for example, merely out of curiosity, a student asked me if there were diamonds to be found within the continental United States. I told him to bring me a map of the United States and I would tell him. He did. After scanning the map, I told him that diamonds could be found in the following states: Washington, California, New Mexico, and Arkansas.

Try this: Suppose that you wanted to locate new silver deposits in the continental United States (or anywhere in the world for that matter). You will need, of course, a map of the area that you are searching, beginning with a large map of the United States. Spread the map out on the floor or table in front of you. You must then quiet your lower mind, clearing it of thought. Then you must have a clear image of the object of your search, which in this case are new silver deposits. This can be done by thinking "silver mines." You will then empty your lungs of air and, holding your breath, take the palm of your left open hand and scan the map. As you come to the area on the map where the new silver deposits are located, you will experience heat generated by that area. As your hand moves away from that area, your palm will cool. It is really that easy but you are not done. A large map of the United States will tell you in what state the silver deposits can be found, but you still need to know the exact location. So now you have to take a map of that state and repeat the procedure. This, of course, will now tell you which county. Now you spread out a county map and repeat the procedure again, locating the specific location of the silver deposits. Of course, in each case, the larger the map the better because larger maps are much easier to scan. This technique can also be used to locate missing people, living or deceased, and even lost or missing pets.

If you are looking to locate an ancient Egyptian tomb, then it would be wise to start with a large map detailing Egypt in the area of the Valley of the Kings. It simply would not make sense to begin your scanning in the Arctic Circle. In fact, a great deal of time could be saved, regardless of what you are searching for, if you could eliminate areas where that object would simply not exist. The procedure to follow, naturally, is the same as what you would employ if you were looking for silver deposits.

Remember, even though the Scanning techniques and principles I am showing you are novice techniques, they are still extremely effective. Once mastered, they are intensely accurate but to master them you must take the time to practice with them.

Q: **Could you please explain the principles of Target Replacement?**

A: The principles of Target Replacement are of paramount importance in circumstances where you not only want to control the disposition of the attacker's weapon (hand strike, kick, et cetera), but of the placement of his body, as well. Remember, where the mind goes the magen goes and where the magen goes the body goes. Whenever an attacker seeks to strike you, it must be understood that it is his mind that moves first. That is, his mind reaches out to select a target—your jaw, stomach, nose, et cetera. His strike is an act of premeditation, an act of overt volition. No matter how little apparent thought he gives his aggressive act, there is still thought, and it is still his mind that moves toward you first. This, as you will see, is an indispensable element in the techniques involving Target Replacement.

Now, suppose that you are face-to-face with someone who means to strike you. In order for him to actually effect that strike, several things must take place, and each of those things must occur in a very definite sequence: First, he must move his mind toward you in order to choose a viable target, which, for the sake of this example, we will designate as your nose. In a way, you can think of it as the radar of his mind locking onto the target—his mind is flowing to the target like a small invisible river.

85

Target Replacement: Facing off (1)

Target Replacement: Straight punch thrown (2)

87

Target Replacement: Sweep hand up and across your body
in an arc crossing in front of your face (3)

Target Replacement: Turning your body to the right, lead strike out and away (4)

Secondly, he must actually issue the order to attack, his weapon (fist) will not and, in fact, cannot move without it. Then, when his weapon first begins to move, it will do so in a priming or negative way. That is, he will first have to withdraw his arm. This act of winding up or withdrawal is termed "moving feminine" or a "feminine prime." As a result of the priming process, his weapon reaches a point where the motion of his arm ceases to move in a feminine direction and is ready to move in a masculine way toward the target. It begins its journey forward as a weak masculine movement, gradually building in speed and strength as it approaches the target. It is this point, during the weak masculine movement of his strike, that lends itself most readily to control. I will explain.

The attacker is throwing a punch to our face with his right hand. While the motion of his strike is at a weak masculine movement, we must do several things and all of those things must be precisely coordinated. First, facing the attacker squarely, we must sweep our hand, palm facing him, in a smooth arc upward from our groin area, past our midsection, past our face, and then outward, away from our face, toward our right side. When we begin to make this sweeping movement, we must simultaneously execute a turning movement with our body. In this case, we will make a turning movement to our right. This turning movement must culminate in a leaning posture toward the right side. This turning-leaning motion will deliver data to the attacker's mind indicating that we are about to take a step to their right. Of course, we are not actually going to take a step to the right, we are simply going through the motions of doing so. Now, once his strike turns fully masculine (i.e., moving toward you at attack speed), it is committed to the target and he will not be able to abort it. He can, however, make certain adjustments that will allow us the control that we are looking for.

Target Replacement: Lead punch (5)

When the visual data that we are feeding him concerning our intention to move to the right reaches his lower mind, he will readjust and look to compensate for that movement so that his strike will still make contact with his intended target. It is very similar to an anti-aircraft gunner firing in front of the plane he is shooting at so that, by the time his shell ascends to that altitude, the target or plane will be where the shell is. This is called "leading the target."

Now, our smoothly sweeping right hand and arm movement must cross our entire body. This assures you that we are sweeping across all possible targets on your body. What occurs when we do this is that, as our hand sweeps in front of his intended target, which in this case is our nose, his lower mind now locks onto our hand. And since our hand is now moving toward our right side, up and away from our body, it will naturally take his mind with it. Since his mind is actually what is both empowering and directing his weapon, as we move his now-captured mind out and away from us, his strike will not have any other choice but to follow this new target, our hand. In other words, our nose will no longer be the target of his strike. It was subtly replaced by our hand. The effect of this combination of movement will place his hand strike outward and away from us, thus missing us completely.

The combination of the turning movement and hand sweep is just one example of a Target Replacement technique. To master this particular genre of technique naturally requires a great deal of practice. Every movement must be executed smoothly and confidently, and everything must be properly timed and coordinated. Move too early and you will fail; move too late and the consequences will not be good. When Target Replacement is mastered, total control over the placement not only of an attacker's weapons but of his body will be made readily available to you. In fact, you will be able to move both his strike and his body in almost any direction you choose—upward, downward, to the left, to the right—any direction.

The principles of Target Replacement are really quite intricate, and they are capable of producing marvelously interesting control results. In fact, when executed correctly, Target Replacement techniques can even allow us the ability to drive the attacker to the ground without physically touching him.

Q: **In Torishimaru Aiki Jutsu, you deal with what you call Frequency Control principles. Could you speak about them?**

A: Briefly, you must understand that everything in the universe is vibrating at a particular frequency, a frequency natural to its particular state and composition. There are no exceptions! From the most basic and subtle constituents of the atom to the largest and most complex structures extant in physical existence, all are vibrating. Unfortunately, it would be too ponderous a task to explain in detail how natural vibrations in each instance produce associative effects on everything around them. It would be infinities affecting infinities and would require volumes upon volumes of explanation. So, for the sake of this discussion, I must necessarily limit my explanation and address only what I call a person's natural operating frequency.

To begin with, you must understand that every person's lower mind has a natural operating frequency, that is, a frequency or magnitude of vibration that is standard and natural for their particular unimpressioned, unsullied, unaffected state of mind. When a person is operating at his particular natural operating frequency, everything appears to be normal, nothing seems out of place or time, nothing appears distorted or convoluted. But when the operating frequency of his lower mind is raised, then everything changes dramatically. Objects appear not only to distort but, depending on how far above his natural operating frequency he is, objects can, and often do, actually disappear to him. Why? Because, when a person's lower mind's natural operating frequency is raised, his lower mind is now moving or operating above what is natural for it. When this occurs, an extraordinary amount of sensory input begins to bombard the lower mind so rapidly that the lower mind cannot process it quickly enough to keep up with it. What results is a sensory input overload, which culminates in what you might think of as a kind of lower mind sensory clog. What this means is that the normal visual, auditory, tactile, and other sensory information that ordinarily gets through to the lower mind when it is in a natural operating frequency state is not getting through to the lower mind while it is operating in a raised frequency state. In this altered state, the sensory input ordinarily offered to the lower mind by the body's senses are either palsied or stopped completely, and this results in time-mind distortions, intermittent or non-existent thoughts, and even physical paralysis.

A person's natural operating frequency is often raised in a very natural way during periods of stress. This, of course, is natural, and everyone has experienced it. There may be a slightly heightened bombardment of sensory input, but it is short-lived and readily handled. However, when a person's natural operating frequency is raised to a dangerous level because of stress, suddenly his lower mind becomes so cluttered with sensory input that he cannot think, or he cannot see, or he cannot hear, or he finds it impossible to stop the voices in his head, et cetera.

Sometimes a person's lower mind creates and perpetuates what I call a "stress loop." This is a stress cycle that, in a sense, turns in on itself like the hollow handle of a Boolean bottle and maintains a constant, unending, self-perpetuating source of stress that a person cannot extricate himself from.

93

When this occurs, if not addressed, it will result, undoubtedly, in the need for psychiatric hospitalization.

Stress loops and associated sensory bombardments are often experienced by professional athletes and are responsible, in large part, for their slumps and inability to perform up to standards. When this happens to public speakers or actors, the effect is called stage fright.

Let me take this just a little further and apply it to a self-defense situation. Should a person's natural operating frequency be raised high enough, anything moving at a lower frequency would literally become invisible to him. That is correct, invisible, and naturally, a person who cannot see an attack coming at him will find it impossible to mount a defense. This, of course, would then allow a person employing the Frequency Control principles to effectively be able to traverse a particular distance without being detected by the subject. The result would be quite predictable.

Whatever the mean operating frequency of a person happens to be at any one particular time determines what is natural for him at that time. In other words, when a person's frequency is raised, whatever is occurring or moving at that same frequency becomes natural for him and not much of a problem. When a person's natural operating frequency is raised, he will be able to respond very well to rapidly moving strikes and objects coming at him. Why? Because fast-moving objects would then seem to be very normal to him due to his raised frequency. In fact, it is now that normal and slow-moving objects would appear to be distorted, odd, or yes, even invisible to him and he would have extraordinary difficulty in dealing with them.

94

You must remember that in order to accomplish sensory distortions or invisibility when you are dealing with an opponent whose natural operating frequency is raised high enough, all your movements must be executed very slowly. That is, you must move much more slowly and at a much lower frequency than that of the subject. Doing this will have you, in a sense, moving under his lower mind's radar.

Try this: Have someone stand in front of you holding a rubber knife. You will stand facing him with your arms at your side. Instruct that person that, should you move in any way, he is to "stab" you in your stomach with the rubber knife. What I want you to do is to move your hands once very quickly to your shoulder level. Naturally, he will stab you, but that's all right, this is just a demonstration. You will then reset, bringing your arms back to your side. Now, repeat the upward movement several times in rapid succession. (The rapid movements of your hands and arms will have the effect of artificially raising his natural operating frequency.) Then, when your hands are at your side, you are ready. Instead of quickly bringing your hands to shoulder height, slowly and smoothly reach out with one of your hands and lightly secure the hand that he is holding the rubber knife with. Not only will he not be able to respond to your movement but, if you have executed it correctly, he should not even be aware of what just took place. Obviously, we do not do this exercise when we are facing a real knife in a genuine self-defense situation. This is simply an exercise to demonstrate how you can artificially raise an opponent's frequency and distort his reality.

I have spent many years developing techniques that will artificially raise an attacker's natural operating frequency to extraordinary levels. These techniques range from very gross, outwardly large movements to movements of such extreme subtlety and sophistication that they are virtually undetectable and, for all intents and purposes, are invisible.

The application of the subtler methods of raising a person's frequency will allow us to increase his natural operating frequency without him even being the least bit aware of it. Remember, if you raise his natural operating frequency enough, you will, in fact, become invisible to him. Imagine the implications of these particular principles not only in the martial arts, but in professional sports: in baseball, basketball, or football, or any competitive sport for that matter. What would it mean to the military?

Q: **Is it possible to actually be able to take the thought of attack away from a person?**

A: Certainly! We do it quite often in Torishimaru Aiki Jutsu. To give you a sense of how this is done, I must first take the time to explain to you, briefly, the mechanics involved in the thinking process.

You must understand that the brain is an intricate part of the lower mind system. It functions as a sort of biological computer that receives its data not only in the form of sensory information generated by the various sense faculties of the body, such as the eyes, ears, nose, et cetera, but receives previously recorded information from the lower mind tape itself. It then takes that data and processes it in a very personal way. Why? Because it is receiving feedback from the lower mind tape and taking whatever sensory information is coming into it, and making various comparisons with personal past events recorded there. As a result, it produces a biased and often muddled output. That new output is also, paradoxically, recorded on the lower mind tape.

Now, in order to produce a conscious thought, the brain requires a certain amount of M'retz Na'she. When the energy needed to give rise to a thought is missing, the thought remains either nonexistent or, at best, vague and

96

unintelligible. The brain must also have the energy necessary to process any incoming sensory data. Without the minimum amount of M'retz Na'she, the brain cannot process that sensory intelligence and, for all intents and purposes, does not exist to it. Conversely, when fully empowered, thoughts are crisp and intelligible and sensory input is received and processed quickly and easily. So again, when the M'retz Na'she powering the brain is low, thinking becomes not only difficult but, at times, nonexistent.

Think back to the times in your life when you were very tired, really exhausted. Were you able to think? If you were, what were the quality of those thoughts? Were they convoluted and incoherent? Have you ever been too tired to think? If you have experienced this, then you know, first hand, exactly what I am talking about when I speak of the brain's response to low-level M'retz Na'she availability.

In Torishimaru Aiki Jutsu, we utilize principles and techniques that allow us to "inject" M'retz Na'she into a person or object, and we also have many principles and techniques that allow us to withdraw that energy, as well. Understand that, in order for a person to attack you, his mind must, necessarily, issue specific instructions to his body to bring that attack about. Those instructions are issued in the form of thoughts. If one were able to draw enough M'retz Na'she from the attacker's brain, then the thought of attack, or any other thought for that matter, could not possibly take place. So it follows that if a person cannot sustain a thought of attack, no attack can or will ensue. Simply stated: With the absence of thought, there are no instructions issued to the body, and when no instructions are issued to the body, there can be no premeditative movement of any kind.

To accomplish the withdrawal of the M'retz Na'she, a psychic gate must be opened between oneself and the opponent. Since this psychic gate already exists between your higher mind and the attacker's higher mind, as it does between all higher minds, there is no need to create one; however, the existing animosity in this case necessarily keeps this psychic gate closed. So, in order to draw M'retz Na'she from him, this gate must be opened. To do this, we must employ principles that we call "gate openers." A gate opener is basically anything that will create a temporary tsuki or gap in someone's train of thought that is immediately filled in or replaced with a new thought or picture that you psychically place there. This process, of course, takes place higher mind to higher mind. But since you have created a tsuki in his lower mind and he is temporarily without lower mind thought, the thought or picture that you transfer to him is readily conveyed to it from his higher mind.

Once the gate has been opened, you must now create within yourself an area deficit of M'retz Na'she. This area of deficit M'retz Na'she is the initial drawing power necessary to begin the process of extracting the M'retz Na'she from the opponent. Although many techniques exist to create a power deficit in yourself, the easiest for a beginner would be to draw his M'retz Na'she to yourself by breathing his M'retz Na'she into your own body through higher mind contact or channels. That is, when you inhale, have the sense of drawing his M'retz Na'she into your own higher mind. Once the process begins, you must continue that flow. Remember, it is through the offices of his higher mind that you will have contact with his lower mind. This, in turn, will afford you access to his physical brain, which is in constant communication with his body. So, in essence, the open gate will give you a psychic influence over his body.

Because of the feminine energy deficit that you have created within yourself, as soon as you open the gate with his higher mind, there will be an immediate discharge of M'retz Na'she from his physical brain. This discharge can be thought of as being very similar to the sudden electrical discharge of a battery. It takes place very quickly. When this discharge takes place, what you are actually doing is removing the M'retz Na'she required by his brain to produce a thought. When no thought is produced, there can be no volitional movements of the attacker's body, so no attack or defense is forthcoming from him. This, by the way, is one of the principles I demonstrated at the neurologic center. The decrease in the brain activity of the subject, lasting fourteen seconds, was recorded by an EEG machine.

Q: **Could you explain how to control an argument? Can an argument be avoided?**

A: Certainly, but first you have to have a clear understanding of just what an argument actually is. Yes, an argument is a difference of opinion between two or more people, but it is really much more than that. An argument is actually a vying for control, an overt attempt at mastership and power. This vying for control, though often beginning benignly as a discourse, has the innate capacity to escalate in seconds into something else entirely, something stronger, louder, and potentially more perilous. Take this case: A husband says something that his wife does not quite agree with. This prompts his wife to state her side. The husband, sensing a sudden loss of control, raises his voice a little higher and a little stronger in order to restate his position. This, of course, prompts the wife, in an attempt to regain control over the argument, to raise her voice and inject more strength into her case. Before you know it, both parties are

99

screaming at the top of their voices in a valiant effort to regain their sense of lost control by attempting to wrench it away from the other party. This goes on for a while and then it happens—it evolves from mere mutual verbal abuse to something physical, something violent. Dishes are thrown, a table is up-ended, doors are slammed, or slaps are exchanged, or worse. I am sure you have experienced this, at least in part, at some time during your life.

There is an old saying among martial artists: I argue with no one, therefore, no one argues with me. What this means is that it takes two people to have an argument. If you choose not to argue, then there can be no argument. The other person, obviously, cannot argue with himself.

If you are unfortunate enough to be faced with a potential argument, more often than not, it can be settled very quickly and rather painlessly. How? Simply by asking the other person if there is any way whatsoever of convincing him that he is wrong. If he says "No!" then there it is. To continue the "conversation," at this point, would only be a waste of time and undoubtedly prove to be both frustrating and, inevitably, anger raising. Now, if the response to the question is, "I think I'm right, but I'll listen to what you have to say . . . try to convince me," then you do not have an argument, what you now have is a discussion, certainly a much more civilized way of dealing with an issue.

Now, since an argument is a vying for control, then it follows that if by resisting—that is, offering opposition— you increase your opponent's strength, then by yielding, you would be able to reduce his strength. In so doing, that is, by yielding, you can avoid the potential for conflict and move yourself stealthily into that position of control. How? Suppose, for example, that your spouse has some very strong feelings about an issue and you know that, in the past, the broaching of this particular subject invariably led to an argument. What can you do about it? Yes, naturally, you can walk away from it, but you know as well as I do that the issue would be far from being settled and would not go away of its own accord any time soon. So, the noble thing for you to do is to yield and deal with it!

Yielding is really very simple to execute, but it does require a bit of self-control. It requires the inner strength to lay aside your ego and cede temporary power over to the other person. Simply stated, to yield, all one has to do is to allow the other person to get his position out on the subject without comment or interference from you. Understand that often, depending on the issue, he may already have been anticipating a strong degree of resistance from you. This anticipation may just cause that person to start off very strongly, perhaps too strongly, thinking that he would need the extra "strength" just to deal with your expected reply. However, once you yield, everything suddenly changes. In fact, the other person may be so taken aback by your response that he may even hesitate to speak for a second or two. It is an interesting phenomenon. That tsuki or gap in the other person's thought process will allow you to slide in and subtly take control. However, once the control is yours, you must be cautious not to press the other person too strongly or else he will realize that you actually have control over the conversation. This, of course, will lead back into the vying syndrome and all is lost. Remember, yielding is not necessarily weakness, it is very often strength, real strength.

101

Q: **What advice would you give someone who is looking to study the martial arts?**

A: There are many wonderful martial arts in the world today for a person to choose from. So many, in fact, that someone seriously thinking about studying the martial arts should really take the time to look into all of the marvelous possibilities. One should think seriously about why he wants to study a martial art in the first place. If that person finds an art that interests him, he should reflect on just what he expects to gain in studying that particular art and whether that art, effectively, has the potential to actually supply those things. Arts, of course, vary widely, from the ultra esoteric to the extremely mundane, and there is, truly, an art to fit everyone. A person seeking to enter the martial arts should try to understand, also, what the instructors of those arts expect from their students, and whether or not he, as a student, can realistically meet those expectations. Remember that whatever the instructors are is what the student eventually becomes. There is an old saying: When two rabbits mate, you can be sure that all of their children, without exception, will also have long ears.

> Listen! A man without shoes is walking down the street one day when he spies a pair of shoes lying by the curb. On closer examination, he realizes that the shoes are very, very expensive, a magnificent pair of shoes. Knowing this, he literally jumps for joy at his wonderful discovery. Unfortunately, when he tries them on, he realizes that they do not fit. "What good are they if they don't fit?" he thinks. "I would rather have found a plainer, old, worn-out pair of shoes that are my size!"

So it is with the martial arts. No matter how fancy the art happens to be, no matter what the particular magnitude of its allure is, it is much better by far to find a martial art that is comfortable and fits than to find one that not only hurts your feet, but can actually cause you great damage. When it comes to the martial arts, one size does not fit all. But when a person does find an art that fits, he has also found a home. He must follow the teachings offered by that art with an open mind and a willing spirit. Further, he must respect and trust his instructor implicitly, because his instructor is the guide on the spiritual path that he has chosen to walk.

Part 2

Meditation
and
the Nature
of the Mind

Q: I've read books on meditation, self-improvement, self-realization, enlightenment, and a thousand other related subjects. Also, I've spoken to what seems to be a thousand "masters," "gurus," and "swamis." As a result, I've picked up a ton of information, but I don't seem to be getting anywhere. How is that possible? What's wrong?

A: A patient is never cured by hearing the medicine described to him. You are like the person who walks into a restaurant, sits down, pores over the menu, orders his food, but does not eat. Reading about the enlightenment experiences of others, no matter how famous or accomplished those others may be, is a lot like standing outside of a movie theater and asking the people exiting that theater how the movie was in an attempt to save yourself the time and effort of actually seeing the movie yourself.

> Listen! One day, during a battle, a man was struck in the chest by an arrow and was borne bleeding to his tent. He was lying on his cot in great agony when the physician showed up and began an immediate examination of his wound. The physician then opened up his medicine case and took out a small blue bottle.
> "Wait!" shouted the suffering man. "What is in the bottle?"
> "The antidote," replied the physician. "You see, the arrow that you were struck with was coated with a very nasty poison, and before I can remove it I must give you the antidote."
> "All right," said the man. "I will take this antidote of yours, but before I do, I want you to answer a few questions for me! What kind of poison is it? Where did it come from? Who first thought of using a poison like that on an arrow? What kind of wood is the arrow made of? Where does the tree grow that produces such wood? Who made the arrow and what kind of feathers did he use? Do the feathers come from a large bird or a small bird? What does the antidote taste like? Who

107

was it that first discovered this antidote? Was he a doctor or a samurai? Why do you keep it in a blue bottle?" Et cetera, et cetera, et cetera, *ad infinitum*.

The man in the story—was he wise or foolish? Foolish? Certainly, he was foolish. Why? Because he was dying slowly of the poison on the arrow but, before he would take the antidote, he had to ask a thousand and one questions. Surely, he would die before all of those questions were answered. Maybe you are like that man. Your life is quickly slipping away right before your eyes and all you do in your quest to achieve realization is to read about the enlightenment experiences of others and ask endless questions, most of them over and over again. Does this sound the least bit familiar to you? If it does, if it is something that you can identify with, then you know that you must exchange that fruitless course of action for a course of action that will bring you to your goal. In essence, you must cease asking your myriad questions and take the antidote! Once you have taken the antidote, only then will you be free to ask your questions. Do you understand? Instead of endlessly talking about taking a spiritual path, or merely reading about that path, you must actually get up and walk the path! Instead of talking about peace of mind, enlightenment, and realization, you must put into effect the right actions that will bring those conditions about! *Eheu fugaces labuntur anni!* Alas, the fleeting years pass by! (Horace). If you do not take decisive action now, you may never have the opportunity to take that action again in this present incarnation.

108

Q: **Is finding a good spiritual teacher the first step in walking a spiritual path? What advice would you offer someone who doesn't have a teacher and wants to meditate on their own?**

A: Finding a wise spiritual preceptor is, of course, a necessity, but it is not what I would call the first step. Confucius said,

"A journey of a thousand miles begins with the first step."
I disagree! A journey of a thousand miles does not begin
with the first step, it begins with the *thought* of the first
step. In other words, just reaching the point in your present
existence where the thought of walking a spiritual path
comes to you is the beginning—an auspicious beginning,
in and of itself.

Once, however, you make the decision to walk a spiritual
path, you must, naturally, seek a wise and competent
teacher. There is an old saying, "If you cannot find a master
or friend to walk the path with you, it is better to walk the
path alone, rather than have a fool for company." The more
competent your instructor is, the quicker and smoother
your journey down a spiritual path will be. An instructor's
wisdom does not come from age, but from an innate
capacity to assimilate the truth of existence and to be able
to bring his charges to that same experience. Therefore,
bearing this in mind, you must exercise good judgment and
choose your teacher carefully.

You must understand that meditating alone, without the
benefit of a caring and qualified teacher, is extremely
difficult, at best. A person genuinely interested in
meditation must make every effort to find a good teacher.
Of course, there are numerous books on the market that
teach meditation. Unfortunately, beginners who are
depending solely on a book will often be totally unaware
during their meditation that they are doing anything wrong.
A competent teacher, on the other hand, will make the
proper corrections at the proper time, smoothly and
succinctly. Also, while the student matures as he continues
his studies, a good teacher may opt to change his meditation
and, in so doing, properly bring him up the meditative
evolutionary ladder toward a valid and lasting fulfillment.
Still, if one cannot find a teacher due to geographical
considerations or logistical problems, and one wants to

meditate, then a good authoritative book or videotape would naturally be in order.

Q: Over the years I have tried to meditate in an attempt to achieve realization and peace of mind, but I always wind up quitting. I don't know what the problem is. I start off fine, but I wind up skipping periods of meditation even though I know I shouldn't. What's wrong?

A: Perhaps you are not quite sure what it is that you want and what you have to do to in order to achieve it! It could also be that you do want realization, but simply do not want it strongly enough.

> Listen! Every morning at dawn, this very famous master would go down to the local lake to bathe. One particular morning, a young man approached him and asked the master to teach him how to find realization. The master rudely turned him down and told him to go away. The young man left dejected and a little bewildered by the master's response.
>
> But the young man was persistent, however, and returned to the lake every morning at dawn for a month to ask the master to teach him. The master, unfortunately, was equally persistent and would always turn him away. Finally one morning, the master said to the young man, "Tell me. Just how badly do you want realization?" Hearing this, the young man suddenly grew hopeful and avidly replied, "Very much, sir! More than anything!" The master said, "That is not enough! It is not nearly enough! Go away!"
>
> Again, morning after morning, for yet another month, the young man would show up at the lake and the master would ask him the same question: "How badly do you want realization?" And, regardless of what the young man would say, regardless of how he responded, the result would

still be the same: the master would rudely send him away.

Then, one morning, the master was quietly kneeling by the lake when the indefatigable young man showed up. Again he asked the master to teach him and, again, the master was dissatisfied with the answer he received to his question. But this time, the master signaled for the young man to kneel beside him by the lake. The young man did as the master requested. The master then asked him once again, "How badly do you want realization?" The young man was just about to answer when the master grabbed him by the back of his neck and shoved his head into the water. The master held the young man's head under the water until he began to feel his body go limp. Then, the master quickly pulled the young man's head out of the water and let him go. Stunned by what had just taken place, the young man sat by the shore coughing, gasping for air, and spitting up tepid lake water. He was both shocked and confused by the master's actions.

While the young man was trying to compose himself, the master asked him, "When I held your head underwater, what was it that you wanted the most? What was it that you wanted more than anything else in the world?" Still coughing, the bewildered young man replied, "Sir, more than anything else in the world, I wanted air! I wanted to be able to breathe, to take another breath!"

"Just so!" said the master. "As much as you wanted air, as much as you wanted to breathe, that is how much you have got to want realization! Do you understand?"

In that one moment, the young man understood. The master, upon seeing this glow of understanding in the young man's face, immediately accepted him as a student.

Do you understand? You must want to achieve realization in the same way that the young man in the story wanted air. You must want it *unguibus et rostro,* with claws and beak—with all one's might. If you did, then, adhering to a program of meditation would not be such a problem. Nothing could possibly interfere with that kind of resolve. What you need to do, then, is to come to terms with yourself and objectively consider just how strongly you really want to achieve realization. That is all.

Q: **You teach a particular concentration exercise that is done with a candle. I understand that this exercise will help prepare a beginner for effective meditation. Could you explain how it is done?**

A: The candle concentration is a Tratrak, or concentration, exercise. It is not a meditation per se, but is one of a number of methods that is often useful in bringing about a special state of mind that we call "one-pointedness." When one practices this exercise long enough, one will be able to take this one-pointedness and apply it to great benefit in various meditations. It is an especially good exercise for the beginner.

In a darkened room, place a lit candle approximately three to four feet in front of you. You may do this exercise in any of the meditative postures or, if need be, while sitting on a chair with the candle placed on a table in front of you. You must now stare at the flame for two minutes. While staring at the flame, you may notice the different parts of the flame as well as the various colors of the flame. You can blink when necessary. After a short while, you will notice that the flame takes on a solid appearance. Continue to concentrate on the flame for an additional two minutes. That makes a total of four minutes in all. At the end of the four minutes, you will close your eyes and lightly cover them with the palms of your hands. You will see the image

112

of the flame in your mind's eye surrounded by a rich field of blackness. This is a mystical image that represents the primordial seed, the universe before creation, and represents the sum total of all existing matter surrounded by the vast eternal darkness of the starless void just prior to the great expansion.

While your eyes are closed and covered, notice the various colors of the image—the yellows, greens, reds, purples, et cetera. Try to keep the image focused and centered in your vision. Should the image begin to rise, which it will, you must concentrate and will it back down. Should the image blur or in some way go out of focus, you must concentrate and will it back into focus. As you continue, you will notice that the colors of the image will change. This is normal. Take note of the various colors as you continue to concentrate on refocusing and recentering the image. Eventually, the image will fade to the point where you think it is gone. When this occurs you must concentrate and try to will it back. You will continue to do this until you reach the point where the image is gone and can no longer be retrieved.

This concentration technique will bring about a marked retraining of your lower mind. When practiced properly, it will promote the one-pointedness so very necessary to facilitate good meditation.

Q: Briefly, could you describe a few meditation postures?

A: I teach five fundamental meditation asanas or positions: seiza, full lotus, half lotus, Burmese style, and lenient. Seiza is the traditional Japanese kneeling posture. In seiza, one assumes a kneeling position, resting the buttocks between the heels. If one is using a zafu or pillow, then the zafu or pillow is placed between the ankles, edge up, and the buttocks placed on that. The knees are positioned two fist-widths apart and the back is kept erect but not rigid. The head is aligned vertically with the chin tucked slightly inward. The hands are placed in the universal mudra—that is, the palm-up right hand is placed on the lap with the pinkie-side touching the lower abdomen. The palm-up left hand is then placed on top of the right hand with both thumbs touching lightly at the tips. When this mudra is done correctly the thumbs will complete an oval, shaped as if you were holding an egg. The eyelids are lowered, but not closed, and the gaze is placed on the floor at a distance of approximately five feet. Just in passing, let me say that students of Torishimaru Aiki Jutsu must become very familiar with the seiza posture. It is a traditional posture in my system.

In the cross-legged postures, it is always best to use a zafu. The zafu supports the spine and eliminates, especially for beginners, unnecessary strain in the lower back area. Also, besides simply being more comfortable, the zafu aids greatly in the promotion of proper posture.

The full lotus or Padmasan is, historically, the most difficult of all the sitting postures. To execute it, the legs are crossed, with the outer edge of the right foot resting on the left thigh, and the outer edge of the left foot on the right thigh. For the beginner, this is normally a very difficult sitting posture because it requires great flexibility in the knee and ankle joints.

In the half lotus, the outer edge of the left foot is placed on the right thigh with the right leg simply folded underneath. I have always found the half lotus posture to be

highly preferable for those students with a reasonable amount of flexibility. For those with less flexibility, there is the Burmese style, in which the legs are folded with both calves resting flat on the ground, one in front of the other. For those students who are truly inflexible and find it much

115

Meditation posture: Seiza (1)

116

Meditation posture: Seiza (2)

117

Meditation posture: Seiza (3)

too difficult to assume the other sitting postures, there is what I call the lenient posture, which is simply sitting comfortably with the legs crossed at the ankles in what is familiarly called Indian fashion.

In all five of these postures, the universal mudra performed by the hands is the same: both knees must touch the floor and all the rules for the proper head and spine alignment also apply throughout.

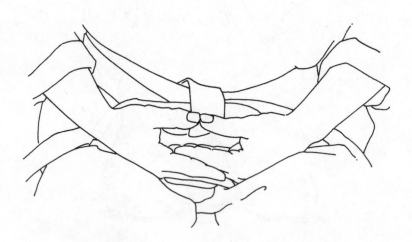

118

Meditation posture: The universal mudra

Meditation posture: Lotus side view

120

Meditation posture: Lenient

121

Meditation posture: Burmese style

122

Meditation posture: Half lotus

123

Meditation posture: Full lotus

Q: **What are some of the potential problems that one must watch out for in order to meditate correctly?**

A: There are several points to be stressed in meditating properly. First of all, the body must be physically balanced, not leaning to the left or leaning to the right, and there should be no struggling in an effort to keep you from losing your balance to the rear. And this is very important: there should be no slouching to the front. You must be especially mindful not to slouch because, for a beginner, this will often occur without one realizing it. You must sit with a sense of dignity, a feeling of great majesty, as if you were a great monarch giving audience to your loyal subjects. Also, you must try to have the sense of supporting the infinite sky with the top of your head and have your chin slightly tucked in.

To find the balanced center of your posture is rather a simple matter. Once you have assumed the meditative posture of choice, simply sway your body gently from side to side in pendulum fashion, slowly coming to a stop in the center. This is followed by a slow rocking forward and backward motion, again slowing until physically centered. It is that simple.

Then you must not fidget or make any extraneous movements. Fidgeting not only throws the body out of alignment but also has a tendency to pull the mind away from the matter at hand. Fidgeting will greatly interfere with a sensation called "body falling away" or Prateyahara, and will impede your progress. Fidgeting is to be assiduously avoided.

124

Finally, you must pay the strictest attention to what is required of you in your particular meditation; attention to what you are doing is of paramount importance to meditation. You must be "there" and "then." If your mind wanders, then you are not doing what you are supposed to be doing; you are doing something else. If you have a teacher and are assigned a particular type of meditation, then you must follow his instructions implicitly; do not vary or deviate from his teaching. What I mean by that is that a student should not experiment or make changes while meditating—no wandering down the fruitless path of invention. Simply do what you are instructed to do. If you listen to your teacher and follow his direction, then all will be well with you and your spiritual progress will be assured.

Q: **Should someone beginning meditation for the first time be taught to count his breaths? If so, how does one go about this type of meditation?**

A: Yes, most definitely! Beginners should always start off by counting their breaths. Why? For two reasons. First, there is a spiritual evolution that must take place in order for one not only to be able to enter into the more advanced stages of meditation, but for one to even entertain the idea of it. Second, a beginning meditator must experience, first hand, the enormous interference offered to him by his ever-loquacious lower mind. By experiencing the magnitude of the problems generated by his monkey-like lower mind, he will subsequently be encouraged to rectify the situation. This experience, for a beginner, is absolutely indispensable. Otherwise, a prime motivational factor, so important for the maintaining of a strict and fruitful regimen of meditation, will be missing, and one's meditation will, inevitably and unfortunately, fall by the wayside.

The technique for the counting of the breaths is as follows: Assume one of the meditative postures—seiza, full lotus, half lotus, Burmese style, or lenient—and place your hands on your lap, forming the universal mudra. That is, place your right hand on your lap with the pinkie side of the hand lightly touching your abdomen. Then, place your left hand on top of your right hand with both thumbs lightly touching at the tips. Perform a gentle rocking motion with your upper body to the left and then to the right, coming slowly to rest in the center. Then, rock forward and back, again slowly coming to rest in the center. At this point your body should be physically balanced. Your nose should be aligned with your navel and your chin slightly tucked in. You should have the sense of supporting the sky with the top of your head. With your eyes slightly open you will place your gaze on the floor approximately five feet from you.

You are now ready to begin to count your inhalations and exhalations. The "sound" of the counting is to be done mentally and in a very particular way. You begin with an inhalation and count "one." It should mentally sound like this: "w-o-n-n-n-n-n-n." On the exhalation you will count "two-o-o-o-o-o-o." On the next inhalation you will count "three-e-e-e-e." Continue in this fashion until you reach "ten." The mental recitation of each number must last throughout the length of the inhalation or exhalation and your breathing must be kept slow, smooth, and silent. Now, all you have to do is count mentally from one to ten, right? It sounds fairly easy, doesn't it? Well, it isn't, especially for beginners. Why? Because of thoughts constantly being generated by the lower mind.

You must understand that singular thoughts that arise in the mind are, in and of themselves, not a problem. If you are in the process of counting your breaths and a random thought does appear, simply allow it to float by like a small puffy cloud in a clear blue sky. Do not attach yourself to it. Just let it float by and allow it to gently dissolve. However, if a thought leads into a narrative or story, such as, "What was that sound? Was it a car door . . . was it my car? . . . I forgot to have the oil changed today . . . I told my wife to do it . . . I wonder what she's making for dinner tonight?" Suddenly, you are not doing your counting anymore. Your mind capriciously wandered from the sound that you had just heard to your car, then to having the oil changed in

126

your car, then to your wife, and then to what you are having for dinner. When you find yourself entertaining any sort of narrative dialogue you must immediately stop your counting and start all over again at one. That is correct, all over again at one. The idea here is to be able to get from one to ten, over and over again, without any such narrative thoughts taking place. I know that, ostensibly, it sounds easy, but if you have never attempted it before, you will find it to be really quite difficult. It takes a great deal of effort, requiring a great amount of discipline, but I assure you that the results will be gratifying.

The insidious machinations of the lower mind will make themselves known to you very quickly during this form of meditation. Once you have mastered counting your inhalations and exhalations, you will be ready to advance to the next stage, which is to just count your inhalations. That is, you will mentally count your inhalations and remain silent on your exhalations. Then, when counting your inhalations is mastered, you will be ready to go on to the next stage, that of counting your exhalations. Once that is mastered, then you have set the stage for your advancement to more sophisticated meditations, such as shikan-taza.

You should never be in a rush to move up to higher levels of meditation. Each step must be taken one at a time. If, in your haste for results, you skip steps, then you will be lost, your progress will be retarded, and you will not have the tools necessary for what I call meaningful sitting.

Q: What about mantra meditation? Is there any value to that particular type of meditation?

A: Yes, of course, there is. Mantra meditation is an extremely valid and useful form of meditation. It offers certain advantages to those who are seeking an immediate sense of peace. It is also one of the easiest and safest forms of meditation to practice, especially if you are meditating without the benefit of a qualified teacher.

A mantra is a word or phrase that has some very special significance to the meditator. In Hinduism, for example, a mantra is considered to be a very special holy word or phrase which, when properly intoned, not only leads to spiritual enlightenment but can instill in the meditator some very special *Siddhis* or powers. The mantra "om," for example, is very dear to Hindu mystics. This word is, in fact, thought of by the Hindus to be the holiest word in creation, and is treated with great respect throughout all of the Vedic literature of ancient India. It is through the constant recitation of the mantra "om" that the ancient Hindu masters say will lead one to enlightenment. In Tantric Buddhism, the mantra "om" became the mantra "aum," and is no less valid.

There are many, many different mantras and each of them has various esoteric as well as physical effects on the meditator. Some are considered to be peace mantras, some power mantras, some merging mantras, et cetera. Clearly, mantra meditation has always been a popular form of meditation. In fact, it is said that Benjamin Franklin used to perform mantra meditation on a regular basis; however, instead of employing a foreign esoteric word that seemed to hold little or no meaning to him, he used to recite his own name over and over.

Of course, mantra meditation is not the ideal meditation for the martial artist, but in certain circumstances it can be useful, especially in starting certain beginners off. It can also be employed with great success as a supplement to the present meditation practices of others.

128

I have always taught meditation based on the ability of the particular individual student to learn, even if it means that all I have him doing, initially, is mantra meditation. As a result, that individual's spiritual progress is almost always assured.

Q: **Suppose I was a beginner and wanted to practice mantra meditation. What should I do?**

A: If you are beginner and cannot find a qualified teacher, you should do the following: First, you should choose a quiet place for your meditation. If you are meditating in your home, choose a room that is free from noise or other distractions. The room should be dark and candle-lit. I suggest burning a lightly fragrant incense to lend an esoteric ambiance conducive to good periods of meditation. If you do burn incense, however, you should make sure that there is adequate ventilation to prevent the fumes of the burning incense from becoming too overwhelming.

Once the atmosphere is in order, you should choose one of the meditation postures that I have already described, remembering, of course, to use a zafu or firm pillow for support. Once you are seated, begin by first closing both of your eyes. Your mouth should also be closed, with your front teeth lightly touching each other. Then, breathe gently and naturally through your nose for a minute or two until your breathing becomes regular and even. Once your breathing has become even, you are ready to begin the recitation of the mantra. I suggest that you use the Hindu mantra "om." The mantra is recited strongly and firmly and must be vocalized in a very particular way. It should sound like this: "O-o-o-o-o-m-m-m-m-m" (pronounced *Oh-em*). The "o" sound should be intoned for a few seconds before gently becoming the "m" sound. The "m" sound should then be held for the remainder of the breath.

There will be a vibration created that will be epicentered around the area between the eyebrows. This area has variously been called the "Star of the East," the "Third Eye," the "Mind's Eye," et cetera. I call it the Daath Gate. However, regardless of its name, it acts as a very special mystical gate. While reciting the mantra, your eyes still closed, you will concentrate your vision in this area, allowing the sound and vibration of the mantra to fill you. Attempt to merge with the mantra until all that exist are the sound and vibration of that mystical word. Do not expect anything to happen. Do not anticipate or look for any mystical experiences. Just recite the mantra, over and over again, getting deeper and deeper into the vibration. If you are waiting for something to happen or are expecting something to happen, then you are not concentrating properly. Remember, all that should exist is the sound and vibration of the mantra, that is all.

At the end of the period of mantra recitation, remain in the meditative position and enter into the silence. Allow yourself to float in that great sea of tranquillity for several minutes, after which time you may slowly stretch your arms and legs and relax for another minute or two. This will end the period of meditation.

A beginner should meditate twice a day, every day; once in the morning and once in the evening. Of course, the times that you choose to meditate are dependent on your particular schedule and lifestyle. Still, you must try to be consistent, choosing your times carefully and trying to sit at those chosen times every day.

In the beginning, it is important that a novice meditator not sit for more than twenty minutes per session. Every two weeks thereafter, the meditation may be increased by five minutes per session until a total of thirty-five minutes is reached. Each of the meditation periods from then on should continue to be thirty-five minutes. Understand when I say "meditation period," I am referring to actual sitting time and not to the sitting time plus all the extraneous time that it takes you to prepare. In other words, sitting time is the time that you actually spend reciting the mantra.

If you are diligent in your meditation, wonderful results are sure to follow. You will find that, as your lower mind becomes quieter and quieter, you will eventually come to the point where you will experience a very great sense of well-being in your life. Of course, the effects of meditation, especially mantra meditation, are cumulative. That is, as you continue, you will find that the calming effects of the meditation begin to overlap from one period of sitting to the next. Your life will change in a very positive way and this change will not only be noticed but appreciated by all those people with whom you have contact. Any proper form of meditation, including mantra meditation, is a wise and noble pursuit.

Q: **What is shikan-taza and how does one practice it?**

A: Shikan-taza is an important form of Zen meditation and has a particular importance in the martial arts. Shikan-taza is just sitting. Of course, when I say "just sitting," I do not mean sitting on a zafu and vigorously trying to make one's mind a blank. That is not shikan-taza. What shikan-taza is is a highly focused form of just sitting, where one must concentrate with all of one's might on one's posture. That is all, just one's posture, making sure that each and every facet of one's posture is correct—from the top of one's head to the soles of one's feet, from the placement of one's hands to the correctness of one's thumbs in the universal mudra. There must be no fidgeting, no daydreaming, and no yielding to the ten thousand concentration-disturbing tricks that one's lower mind is liable to play. So when I say "just sitting," you must realize that for a novice or beginner there is really a great deal to do.

Of course, breathing in shikan-taza is very important and should be done in a very particular way. The rule is that the exhalation should always be longer than the inhalation. That is, one should take in a normal inhalation, but the exhalation should be protracted and silent. The longer the exhalation the better and, of course, all breathing should have its origin in the tanden, that mystical area of power located approximately two inches below the navel. This is also the area that is called the Sh'ar Ha'ar or "gate of glory." A light pressure exerted in that region by the edge of the small fingers in the universal mudra should mark the area for you. Never should you breathe through your mouth, always through your nose.

When you are sitting in shikan-taza and thoughts come to you, simply allow them to float by. Do not attempt to stop them, just do not hook onto them. Just let them float by and dissolve. As one's evolution in this meditation continues, there is less and less to do, until at last just sitting is realized. At that time, just sitting really is just sitting. It is being in the here and now with no thought of yesterday or tomorrow, two minutes ago or two minutes from now. It is focus without focus. It is Ku, or emptiness. But do not be misled. The emptiness of which I speak is not nothingness, it is an all-inclusive everythingness with nothing superfluous or lacking. In this state, all is well and everything, without exception, is in its place.

Q: **Why is it so important to keep the eyes open during shikan-taza and other Zen meditations?**

A: It is best to keep the eyes open for a couple of very important reasons. First, when the eyes are closed there is a great tendency to become drowsy. Drowsiness produces inattention, and inattention, wasting valuable time, is to be painstakingly avoided.

Second, closing one's eyes during meditation is a clear attempt to shut the world out and in so doing you are artificially creating a duality, a separateness that has as its basis pure illusion. We must not place ourselves in a position where we are looking to run from the world. It is very easy, almost too easy, to be calm and experience great peace while sitting securely at home in a semi-dark room burning incense and candles. It is even easier to find peace sitting cloistered in some ancient monastery on some obscure mountain peak in the middle of the Himalayas that only a Sherpa guide or mountain goat could scale. But you can no more run from the world than you can run from yourself.

In the absence of wind, a pile of cotton can think itself to be as strong and steadfast as a great mountain, but open a window, even just a little bit, and that pile of cotton that had thought itself a mountain is soon blown willy-nilly all about the room. To be a real mountain is to live in the world, unscathed, untouched, and unencumbered by the vicissitudes of life. To be able not just to see but to experience the underlying peace that exists within even the most chaotic of situations, that is true peace. To run from the world is a fool's errand, at best. One must learn to live in the world, but not be of the world.

Q: After meditating twenty-five to thirty minutes, I feel as if I am going to float away. The feeling frightens me and I always stop meditating. Could you explain what it is that I experience? Is it something to worry about?

A: The experience that you are speaking of is what we refer to as "body falling away." It occurs when your body is in perfect balance and you are executing proper concentration. It is a condition that, in fact, tells you that you are doing everything correctly, and normally occurs, as it did with you, approximately twenty-five to thirty minutes into the meditation. There is an old Zen story that describes the situation you are speaking of.

133

Listen! One morning, during a period of intense meditation, a novice Zen nun suddenly bolted to her feet and began to run around the meditation hall screaming, "I have no head! I can't find my head!" She ran around the room in an absolute panic. Eventually, she ran up to the Zen master.

The master asked her what the problem was. "Master, I cannot find my head! I have no head!" she screamed.

At this, the master calmly raised his right hand and slapped her across her face, and said, smiling, "Why all this fuss? There is your head on top of your shoulders all the time!"

What this novice nun experienced during her meditation was "body falling away" and it had caused her to panic. She was distraught because she did not understand the experience. She did not understand that "body falling away" was not only a harmless but necessary step in the evolution of one's meditation. All the master did was to prove to her that everything was all right and that, in fact, her head was still attached to her body.

In reality, "body falling away" is actually a very pleasant, blissful experience and one not to be avoided. The next time you meditate and experience this, you must not panic and break your concentration. You must press on. If you do, you will come to understand the beauty of this event and the great serenity that it promotes.

You must persevere and pass through this little gate of "body falling away" and out into the unfathomable and mysterious depths of meditation beyond. When the body falls away, the lower mind, the higher mind, and you are left; when the lower mind falls away, then only the higher mind and you are left. And then, when the higher mind finally falls away, only you are left! That is the miracle.

134   Q: When I meditate I sometimes have visions that seem very real to me. They are sometimes silly, sometimes frightening. Is this normal?

A: The visions you describe are called *makyo* or illusions. They are sometimes encountered in the more advanced stages of meditation and hardly ever to beginners. Even so, they are totally harmless and will eventually leave. Do not act upon them. Just let them go.

Listen! One day, during a period of intense meditation, a young monk noticed a tiny spider suspended by a very thin strand of silk some five feet in front of him. He closed his eyes for a few seconds and thought nothing of it. Then when he opened them again, he observed that the spider had grown to the size of a small bird. He closed his eyes again. When he opened them just a few seconds later, to his horror he saw that the once tiny spider had now grown to the size of a large dog. This frightened him so much that he ran screaming in terror from the meditation hall and into the kitchen of the monastery. The master happened to be in the kitchen at the time and noticed that the young monk had grabbed a large sharp knife from the table and was about to return to the meditation hall with it.

"What is this?" asked the master, pointing to the knife. "What are you going to do with that?"

"I am going to kill a spider," said the young monk.

At the master's request, the young monk explained to the master what had taken place during his meditation.

"I must kill the spider, master," he said, again.

"Nonsense!" said the master. "Give me the knife! I have something much more effective than that. In fact, what I have is perfect for you to use against such an enormous spider."

Taking the knife, the master handed the young monk a small piece of chalk.

"What could I do to that monstrous spider with just a piece of chalk?" asked the puzzled young monk.

"The next time you see that nasty spider," said the master, "take this piece of chalk and place a large X on its abdomen. If you do this, I promise you that this spider will never bother you again."

Trusting in the master's wisdom, the young monk returned to his seat in the meditation hall. He searched high and low, but the spider was nowhere to be found, and so he returned to his meditation. Sometime into his meditation, he opened his eyes and saw the tiny little spider in front of him once again. And each time he closed and then opened his eyes, the spider grew larger and larger and he, again, became more and more frightened. Then, when the spider reached the size of a large cow, the young monk nervously closed his eyes, reached out with the piece of chalk, and placed a large X on the spider's abdomen, just as the master had instructed him to do.

When he finally found the courage to open his eyes, to his great relief, the young monk saw that the spider had vanished. Not even the little spider remained. He was so happy that he couldn't wait to tell the master what had happened, and so the young monk ran as quickly as he could to relate the story of his ordeal.

"Master! Master!" the young monk shouted. "I did as you said and the spider is gone!"

"I see," said the master. "You placed the X on its abdomen, then?"

"Yes, master, I did!"

"Are you sure?" asked the master.

"I am positive!" said the young monk.

The master then directed the young monk to lift up the front of his robe. When he did, the young monk found, to his amazement, that there was a large X drawn in chalk on his stomach.

136

The point of the story is that there really was no such spider to begin with. The spider that was plaguing the young monk was makyo, or illusion, and was generated by his own lower mind. Imagine what would have happened if the master allowed the young monk to stab the spider as the young monk had first wanted to do. Yes, it is just a story, but if you are involved in certain types of meditation, it is one that you should understand and remember.

Not all makyo is unpleasant, however. Sometimes the illusions created by the lower mind are really quite pleasant—the scent of roses, the odor of roast beef, the sight of a pleasant hill under a warm summer sun—many, many possibilities. The point is that, pleasant or unpleasant, these makyo are all short lived and harmless and are to be ignored when they occur. Once you pass through this makyo-laden advanced stage of meditation, you can rest assured that they will never occur again.

Q: **What is a koan?**

A: A koan is an enigmatic, seemingly paradoxical question transmitted from a Zen master to a student. It is a question that concerns itself with some vast eternal truth of existence, a question transcending the minor limits of logical thought and solvable only within the infinite arena of the higher mind. It is a riddle, if you will, which must be worked on incessantly in order for it to be resolved.

A classic koan, and one that many people have heard before, is "What is the sound of one hand clapping?" If I were to pose this question to you, how would you answer? What would you say? But understand that any delay whatsoever in your response would immediately tell me that you do not know the answer. Why? Because a delay in your answer would indicate that it was coming from your lower mind. This is wrong. The answer must come spontaneously from the depths of your higher mind. Any true master would be able to tell the difference right away and would never accept an answer, regardless of how correct it sounded, if it is the product of reason. But then, that is the whole point of the koan, to transcend reason.

137

To solve a koan, you must probe its depths twenty-four hours a day, three hundred and sixty five days a year, year after year, exhausting every avenue of logical thought until, at last, the answer breaks forth in one great luminous flash of knowing. Still, when this occurs, you will have only a glimpse, a momentary insight into the "truth" of the nature of the illusion of the world.

With all of that, in essence, understand a koan to be an esoteric tool used by a number of Zen masters, especially of the Rinzai school of Zen, to bring about certain realization experiences in their students.

Q: **Could you speak more about the natures of what you call the lower and higher minds?**

A: The lower mind is the mind that the average person is used to dealing with. It is the calculating, reasoning, discriminating, fearing, hating, loving, and conniving part of you and is, for the most part, the loathsome culprit responsible for the general misinterpretation one has of the exterior world after processing the input supplied to it by various inferior sense faculties. Unenduring, it is born with the body and inevitably passes away with the body and, unlike the higher mind, which is of infinite capacity and exists eternally in nature, it is limited by varying capacities, endowments, potentialities, and wide-ranging perfidious magnitudes of untrustworthiness.

How we think is how we make the world. This is an indisputable fact. After all, if several people were to simultaneously view the same event it would, more than likely, result in several different perspectives and interpretations, all of which have their genesis in their individual lower minds. In fact, it is the arbitrary interpretations that the lower mind is subject to making that result in the cloudy obscuration of the fundamental truth of a subject, and it is these cloudy obscurations that cause so many of the problems humankind is plagued with.

It is the lower mind, in its egotistical self-righteousness, that produces an unending stream of arbitrary judgments and vain speculations concerning the many objects and events that it comes into contact with. Often, this is done in such a blatantly cavalier fashion that deep confusions arise not only between individuals but within the mind of the observer, himself, causing misunderstandings, strife, and an unsettling chaos-producing separatist view of the world. So, we see that wisdom is not exactly the lower mind's forte.

The unrelenting prideful view that the lower mind has of itself and the world around it is absolutely astounding! I find it further astounding that those who voluntarily impose upon themselves the task of investigating the nature of the matrix of existence should make the grievous error of doing so by utilizing such an inferior instrument. Why is it such a grievous mistake to charge the lower mind with such an ambitious task? Because the inquiring lower mind simply does not know how to go about it. The lower mind, so intent on discovering the unity of existence, recklessly selects to go about it by unremittingly dividing that oneness up into an infinite number of component parts. It works backwards. That is, it begins with the macrocosm in an attempt to understand the microcosm. Strange logic!

The lower mind errs when it receives sensory information. For example, when the eye first perceives an object, it does so quite without prejudice. That is, it takes in the raw image of the object without predilections or discrimination. The eye is seeing the pure object according to its particular physical ability, devoid of labels, descriptive colorings, introduction of past correlative associations, and biased historical or personal aversions or attractions. Once, however, the image enters the lower mind for interpretation,

139

the expansive journey away from the pristine truth of the object begins, ending inevitably in a subtle micro-flash of manipulative distortions and beguiling half-lies.

How this happens is really not difficult to understand. The eye sees an object or event and delivers that image to the lower mind. However, the lower mind, instead of just acknowledging it, takes that unpredicated image and interprets it in a very personal way. That is, it takes the raw image presented to it and paints or distorts it according to its own individual innate prejudices. It is the painting of these images that leads us unsuspectingly down the dark and ominous corridors of illusion and into the murky, often frightening world of ignorance.

The old adage that tells us "beauty is in the eye of the beholder" is irrefutably true but, unfortunately, does nothing to explain that everything seen is interpreted by the mind not only as beautiful or ugly but also as frightening, not frightening, comforting, not comforting, funny, not funny, somber, not somber, melancholic, not melancholic, et cetera, *ad infinitum*.

To understand this better, suppose that several people were looking at a baby—the parents of the child, a female friend of the parents, a single male friend of the parents, another child, a barren woman, a pediatrician, and a man who has many children. Each of these people, although seeing the same child, perceives the child in a very different way. The parents, for example, see the child as the central portion of their lives. To them, the child is their joy and serves to supply for them the once-elusive answer to the riddle of purpose. To them, the child is a limitless source of pride and love and from these parental emotions issue forth descriptions of the child that are biased and opinionated sometimes to the point of agitating the people they are describing their child to. To the doting parents, the child is the absolute epitome of beauty, intelligence, and talent personified. Moreover, they carry an enormous array of pictures of the child and force the introduction of those pictures into every conceivable social and business event they are privy to.

The female friend of the parents perceives the child as cuddly, warm, and utterly adorable. She finds herself instinctively needing to hold and fondle the baby. The child conjures up visions in her of her own possible future as a warm and loving mother.

The single male friend of the parents may, at best, exhibit merely a passing interest in the baby. He sees the baby as something small, pink, and weak. He may, of course, raise an occasional eyebrow toward the doting parents in an attempt not to offend them, and may even offer a further vagrant smile in tacit agreement to their "ridiculous" parental adulations.

To another child, perhaps a sibling, the baby is an absolute enigma. It is something to be wary of in terms of how much less attention he or she will receive as a result of the birth of this half-welcome interloper.

To the barren woman, the baby is something to be coveted. She looks at the baby with consummate envy, while simultaneously cursing her own miserable fate. To her, the baby is perceived with an unquenchable sadness.

To the pediatrician, the baby is simply another potential patient and he looks at the baby in a very clinical way. He sees the baby's coloring, weight, length, and considers its general health. He looks at the baby as dispassionately as a veteran auto mechanic would look at an automobile.

Finally, the man with many children looks at the baby **141** and sees all the bills that the new baby will incur. He groans and grimaces and views the baby as an incredible economic burden, while thanking his lucky stars that the pink little tyke isn't his.

Naturally, there are an almost infinite number of possible perceptions relative to each one of these viewers; however, the idea should be clear to you. The lower mind colors the perception of the baby according to the individual's personal biases. As a result, various responses to the same object, namely, the baby, not only occur but are inevitable.

Things are what they are. Profound? I think so, and also so very basic to a true and accurate understanding of the nature of the matrix of existence. If you have ever been repulsed at the sight of a spider or a snake, for example, you shouldn't be too surprised to learn that there are people in the world who would view these animals as creatures of great beauty and majesty (i.e., entomologists and serpentologists). Why are you repulsed? Maybe you are not seeing clearly the true nature of these creatures. Maybe you are viewing these creatures through lenses tinted and distorted by the fear-based biases and arbitrary concepts of beauty presented to you by your lower mind.

The lower mind is, in fact, a skillful yet more often than not nefariously talented artist and through its vigorous and colorful artistic machinations it creates a world of love, hate, greed, covetousness, violence, repulsion, folly, and fear. It creates your world, the one that you alone call your own.

Actually, the differences between apparent opposites, such as loving and loathing, attractiveness and revulsion, merely lie in our perception of the object or event relative to how we paint it. Understand that the choice of paints we use to color our world is based solely on the variety of pigments available to us on our individual palettes. But just where do these paints come from, and how did they wind up on your palette? This I will answer, but first let me say that the lower mind should be thought of as a sort of sophisticated cassette tape. It is born with the body and inevitably dies with the body. It begins recording at the very moment of conception and continues, nonstop, until death. It records all of our life experiences, good, bad, or indifferent, and what it records becomes a good part of the various paints on our palette.

How much information the lower mind can record naturally varies from person to person. Some people have, for example, 60-minute tapes, some 30-minute tapes, some 90-minute tapes, and some 120-minute tapes, et cetera. This accounts for a number of phenomena, such as the differences in intelligence and the ability to retain information.

The countless objects taken in by our senses and the plethora of experiences we have had—good, bad, or indifferent, since conception—are recorded on the lower mind tape. Along with these objects and experiences are recorded our reactions to them. If our reactions to an event, due to particular circumstances, were pleasant, then it is recorded in just that fashion and immediately colors or paints our anticipative reactions to any similar future events. For example, parents make a birthday party for their child when he turns five. The child has such a pleasant, positive experience at that party that he not only looks forward to his next birthday but automatically expects a similar positive experience at that party. So, his positive experience has become a dab of light paint on his lower mind palette. Should he ever suffer a negative experience at a future party, then that experience becomes a dab of dark paint on his palette. The problem is when dark paints are added to one's palette that already has light paint on it relative to a particular object or event, it offers the lower mind a choice, light paint or dark. Should the light paint option be used, then the child is liable to suffer a letdown, even if the two birthday parties are exactly the same. This occurs because it is the nature of the lower mind to amplify both positive and negative experiences irrationally to the point of non-reality

143

and, as a result, the child will more than likely be disappointed with the experience of the second party. Through the natural amplification process instinctive to the lower mind, it produces an anticipated response to an event that becomes difficult or even impossible to satisfy because it actually employs brighter paints than were created by the original birthday party. The lower mind's influence in this and similar events ultimately leads to a life of unbounded disappointment and endless anguish.

Now, should dark paints be used by an individual's lower mind to color an event or object, that event or object is again tainted, and when an opinion is verbalized, that person might very well be viewed by others to be morosely pessimistic and negative.

The lower mind's use of dark paints creates many problems by immediately precluding even the vaguest chance of happiness concerning future events. In the case of the birthday party, the use of dark paints in the memory of that party has the child already anticipating disappointment. This, of course, influences the child's attitude at the actual event itself and conjures up images for the child that ultimately destroy the possibility for enjoyment and happiness.

A person who constantly uses dark paints to color his world sets himself up for a life fraught with disappointment and misery. Every thought concerning the future for this person becomes a grueling, ponderous, self-fulfilling prophesy. This only reinforces the use of dark paints because his life and his world have become dark and foreboding. Ironically, this causes him to increase the quantity of dark paints on his palette. Eventually, his palette becomes so full of dark paint that his lower mind has very little choice but to employ them and the world is painted grim and foreboding and his life becomes one of abject and needless suffering. This is the unfortunate circumstance of a

144

person who is subject to the arbitrary picture painting of the uncontrolled lower mind.

If you want to know when you, yourself, are painting, it's easy. One of the most salient warning signs to look for is the tell-tale arbitrary opinion. Basically, an arbitrary opinion is an opinion about an object, person, event, past, present, or future that you create about those things based on the use of the paints on your palette. An arbitrary opinion becomes apparent when you vocalize your thoughts concerning a person, place, or thing to someone else without being asked. For example, suppose that you are standing on the street corner with your friend when a dog wanders by. Without being asked by your friend, you turn to him and say, "Boy, is that one ugly dog!" That is an example of an arbitrary opinion. Nobody asked you for your opinion, and yet you took up your brushes and started painting anyway. You arbitrarily painted the dog ugly. Even though it may have been ugly to you, your arbitrary opinion has just distorted the very essence of the dog. Also, what you have done was to assist your friend in painting a picture of the dog, thereby interfering with his ability to see clearly for himself the true essence of the animal. This makes you guilty of two spiritually criminal acts; namely, painting in the first degree and the aiding and abetting of a fellow painter.

You must assiduously and systematically get rid of all your arbitrary opinions or you will be doomed to a life of fear, anger, greed, chaos, and misery. In order to help you to help yourself do it, try this little experiment: Keep a small notebook and pencil with you at all times and, should you come up with an arbitrary opinion, place a check mark on the dated page. Each evening, just before bedtime, see how many check marks you have accumulated during the course of your day. Compare that with the next day's check marks. Understand that there is no passing or failing. Be honest with yourself and place a check mark when appropriate.

145

This little exercise will help you to monitor your lower mind. It will show you just how many times during the course of a single day you take out your pigments and brushes and paint the world. Oh, by the way—if you just thought to yourself that this exercise is silly or pointless or even good or wonderful, then I have got you . . . you just produced an arbitrary opinion, so give yourself a check mark!

The higher mind, on the other hand, does not paint pictures. It produces no arbitrary opinions to obscure one's vision of the true nature of the world. It is what you are . . . original mind. It is the part of you that has always existed and is your pristine link both with God and the universe. The higher mind has been recording information relevant to your existence and its experiences since time immemorial. Further, the higher mind is incapable of making a mistake, and has the capability of securing all knowledge. That is, it has an unerring ability to tap into the vast knowledge available to it concerning the past, present, and future.

Just as the lower mind tape is limited, both in capacity and ability, the higher mind tape is infinite in both capacity and possibility. Not being subject to the emotional pettiness that plagues the lower mind, the higher mind has the faculty to see clearly—without bias, without preconception, without comment, without debate—and while the lower mind is self-serving in a world of its own creation, the higher mind functions flawlessly in a world it sees without illusion.

146 Q: **What about animals? Do they have higher and lower minds?**

A: Yes, they do. They have both a lower mind and a higher mind, but the magnitude of combination of the two minds can vary widely from species to species, depending on where they stand on the evolutionary ladder. You could say that the input coming from the higher mind is inversely proportional to the degree of development of the lower mind. In other words, the more developed the lower mind, the louder it is, and the louder it is, the more difficulty the higher mind has in being heard. You can also say that we, as human beings, are the loudest thinkers in the animal kingdom and so are the least able to operate on an intuitive level then everyone else in the animal kingdom.

Human babies, for example, are very intuitive because their lower minds are just developing. That is, they have very little information accumulated with which to clutter up their lower minds. However, as time passes, they take in more and more sensory information, as well as developing even more information based on that accumulated sensory input. They are fed information from everyone and everything in their environment. And so, as the human baby matures, its lower mind grows louder and louder until, at last, it becomes so loud that input from the higher mind is all but drowned out. Ironically we, as a species, as evolved as we are in most areas, are on the very top of the lower mind ladder and, at the same time, on the very bottom rung of the higher mind ladder. This gives the other members of the animal kingdom certain advantages over us.

Listen! Once I had a cat that had never had kittens before. She had wandered out of the house one evening and spent what could only be described as a wonderful night of feline indiscretion. As a natural consequence of her night on the town, she became pregnant. The weeks passed and when she knew that her time was near, she began to search for the right place to have her kittens. She found that place on the carpeted floor in a very cozy spot in my bedroom closet. There she made her little cat nest.

When the big day arrived I had the opportunity to observe the kittens being born. The mother laid there without a whimper, without a worry,

without a midwife, and without a copy of a
Dr. Spock manual, and had her kittens.

When the first kitten was born, the very first
thing she did was to remove the afterbirth and
other material from the kitten's mouth and nose
area so that the kitten was able to breathe
unimpeded. She then proceeded to meticulously
clean the rest of the kitten's body. It was not until
the first kitten was totally taken care of that she
allowed the second kitten to be born. She did this
for all four kittens. No one had to teach her what
to do or how to do it. Why? Because it came to
her in the form of ancient cat memories that were
recorded on her higher mind tape. They weren't
the collective memories of her species that came to
her genetically from her parents, they were
actually her very own memories.

Let me explain. Animals, like humans, also reincarnate.
And, just like humans, animals always reincarnate within
their own species. In other words, my cat was always a cat.
The ancient memories that taught her what to do in giving
birth and tending to her kittens' needs were her very own
memories, based on her very own experiences. Do you
understand? She had her kittens without benefit of books,
veterinarians, or midwives. Because of the eternal nature of
the higher mind and the ever-ongoing reincarnation of
animals back into their particular species, there is no need
to teach a pig to be a pig, or a dog to be a dog, or a tiger to
be a tiger . . . they are in the present what they have always
been in the past.

148

As you descend down the evolutionary scale and enter
into the world of the insects, you will find that their lower
minds are so quiet, so tenuous, so subtle, that their lower
minds, for all intents and purposes, can be considered
negligible, but they are still there. Bearing this in mind, let
me say that the more developed the lower mind is, the more
of a sense of "I-ness" there is. In the Bible, King Solomon

advises the sluggard to go to the ant and consider her ways. What Solomon was saying was that the industrious ant works from dawn to dusk without the slightest complaint or debate. The ant works not for herself but for the welfare of her queen and the good of the colony. This phenomenon occurs because the lack of a loudly functioning lower mind offers the ant almost no sense of "I-ness," and so the ant is self-sacrificing nearly to a fault, all for the good of her compatriots and her species.

Ants are also fearless creatures! They are admirably courageous because fear and other emotions only exist within the nebulous climes of the lower mind. Further, the ant has tremendous physical strength, which is also indicative of the presence and predominance of the higher mind. In fact, as soon as they are born, the ants, without hesitation, go right to work in support of its species. There are no ants in the colony in training to be ants; there are no ant schools. They are born with all the necessary ingredients for full and unobstructed anthood.

Another example one might consider would be the spider. As soon as they are born, they are literally on their own. They leave the nest and, without the slightest instruction, find a suitable place to construct their own intricate webs. The webs that they construct are considered by even the most casual observer to be some of the most creative wonders of the natural physical world. They construct their webs, not only with uncanny precision, but according to a particular plan and design. That plan and design comes from the ancient memories stored on their individual higher mind tapes. They are as they always were . . . spiders.

So it is, throughout the animal world, from the highest to the lowest, without exception, each animal bringing into their present life the necessary tools and information required for them to both survive and flourish. All the patterns or standards of behavior of each particular animal has been recorded on their individual higher mind tape for use in each and every incarnation.

Q: Are there different types of ancient memories?

A: Yes, there are. In fact, over the years, I have created a system to explain them. Briefly, ancient memories can be divided into two major types: common ancient memories and personal ancient memories. Within each of these classifications are further divisions that explain just how those ancient memories behave. I call them recessive ancient memories, dominant ancient memories, and sporadic ancient memories. Of course, I have made further divisions within the areas of recessive, dominant, and sporadic ancient memories, but they are not necessary to explain at the moment.

Common ancient memories, or CAM, are those ancient memories mutual to all of humankind and are, on the whole, generally responsible for how we behave as members of the human race. They are memories that have been recorded on our higher mind tapes not only since our first incarnation into this world but memories, you'll be surprised to learn, that have been recorded prior to our initial incarnation. They are memories that are shared by or common to all immediate members of the human family.

Examples of common ancient memories are the physical death process experience, the birth experience, associative experiences such as collective defense, sexual imperatives, et cetera.

Personal ancient memories, or PAM, are those memories that have been recorded on our higher mind tapes that are of a personal nature. That is, memories of specific events that have occurred in our past lives that have affected us in a very personal way. Events such as personal encounters with great danger, happy events, traumatically sad

150

occurrences, and even our own personal deaths relative to the particular circumstances surrounding those occurrences throughout our many lives.

Recessive ancient memories, or RAM, are those that, although existing intact on our higher mind tapes, do not manifest themselves in terms of overtly influencing our current lives. Yes, they are there, but however fortunately or unfortunately they would or could influence us, they remain relatively dormant.

Normally, recessive ancient memories are minor in nature and may never surface during a person's life unless triggered, usually by either some vast traumatic event or by an odd, quirky incident. An example of recessive ancient memories may be a pre-modern human pattern of behavior such as cannibalism. Those extremely rare cases of cannibalism not generated by survival-related situations, such as was the case with the unfortunate Donner party in nineteenth-century America, find their genesis through the mechanism of a trauma-trigger, such as is the case in serial-killer instances of human flesh consumption.

Dominant ancient memories, or DAM, are those ancient memories that have a constant and profound influence on our behaviors as individuals as well as a species. The need to procreate and the need to survive, as well as the acquired skills with which to assure survival, are examples of dominant ancient memories.

Finally, there are sporadic ancient memories, or SAM. They are those ancient memories that, from time to time, appear in our lives and affect us either negatively or positively and seem to be beyond both our control and generally beyond the average person's understanding. Sporadic ancient memories lack the benefit of predictability and so often make their appearance at odd moments, sometimes creating great stress in a person, sometimes great elation. It really depends on a person's past history. An example of a sporadic ancient memory may be found in the random homosexual feelings that a person may have which, of course, are directly related to those infrequent times when in former lives they were a functioning member of the opposite sex. This sort of sporadic ancient memory will generally make its appearance in the form of a fantasy during masturbation episodes or even during sexual union with a member of the opposite sex.

Ancient memories, both common and personal, are at work in our lives all the time. In fact, it is the ignoring of the existence of ancient memories by the psychologist and psychiatrist that will forever relegate their efforts at understanding human behavior to abject failure. Until they recognize and understand the relevance and impact of ancient memories in the present life of human beings, their science, based on a lack of information, will be ever incomplete and their patients, as well as society, will suffer unnecessarily as a consequence.

Q: I've heard you use the term "seepage" in reference to ancient memories when you address your class. What exactly is seepage?

A: At various times throughout a person's life, his higher mind exerts itself and subtly influences his lower mind. If, for example, a person was traumatized by a snake in one of his former lives, that traumatic experience, recorded on his higher mind tape, may seep or trickle into his present life in the form of a phobia relating to snakes. If a person's present-life phobias cannot be adequately explained by any of his present-life experiences, then where could those fears have come from? Yes! They came from one of his former lives.

Seepage is exactly how your ancient memories, those memories recorded indelibly on your higher mind tape, come to influence almost every facet of a person's life. Fears, family relationships, loves, hates, attitudes, and aptitudes are the result, to a great extent, of a person's past-life experiences seeping into their present life.

Q: **What about plants? Do they have a higher mind and a lower mind? Can they think?**

A: Plants have a higher mind but not a functioning lower mind. Because they lack a functioning lower mind they do not think the way we do; however, they do think! That is, they think on a higher mind level. It is well known, of course, that plants react to their environment. That is, they bend toward sunlight, lean away from cold, et cetera. In fact, there are plants in existence that are actually carnivorous and have devised some very ingenious ways of capturing their prey. This is, of course, indicative of some sort of mind involvement. This thinking takes place on a higher mind level and is called "thinking without thinking," which is, mystically speaking, the highest form of thought. It is pure thought.

Since plants do have a functioning higher mind supplying them information, unimpeded by the presence of an interfering lower mind, and since all higher minds are mystically linked, you might find it interesting to learn that plants are great receptors of thought. That is, they are truly masters of extrasensory perception and can receive the thoughts of not only other plants but those of humans and animals in their vicinity, as well. In fact, plants cannot only receive a person's thoughts but, depending on the nature of those thoughts, will actually react to them, either positively or negatively. This is one reason why many experienced home gardeners have found that by speaking kind and loving thoughts to their plants, their plants actually respond in a very positive way and flourish.

A plant picking up the nonviolent, beneficially oriented thoughts of the gardener opens up its higher mind gate with

153

that gardener, and a higher mind link is created between them. This higher mind link allows a flow or exchange of M'retz Na'she to take place, permitting the plant to draw extra M'retz Na'she, which, of course, in turn, sustains the plant's good health and encourages its growth.

As I indicated, plants are extremely intuitive and very often react not only to human thoughts of love and kindness but to human thoughts of violence, as well. In fact, you may find it interesting to know that plants have a great aversion to violence, especially violent acts or thoughts of violent acts that may involve them directly.

> **Try this:** If you have plants in your home or business, step into the room where you keep your plants and with a lighter or matches in your hand, entertain the thought of setting fire to the room. You needn't light the lighter. It is just the thought of fire that is required, not the action. What will happen may surprise you. Just the reception of your thought of setting fire to the room or building by your plants will actually be enough to send them into shock, often deep shock. If this experiment is carried out on a continuing basis, your plants will wilt and die. I know how this may sound, but it is true. If you had an EEG machine attached to your plants you would actually be able to record their reactions to your various thoughts. To quote Shakespeare: "There are more things in heaven and earth, Horatio, than are dreamt of in your philosophy!"

Q: **What part does the lower mind play in meditation?**

A: The lower mind is actually the reason for our having the need to steep ourselves in meditation in the first place. It is not only the major cause of most of our problems, but is undeniably the villainously stealthy culprit solely responsible for their flourishing. The lower mind is very much like a spoiled child and does, from moment to moment, whatever is expedient and self-serving. It is the source of our greeds and hatreds, angers and attachments. In meditation, the idea is to quiet the lower mind and to end, once and for all, the self-imposed, self-generated, self-sustained negativity that plagues us in our daily lives.

But the lower mind is very clever and proves itself a redoubtable master of shrewdness and calculation whenever we attempt to bring it under our control. For example, you may, on a particular day, be looking forward to entering into a period of quiet meditation. All day long you find yourself unable to wait for evening, when you can light your candles, burn your incense, arrange yourself on the zafu, and meditate. Throughout the day, the lower mind may have been in perfect accord with this idea. In perfect accord with this idea, that is, until it actually comes time for you to sit. With a smile on your face and determination in your heart, you arrange the room, place your zafu, sit down, center your physical posture, close your eyes, and then it happens! Suddenly, the lower mind says to you, "I'm hungry," or "I'm tired," or you suddenly find yourself scratching, first here and then there, and then over there. Everyone who has ever embarked on a regimen of meditation has experienced one or, more than likely, a vast number of these annoyances.

What is happening is that these are actually illusions that the lower mind creates in order to interfere with your meditation. These are the insidious ploys it makes use of to sabotage your efforts to attain true peace and happiness. Why? Because the lower mind is frightened. It is terrified of the unknown and wonders what would or could happen to it if it relinquishes even the minutest control to you. It conjures up all sorts of bleak and ominous scenarios and frightens itself for no reason. So, in short, the lower mind plays the part of the sneering, untrusting villain or antagonist in your meditative efforts. This, in fact, is precisely the reason why meditation is so very important. We need to wrench the control that the lower mind has over us and our lives and, by so doing, remove the source of many of our miseries.

Q: **Sometimes during meditation my mind is jumbled and wanders. At those times, I am bombarded by thoughts and can't seem to stop them. What should I do when my lower mind persists in interfering with my meditation?**

A: There is a definite connection between our breathing and our ability to produce thoughts, between our breathing and the current state of our lower mind. For example, when the lower mind is agitated and our thoughts are jumbled, our breathing becomes rapid and shallow. Conversely, when our lower mind is quiet, our breathing is correspondingly slow and even.

If a jumbled mind, as you call it, exists prior to meditation, then you must enter into a breathing exercise in order to bring it into a state conducive for meditation.

Try this: Exhale as much air out of your lungs as possible. Once this is done, hold your breath for eight to ten seconds. When you hold your breath in this way, you will notice that your thoughts will quickly diminish and eventually stop! Now, once your thoughts have stopped and you are ready to inhale, you will breathe in a slow controlled manner, and exhale even more slowly. This will bring you into a state where your mind is quiet and prepared for meditation.

The lower mind has a tendency to put up roadblocks when beginners start to meditate. It does so by doing what it does best. That is, it creates a deluge of thoughts specifically designed to distract one from the work at hand. It will often have beginners facing thoughts of past and future events in their lives in an attempt to enmesh them in the mundane. Guile is the forte of the lower mind and so will also create illusions centered around the needs of the body—lack of strength, hunger, pain, itching—many things. One must see these things for what they really are, illusions, and not fall prey to their influence.

Should you begin to sit, for example, and the lower mind begins to interfere with you by generating thoughts of hunger, simply say to it: "Excuse me, I am meditating right now. As soon as I am finished, I will eat." You must be gentle yet firm when you say this to yourself. The firmer you are, the more the lower mind will realize your seriousness over the matter and will quietly relent.

If the lower mind informs you, suddenly, how very tired you are, then, if you must, go to the sink, wash your hands and face, and refresh yourself. Never give in to this clever ruse. If you do and forego your meditation, telling yourself that you will meditate twice as long tomorrow to make up for not doing it now, you are just fooling yourself. You have been taken in by the insidious machinations of the clever little lower mind. Why are you being fooled? Because missing a period of meditation is very much like missing lunch, thinking that by eating two lunches tomorrow you will make up for the lunch you missed today, and that reasoning is non sequitur, illogical. If you do not yield to the lower mind's interference, the lower mind will have to rethink its strategy. It will have to think of something else, and then something else again. In time, the lower mind will relent, finally giving up its foolish attempts at interference, and will cede control over to you.

The firmer that you are in your dealings with the lower mind, the more the lower mind will allow you to do what it is that you have to do. You must persevere, however, and not give up. Never give up! Remember: The monkey who misses his branch, and the man who misses his opportunity, are both irretrievably lost. Of course, if you yield to any of the myriad of devious suggestions offered to you by your lower mind, you will not be sitting that day, and probably not any other day either.

Q: **It seems that when everything is going right in my life, suddenly everything spontaneously disintegrates right in front of my eyes. Sometimes I think that I bring it on myself. Could it have something to do with my lower mind?**

A: The fact is that there exists in the lower mind a mechanism I call the self-destruct button. It is a device so ominous, so insidious, and yet so alluring that, when the button is pressed, it causes our present happiness to quake, crack, and ultimately burst, sublimating into small dark nuclear micro-clouds that loom opaque in our mind's sky and obscure our positive views of life. You know exactly what I am talking about because, at odd times during your life, you have pressed it. That's right . . . you pressed it! Think about it.

The most obvious warning sign, one that should alert you that your hand is approaching your self-destruct button, is a sudden inordinate propensity toward superstitious behavior. You may, for example, find yourself rejecting wishes of good luck, or you may think that "things are going too well . . . I better not press my luck," or you may refuse to talk about some good future event because you feel that if you do, it will cause that good occurrence not to take place. Nonsense!

In reality, when you become superstitious, you are laying the groundwork for your own destruction. You do this by literally creating your own negative future, your own evil eye. Blindly, you are actually instructing your lower mind to become so cautious, so meticulous, so fearful of failure, that your actions become restrictive to the point that the very disaster you once dreaded has now become a self-fulfilling inevitability. Why? Because of the existence of your higher mind. You must understand that your higher mind, which is in communication with other higher minds, transmits to others those negative images created by your lower mind. It enters the lower minds of others in the form of an intuitive knowing. It then becomes your downfall when dealing with those people and, before you know it, that big business deal falls through, your boss fires you, you fight with your spouse, et cetera.

Have you ever gone bowling and thrown two strikes? Assuming that you are not a professional bowler, what thoughts do you entertain when you go up to the line to attempt to throw the third strike? Is there a change in your thinking? Do you get nervous? Do you think that it is impossible to achieve the third strike? Do you become superstitious? How often has your lower mind actually interfered with the achievement of that third strike? If it has, then you have experienced exactly what I am talking about—you have experienced the pressing of the self-destruct button.

What you should understand is that you have the power to avoid pressing your self-destruct button. How? By understanding that your very own lower mind has a way of actually bringing about the things that you fear. It has the very real potential for setting in place the groundwork leading to misfortune. To prevent this from occurring, you must act preemptively, with self-assurance and without fear. That is, as soon as you recognize the appearance of superstition in your life, you must dismiss the superstition as complete and utter nonsense and replace it with a positive thought, a productive thought, a thought that epitomizes the ultimate expression of confidence that you

159

have in your own innate abilities. You are more than you think you are! What will be, will be! The results generated by your newfound confidence will surprise you and you will find that your self-destruct button will remain inviolable from all negativity. Positivity breeds positivity, positively!

Of course, the best and most enduring cure for the uncontrolled, self-destructive nature of the lower mind is to enter into a proper regimen of meditation. A good regimen of meditation will eventuate in the natural destruction of the destruct button by automatically instilling in you the confidence that you need to succeed in all of your endeavors. It does this by freeing you from the oppression that is so often imposed on a person's life as a result of the capricious and often wildly licentious lower mind. Meditation, confidence, and the correct knowledge will not only change your life but will prove to be, themselves, the tools that you need in order to take control of your life.

Q: You teach non-attachment. To me, that conjures up strange images of a guru giving up the world and sitting in deep meditation in a monastery somewhere in Tibet. Could you speak of non-attachment?

A: Non-attachment is really a very simple concept to understand and yet people, in general, almost always miss the point. To begin with, let me say that, in truth, no one owns anything. Everyone comes into this world with nothing material and exits the world exactly the same way, without anything material. In between their comings and goings, all a person really gets to do is merely use those objects. When it is time for that person to leave, all the objects of his attachments, without exception, remain behind.

The pharaohs of ancient Egypt went to extraordinary lengths in order to take their most prized possessions into the next world with them. They had massive stone pyramids erected, replete with elaborate and arcane passageways, in order to safeguard those possessions. But, as we know, the legendary wealth of those pharaohs can currently be viewed in all their pristine glory in the public galleries of various museums of antiquity around the world.

At best, all the material objects of a person's life are leased, and without the remotest possibility of ever being owned whatsoever. This is an immutable truth and forms the basis leading to the wisdom of non-attachment.

Of course, the real issue when it comes to non-attachment truly has nothing to do with the objects themselves. That is, non-attachment should never be understood to imply the "not having of things." In fact, this could not possibly be further from the truth. What non-attachment means is that these things, whatever they are, should not have *you*. Do you understand? A poor man, without any physical or financial assets, can still be caught up in the insidious web of attachment, while a rich man, with more money then he could spend in a dozen lifetimes, may be utterly free from attachment.

Attachment to material objects is a common insecurity that has its genesis in the lower mind. It is the lower mind, in its ignorance, that thinks by possessing material things one could be spared from infirmity by the ever-outstretched and threatening talons of grief and disaster. Also, it is the belief of the lower mind that life without "ownership" is, at best, an utterly useless life, and so it goes on acquiring, hoarding, scratching, conniving, and wheeling and dealing for not only physical possessions but for a place of honor and stature in the world of humanity. Believing that a successful life is measured in financial success and status, the lower mind connives, schemes, lies, cheats, and steals, if necessary. It conjures up idle visions of "success" such as fancy cars, expensive homes, political office, beautiful women, power over others, et cetera, and becomes attached

161

to those visions to the point that all of its happiness in life is dependent solely on the attainment of those objects. Very rarely, if ever, do the attainment of such attachments culminate in a lasting happiness. This is the way of things.

Ask yourself this question: If you were cast into the sea, what would you look to hold onto—a bar of gold or floating debris? Well, obviously, if you held onto the bar of gold your chances of survival would be very suspect, indeed. The floating debris would be a more suitable choice, wouldn't it? Of course, you can argue that the question is non sequitur and does not apply to you. Yes, you could think that, but you are wrong. It does apply to you. It applies to all of us. We are all cast into this great ocean of universe, life after life, and what we cling to will prove to be, in the final analysis, of great importance. What we cling to in life will either help keep us buoyant or bring us down.

In October of 1929, there was an incident that shook the very foundations of the financial world . . . the stock market crash. When this occurred, people were hurling themselves out of skyscraper windows, swallowing poison, shooting themselves, and hanging themselves in the bedrooms of their homes. Those who took such drastic action did so because of their attachments to many of the material things I mentioned earlier. Were their suicides really necessary? Were these people wise or foolish? What would you do if you lost your wealth? The point, when it comes to attachment or non-attachment, is this: Who possesses who? Do you possess things or do things possess you? It is that simple. There is nothing complicated, nothing abstruse, nothing difficult to understand.

162

Attachment comes in many forms. People, as I have indicated before, form attachments to physical objects, but attachments also exist to immaterial things as well— immaterial things such as ideas. What kind of ideas? Ideas that people entertain about themselves, other people, places, things, events, futures, pasts, rights, wrongs, et cetera. Their attachments to those ideas have a price and cost them dearly. What price? A life of misery because, inevitably, clinging to such ideas forms unfounded biases, inane discriminations, passionate hatreds, and unending unresolvable conflicts. All such attachments are based on erroneous notions of reality, a reality that has no basis in fact.

Further, attachment to ideas induces people to develop personal principles that are, at best, self-serving and egocentric. In fact, if you take the time to think about it, every war that was ever fought was fought over such self-serving principles. Adolf Hitler, for example, marched arrogantly into Austria with his army operating under the "principle" that the Austrians were actually Germans, and that Germany should be united. He then went to war with and conquered Poland under the "principle" that he was insulted by the Polish government, and the honor of the German people was at stake. What foolishness! Yet that foolishness spread among his followers and became the basis of a world war.

Hatred, envy, greed—in fact, many of the baser emotions—have their genesis in the womb of the lower mind and its attachments. They are all born of ignorance. To hate someone at all, let alone for ridiculous issues such as the color of his skin or her particular religious affiliation, is pure folly. How can you hate others for what they are when you do not even know who and what you are? Do you understand?

To truly comprehend the concept underlying the practice of non-attachment is really not difficult at all. It is just letting go of attachment to material things and erroneous ideas! Of course, understanding is very easy, but it is the actual practice or implementation of non-attachment in a person's life that is very difficult. Why? Because of the ignorantly acquired habits of not only this present life but

163

of all a person's previous lives. This brings up the concept of attachment as a seed existing in the higher mind from a person's distant past that sprouts insidiously in the lower mind created in each of a person's subsequent incarnations. This, naturally, means that attachment to things and ideas is so ingrained, so entrenched in a person's existence, that it cannot be extricated by merely attempting to reason it out. Attempting to reach detachment through reasoning, in essence, would be like asking the clever little fox of our lower mind to watch over the tender chickens of the coop. If we did let the fox guard the chicken coop, we should not be at all surprised in the morning to find a few of the tenderest chickens missing, and the "innocent" little fox standing there with a fistful of feathers in his mouth mumbling something to the effect that "Everything is all right, boss. You can trust me!"

The only way to end attachment successfully is to destroy it at its roots, and to reach those roots—that is, the higher and lower minds—one must meditate. Without meditation, non-attachment will remain nothing but a pleasant philosophical idea whose successful implementation would be, at best, sporadic and meaningless. To employ a philosophical type of detachment would be like trying to get rid of weeds by simply mowing them down. Doing this, all you would be doing is getting rid of the appearance of the weeds, thinking that if you do not see them, then they are not there. Destroy attachment at its root, and all will be well.

Q: "To be in the world, but not be of the world." What does that mean?

A: It means that while you are living in the world you should not be taken in by the endless multiplicity of things, the innumerable illusions of the world. It means to become aloof and inviolable from the insidious cravings of the lower mind that have you grasping for things that are, in the final analysis, ephemeral and ultimately unimportant. It is the understanding and patient acceptance of the fact that the lower mind is caught up in the illusions of the material world and that, being caught up, confuses that which is real with that which is unreal. It is the knowledge that one must not ignore the truth of the unreality of things, places, thoughts, and existence. It means to be free from the illusions that motivate a person into the voluminous attachments that lead to a life fraught with unnecessary stresses and ultimate futility.

When one understands the true nature of the world, one cannot help to be not of the world. In a very great sense, not being of the world is not an option at all, but is a natural evolutionary consequence of walking a true spiritual path.

Q: **Could you tell us more about emptiness?**

A: I can, but you must be warned that whatever I say on the subject cannot be nearly half the truth. Words on or about the subject are, in the final analysis, nothing but fodder for the voracious appetite of the lower mind. In Japanese, emptiness is called "Ku." You must understand that filling the lower mind with explanations of Ku, no matter how well expressed, is like casting pearls before swine. Swine cannot appreciate the beauty or value of pearls; they do not understand what they are. To swine, a pearl is nothing more than just another stone—shiny, yes, but just a stone nonetheless and something to be discarded or ignored. The only way for a person to truly understand Ku is to experience it for themselves and not just read about it, or listen to it explained by someone else. Even so, for the sake of this particular forum, I will address the subject.

Ku or emptiness, as I have said before, is not nothingness, and it is not experienced by those who fall into an abysmal stupor because they are practicing meditation incorrectly.

That is, some people practicing meditation incorrectly experience what is termed a negative samadhi or negative state of consciousness that they believe, ignorantly, is Ku. It is like mistaking brass for gold and that is a grievous error.

Being unconscious or dead to the world is not Ku, either. However, being unselfconscious, now, that is a great leap closer to it. No, it is still not Ku, but it is a necessary element required on the path that leads to the elusive Ku experience.

In order to experience Ku, the lower mind must be quiet. It must be made so quiet, so still, so silent, that the higher mind, in one great mystical bound, leaps forward across the infinite sea of eternity to settle gently on the other shore. This must be done because it is the very nature of the lower mind to not only be loquacious to a fault but to assiduously take great pains in separating itself from everything else. The lower mind prides itself on its "great" ability to reason and, while doing so, looks for oneness or unity in a universe that it is constantly dividing up into an endless number of infinitely small pieces. How odd this sort of reasoning is.

The higher mind, on the other hand, does no such thing. It does not discriminate between this and that, high and low, good and bad, great and not great, et cetera. The higher mind both exists and functions beyond all qualities of discrimination and so can experience "reality" without the least vestige of conflict, predilection, or debate. It alone can experience Ku. But, to bring this about, you must valiantly throw yourself away and, once thrown away, the question arises . . . who would be left to experience it?

166

Ultimately, if I were to say that Ku is this, or Ku is that, I would ignorantly be placing limits on the limitless; I would be attempting to give form to that which is ultimately formless. Suppose, for example, that you meet a man who has never tasted lox before and this man asks you to explain what lox tastes like. How would you go about it? How could you explain it to him and actually have him know what lox tastes like? Think about it.

If you give it just the slightest thought, you will come to realize that no matter how many words you use, no matter how well you use those words, there is no adequate way to explain it. But, if you tell him where to buy the lox, how to prepare the lox, and then have him eat it, what would result? His own personal experience would totally and fully explain to him what you could not. Then, and only then, would he truly know what lox tastes like. Later, of course, should you run into him again, you may ask him, "Well, what does lox taste like?" He may smile, and in that cryptic smile, without a single word spoken, you will have your answer. Why? Because it will be a smile of knowing, and in that one knowing smile, ten thousand words of explanation are exchanged.

So, to truly know Ku, you must do your meditation. Sit! Sit! Sit! The true answer to what you are seeking will come from the depths of your own soul. Then, one day, we may meet, and I may ask you what Ku is. If you smile a knowing smile, then I will know that you know. That is all.

Q: I've heard you speak of impermanence. What do you mean?

A: In the art of Torishimaru Aiki Jutsu, we call it *mujo*, a Japanese word that means "impermanence." That one word tells us that nothing stands still, everything is in motion, everything is breaking down, everything is impermanent. Mujo or impermanency is the natural state of things in the manifest universe. When one comes to realize this, then one has realized a great deal. Then, each and every time one sees or comes into contact with an object, however briefly, it takes on a new look, and you, the looker, take on a new, true, and invaluable perspective.

Oddly, even though your lower mind bears witness to the workings of impermanency every day of your life, it has the

167

unfortunate tendency to ignore it. It sees impermanency all around it and yet learns nothing from it. However, on those rare occasions when it does manage to learn something of impermanency, it takes that information, processes it in its own special way, and turns it into nothing more than a vain and useless philosophical idea. Then, having reduced mujo or impermanence to just a mere philosophical concept, it believes, in its ignorance, that it really knows just what mujo is.

Understand that whatever I say about mujo can be only the thinnest sliver of the truth of it. For you to know it, for you to know it intimately, you must meditate. Only through the practice and discipline of meditation can the truth of mujo be truly known, and this type of knowing travels light years beyond the brazen grip of mere egocentric philosophical rhetoric. Through meditation, mujo makes itself known in the deepest and most arcane recesses of your being. When this occurs, then and only then will you realize that everything is correct, everything is in place, and everything is as it should be . . . mujo.

Q: You have mentioned the term "priorities." What exactly do you mean by that?

A: It is really very simple. As I have mentioned earlier, people, in their ignorance, live their lives as if they were permanent residents here. Living that way naturally not only affects the way they think about the world and their place in it, but how they carry on their day-to-day affairs. They do so many things in their attempts to achieve happiness based on the idea of permanent residency that they almost invariably fail. It really, in large part, comes down to a question of priorities or the things that we deem important in life. Yes, everyone has them, even you. Of course, your priorities are set and currently direct your life, but suppose that something occurs in your life that would give you cause to

168

reconsider what is truly important. Suppose, for example, that you received from your physician the unfortunate news that you had only three months to live and that there was nothing medically that could be done to alter that grim prognosis. What would your priorities be then? Would they change? Would you change? I am sure that both you and your current priorities would change.

Think about it. Having three months to live, what would you worry about? Would you worry about your telephone bill, car payment, dental bills, credit card balances, bank interests? Would you worry about who will win an Oscar for best supporting actor next year or who will win the baseball World Series in the fall? I don't think so. Suddenly, you will come to the shocking, eye-opening realization that a brand new list of priorities is in order, and that list would be comprised of what is currently truly important to you.

Well, in point of fact, not many people know exactly how much time they have left in this present incarnation. *Incertum est quam longa cuiusque nostrum vita futura sit;* It is uncertain how long the life of each one of us is going to be. If the statistics show that a man living in the United States will live to the average age of seventy years, and a woman about seventy-five years, the question is, how old are you now? Are you thirty-five, forty, fifty? Think about it! If you are forty, statistically, you only have thirty years left to live, and that is not a great deal of time, is it? If you are fifty, then statistically you only have twenty years left. Of course, there is no guarantee that you have even one day left. Knowing this, don't you think that it may be in your best self-interest if you change your priorities now? After all, happiness is something that should not be put off for some distant tomorrow, that "someday" just beyond the horizon. That "someday" may never get here.

To acquire true happiness requires, more often than not, that the priorities a person currently has in life, and which have not brought them happiness throughout the years, be changed. The present moment is really all that exists in your life. Tomorrow will always be tomorrow. That is, it will always be coming and never arriving. If you had to eat every meal tomorrow, you would undoubtedly starve to death, wouldn't you? It is not any different when it comes to happiness. If you always delay your happiness until tomorrow, you would never achieve happiness at all. Do you understand?

Similarly, yesterday is forever gone and cannot be brought back. Yesterday is like a vision, or a memory of a memory, a dream in reverse. Those who live in the past are forever blind to the present. They live steeped in the abysmal mire of an ancient time and place.

If I were to ask you how much money you currently have in your pocket, I am sure you would be able to tell me without looking, within a few dollars, what that amount is. And yet, if I were to ask you how much time you have left in this incarnation, you could not even begin to venture a guess. Isn't it strange that a person who knows how much money he has is so very careful about the way that money is spent? He makes sure that he does not overspend, and painstakingly guards his money like he guards the pupils of his eyes. Yet, paradoxically, that same person who does not know how much time he has left will frivolously squander his time away in the idle pursuit of things that are ultimately unimportant and of no lasting value to him. Isn't it odd? A person who can always make money spends it so cautiously, while that same person who lacks the power to create time does not care at all how he spends it. Do you understand? If you do, then you know what I mean about priorities.

Life is so very short and to spend it in idle pursuits of mundane acquisitions is to fritter that life away. To spend one's life chasing after shadows is sad, very sad. Why do what you will regret? Determine what is real and what is not real. Reconsider your priorities and you will be guaranteeing your own happiness.

Q: What is "nowness"?

A: Nowness is the state of ideal attention. That is, it is a state of being where all that exists is the present moment, without any thought of past or future. It is paying total attention to what you are doing in the moment that you are doing it. If you are eating, for example, just eat. If you are reading, just read. If you are eating and you are thinking about your bills, or what is on television tonight, then you are not in a state of nowness. If you are reading and you are not totally concentrating on the act of reading then, again, you are not in the present. Regardless of what you happen to be doing, if you are thinking about something else, then you are not attentive and not in a state of nowness.

When you are not attentive, not here and now, your present peace of mind may be disturbed by some oncoming future event for no good reason. For example: Remember when you were in high school and you had a very important test coming? It was Friday and the test was to take place on Monday. That night you went to a party and enjoyed the evening for several hours when it happened! What happened? Suddenly, thoughts about the impending test darted across your mind and your night was ruined. You tried not to think about the test but to no avail. Your present happiness was destroyed by the thoughts of a future event.

Understand that if I were to ask you how you feel, I am not asking you how you felt yesterday or how you believe you might feel tomorrow. I am asking you how you feel at this very moment. If you were to answer me by saying, "at the present moment I feel fine," then you are fine. You are

171

fine because now is all that exists. Tomorrow will always be beyond your grasp and yesterday is forever gone. All you have is now. It is the only reality.

Q: **Could you explain more about the higher mind's role when it comes to ancient memories?**

A: In life, what a person likes or dislikes or is drawn to or repulsed by is not necessarily a lower mind choice. You must understand that one's likes and dislikes from innumerable past incarnations are also recorded on one's higher mind tape and are not, necessarily, the result of present-life circumstances or experiences. If, for example, a person has a fondness for eating a certain type of meat, or a child rejects, out of hand, a certain type of food, this may not be just a spontaneous subjective response to the way the food was prepared, the way it looks, or the way it smells. It may be directly related to past-life memories, negative or positive, of that person's experience with that particular food that causes them to react for or against the eating of it. Remember, the higher mind tape has been recording throughout all of a person's many past incarnations, and so a person enters into this present life already predisposed to particular things, things such as certain forms of music, art, science, athletics, particular foods, et cetera.

A person's leanings toward or away from something, or even their skills in their present life, may often be quite surprising to many people—such as in the case of a five-year-old piano virtuoso, seven-year-old mathematical genius, or six-year-old artist. Those who know about the nature of the higher mind, of course, are not that surprised because they know that the various talents of these geniuses were already there, preexistent on their higher mind tapes.

Take this case: A mother gives birth to twin sons. They are raised exactly the same way, go to the same schools,

172

have the same friends, and are exposed to the same influences. One son, however, passionately detests school and would rather spend his time fishing or playing baseball, and the only music that he can produce comes from his acquired ability to turn on the radio or CD player, while the other son seems to be diametrically opposite in that respect. He not only loves school but even entertains the lofty ambition of becoming a hypothetical physicist when he grows up, and finds baseball and fishing boring. He, rather than playing a CD, would rather spend hours at a time practicing the violin. This scenario is, of course, very common.

What gives each of these boys their different propensities in life is not attributable to anything biological, nor is it necessarily based on their particular present life exposures. It is very often what comes to them from their individual pasts. So, clearly, there is more to a person's leanings and talents than is at first sight outwardly apparent. Their leanings, aversions, and "depth" are more likely than not the result of what happens to be recorded on their higher mind tapes since time immemorial.

Q: **Often, I've had the opportunity to do some exciting things, important things, but for some reason, when the time came, I never quite had the courage to actually do them. Is that normal? What can I do about it?**

A: Yes, it is very normal. In fact, you may take some comfort in knowing that many people over the years have come to me with precisely the same problem. What you are asking about is a very common problem and one that is not so difficult to overcome.

173

> Listen! One day, in the wilds of New Jersey, a large contingent of farm animals decided that they were going to go on a little hike. Although it was the dead of winter, they were not in the least bit

deterred from their outing. Walking Indian-file on a very narrow, winding path through a large section of woods, they came to the edge of a vast frozen lake. Undaunted, the first animal, a large cow, deftly trotted across the ice. She was followed by an enormous bull, a mule, and then a horse. Next in line was a little fox who, instead of crossing, just stood there staring at the ice-covered lake. "Let's go, Mr. Reynard! Why are you waiting? You're holding up the line!" shouted the rooster, standing impatiently behind him. Looking at the ice and then turning to the rooster, the little fox said, "Oh no, not me! I'm not going to cross the ice until I see an elephant cross it!"

Needless to say, there are no elephants to be found in even the wildest unsettled sections of New Jersey. So? So, twenty years later, there could be found a little fox skeleton still on the wrong side of the lake. Clearly, even having witnessed much larger, heavier animals cross the ice safely, the little fox should have known that it would have been safe for him as well, but why was he still afraid to cross? It was simply out of fear. Logically, of course, after having witnessed 1500-pound animals cross the ice, the little fox, weighing all of 15 pounds, should have deemed the crossing safe, but he didn't, and so he died without ever having explored the wonders awaiting him on the other side of the lake. You see, fear frequently transcends logic and, more often than not, interferes not merely with our need to learn as much as we can about the world around us but very often undermines our lives to the extent of actually limiting our ability to enjoy peace and happiness while we are here.

How many times has the little fox of your lower mind prevented you from doing the things in life that you have wanted to do? How many opportunities have you missed because of fear? Even though you know that others have crossed the ice with much success, why have you faltered? Fear of change? Fear of failure? Fear of . . . ?

A wise man lives bravely and without regret. Do not be someone who, out of fear, misses the wonderful opportunities available in life. If you are able to read this book, and obviously you are, then it is not too late! It means that you are still alive, still subject to opportunity! If there were things in life that you have always wanted to do, but were afraid to, stop, and reconsider the fate of the foolish little fox. My advice to you is to cross the ice and begin to live your life to the fullest and without regret! Don't spend all of your time thinking about it. Just do it! Time is fleeting!

Q: Could you explain dreams?

A: Dreams have their origins in one of three places: the lower mind, the higher mind, or the soul. Dreams that have their genesis in the lower mind have as their basis events recorded on the lower mind tape. Generally, the main factors that constitute the salient elements of lower mind-based dreams are emotion-connected. That is, they are created and brought to the surface in order to resolve some unfulfilled emotion that simply should have been dissipated at the time the actual event took place, but for one reason or another wasn't. When, for example, an event takes place in a person's life that has an emotional element connected with it, such as a hate element or a fear element, and the working out of that emotion and its associated energy wasn't totally fulfilled at the time of the occurrence, then it is brought to finality by being dissipated through the various machinations of a dream. Often, the dream is more horrifying than the original real-life event, and at times it is much less so, the quality being determined by the amount of emotional energy needing to be dissipated. Sometimes the

175

dream is happy, sometimes sad, sometimes sexual, sometimes not. Whether the dream is happy, sad, sexual, or even terrifying in nature, it is a perfectly normal and healthy event. You could call a dream an emotional safety valve that very often resolves emotional events and may be responsible for ultimately assuring a person's mental health.

An example of a lower mind-based dream would be one that is sexual in nature. Here, as in the case of a male or female lacking a physical release of sexual tension, a sexually stimulating dream would be produced by the lower mind in order to fulfill not only an emotional need but a physical need as well (if uninterrupted, the dream will almost always culminate in ejaculation or orgasm).

Without lower mind-based dreams, the attendant emotion will remain unfulfilled. It will abide alive and active on the lower mind tape and be a constant drain of a person's feminine energy. If there are enough unfulfilled emotions, then the drain of a person's feminine energy could reach levels so critically low that it interferes with the ability for that person to function properly during the course of his day, and may produce an insidious cycle of events culminating in a state of depression.

Again, you can think of lower mind-based dreams as a sort of safety device designed to preclude any unnecessary loss of energy by the body. One should not pay too much attention to them when they occur. You must understand that these particular dreams, which have their origins in the lower mind, are not prophetic in nature and have no hidden good or evil omens whatsoever inherent in them.

Unfortunately, those who do consider them as prophetic are going to be greatly disappointed when those dreams, if they promise good things, aren't fulfilled. Moreover, they will condemn themselves to suffer needless anxiety if those lower mind-based dreams have negative elements associated with them. Again, lower mind-based dreams are just an emotional safety valve, that's all.

Higher mind-based dreams are really very similar to lower mind-based dreams except that the unfulfilled emotions generally have their genesis as a result of events that have taken place in former lives, past incarnations. It is the valiant attempt of nature to resolve past emotional issues and finally lay them to rest. Again, as in the case of lower mind-based dreams, there are generally no prophetic elements in them. However, there are odd exceptions to that rule and the higher mind does, in fact, take on the mantle of seer and prophet. At those rare times, the higher mind receives prophetic information coming from the soul that it presents to a person in the form of a dream. This is not so strange when you consider the fact that the higher mind is the link between the two worlds, that of the mundane physical world of the body and that of the mysterious ethereal world of the soul.

Soul-based dreams are of a different character altogether. They are generally prophetic in nature but can also be learning oriented, as well. Because the soul is one with God and has the attributes of God, the amount of information that it is privy to is unlimited. Soul-based dreams cannot only tell you about the infinity of past, present, and future events, but can also teach you about the nature of existence by bringing to your attention what it feels you need to know in order to aid in your spiritual evolution. Even so, parenthetically, you must understand that each soul, with its vast store of arcane knowledge and with all of its inherent abilities, still lacks certain elements that will eventually lead to its emancipation within the context of God's redemption. For this reason, the impetus that is responsible for one's taking of a spiritual path originates in the soul and not in the lower or even higher mind.

The real problem in determining exactly where a dream has originated is that all three are projected on the lower mind screen. Higher mind-based dreams seep into the lower mind; soul-based dreams seep into the higher mind and are subsequently passed on to the lower mind for review. For this reason, interpretation of dreams is very difficult unless the interpreter is extremely experienced in being able to differentiate their origins. Clearly, dream interpretation becomes even more difficult when, for example, the dream is soul-based and then passed on to the higher mind. When this occurs, the higher mind is stimulated and adds or superimposes information of its own on that soul-based dream, information that may, in fact, have relevance to a past event or situation as yet unresolved. Should this occur, then the higher mind passes a cloaked dream onto the lower mind, and more mischief in all likelihood may take place. The lower mind, through its rather unsophisticated machinations, now takes that already impure soul-based dream and again superimposes on it current emotion-based information, further distorting the original prophetic soul-based dream. This is the way of things. Very rarely would a person receive a pure, untainted soul-based dream. Only an expert well-versed in the nature of lower mind, higher mind, and soul-based dreams could make an accurate determination and subsequent interpretation.

Q: I have been angry on a number of occasions and I sometimes let it get the best of me. When this happens, I almost always get myself into trouble. What are your feelings about anger?

A: At one time or another everyone gets angry. Wise men get angry and fools get angry. A wise man's anger, however, lasts for a very short time and he does not act on that anger. He waits patiently until it safely subsides. A wise man waits patiently so that, if he still feels the need to act, his actions are not dictated by that emotion. He does so because he understands that a man who acts out of emotion tends to overreact. He knows that he may not possess all the facts necessary to make a truly wise and prudent decision and so guards himself from acts of foolish violence and unnecessary cruelty. A wise man knows that violence is something to be assiduously avoided.

Sometimes anger comes from a sense of frustration, sometimes from the sense of being wronged, sometimes from fear, and sometimes anger arises from the insidious nature of one's personal inner insecurities. If you are a person who is prone to anger, then you must come to understand how truly destructive it is. When you are angry to the point of saying or doing something that you may regret later, then, if circumstances permit, you must remove yourself from that situation and not return until you are calmer.

Angry words hurt, and that hurt may very well come back to you; it may rebound. Once angry, hurtful words pass your lips, they cannot be recalled and the damage that they do to others can be long-lasting. When you are in the throes of anger, it is often better to say nothing and remain mute until the anger passes.

Whenever anger leads to acts of violence, then, clearly, nobody wins, nobody has the chance to win. When you feel that you have been wronged by another person and anger wells up inside of you, you must learn to let go of it. You must release it as quickly as possible because the lower mind, if given the time, has a great tendency to embellish the facts that led to that anger and what you will have is an exacerbation of anger based, for the most part, on false imaginings. In fact, at times, your anger may even be triggered and/or increased by particular events that may actually have taken place in your past and have little relevance to your present situation. Even so, you must let go of it. You must always let go. Why cause harm or injury to yourself or others? You must make every attempt to always be harmless and blameless in all things. *Est innocent adfectio talis animi, quae noceat nemini;* Let go of anger and live in peace!

Q: **What is fear and how does one overcome it?**

A: As you must already know, fear is a natural lower mind reaction to danger, potential danger, and even imagined danger. When present, it can either be a noteworthy ally or an insidious foe; it can save your life or cause you great harm. When, for example, there is a legitimate reason to be afraid, such as in the case of a forest deer suddenly becoming aware of the presence of a mountain lion, that fear will trigger a flight mechanism in the deer and it will flee for safety into the forest. Certainly, if deer did not possess this quality and nature had erred by making them fearless, the entire species would have become extinct many millions of years ago. In this case, fear acts as a life-preserving ally which, needless to say, is of great benefit to the individual deer. If it did not exist, deer would have stood their ground against mountain lions and other predators with obviously catastrophic results.

However, not all fear is grounded in reality. The lower mind often has a tendency to embellish the sensory information coming to it by superimposing on that information any one of a combination of things including, but not limited to, one's own personal past experiences, the past experiences of others, or even the various experiences that have happened to fictional characters in a movie, television show, or book. Remember, the lower mind tape is constantly recording all of the sensory input it receives and it plays that information back, often irresponsibly, whenever and wherever it wants to. It can, for example, take what is essentially an innocuous situation and transmute it quite easily into an event of great weight and immanent peril.

You must understand that when this occurs, it is both real and unreal at the same time. It is unreal in the sense that the benign situation became perilous only by reason of the intervention of the lower mind's capricious machinations, and it is real in the sense that the person experiencing it cannot perceive the reality of its non-reality.

When the lower mind embellishes a particular situation and produces fear, it causes that person to overreact, and the results of that overreaction may actually precipitate violence or, at the very least, cause an unwarranted escalation of lesser hostilities.

To make this easier to understand, I will give you an example of just how the lower mind mishandles sensory information and creates non-reality. It is a common circumstance, one that I am sure you can identify with. Have you ever been in a situation where you are very angry with a particular person, say, a car mechanic or plumber? If you have, you may have noticed that as your anger escalated, you found yourself reaching the point where you started to become fearful. That's correct, fearful! *You* were the one who was angry and yet, at some point, that feeling of anger simultaneously co-existed with a growing sense of great fear. Why? Remember that I told you it is the nature of the lower mind to react to the sensory input coming into it? Well, aside from the obvious sensory information coming to it from the outside, there is also an enormous profundity of sensory information coming to it from the inside. Understand, anger is a very strong emotion and causes a number of natural physiological reactions in the body. One of those reactions is to trigger the stimulation of the adrenal glands which, in turn, causes the glands to pump adrenaline into the blood stream. The infusion of the adrenaline results in various symptoms such as sweaty palms, dry mouth, and tense muscles. When muscles are tense for any length of time, micro-spasms or shaking results. Think about it! You

181

are the one who is angry, but your palms are sweating, your mouth is dry, and your hands, legs, and body are trembling. Aren't these exactly the same symptoms that a person in great fear would have? Of course, they are!

What happens is that the lower mind takes the sensory information coming to it from the body—that is, the dry mouth, sweaty palms, and muscular trembling—and immediately associates it with fear. Why? Because fear is a more natural instinct than that of anger and leaves a larger and louder imprint on the lower mind tape. So, when the lower mind becomes aware of the symptoms, it recklessly rolls back the tape and blindly associates it with the most salient corresponding set of causes. This causes the lower mind to enter a fear mode. It is snared by the adhesive web of egregious illusions spun by its own machinations. It is that simple.

Another example that you might identify with, and one that is really very common, occurs when you go to the movies. If you have ever seen the movie "Jaws," for example, you probably remember the scene where the pier broke and a fisherman was dumped into the water. You knew what was going to happen next. Right? Of course! There was the poor man in the water some distance from the shore when, suddenly, you heard the low, driving beginning of the haunting musical strains that told you not only that the shark was in the vicinity but that the shark was coming to dine. How did your body react? Did your heart race? Did you feel your pulse quicken? What did you experience as the music began to get faster, louder, and more intense? Do you remember the man's friend on the shore calling out to him "Don't turn around, just swim"? Did you find yourself screaming "Swim . . . don't turn around" or, perhaps, suddenly, it was *you* in the water and, without a conscious thought, you found that you were beginning to move your hands as if you were swimming?

If you think about it, you walked into the movies knowing all the time that it was just a movie . . . professional actors, water, and a rubber great white shark projected on a silver-tinted screen in glorious cinemascope and living color. There was absolutely nothing real about any of it, right? Right—that is, until it happens! What happens? Until you remember that you are just watching a movie, you start reacting to everything you see on the screen as if it were real and actually occurring. Of course, when you catch yourself reacting this way, you try to settle yourself down and remove your fear by repeatedly telling yourself that it is just a movie, an illusion, and that, in reality, no one is being killed or injured. But does seeing the truth of the cinematic deception remove your fear, or do you find yourself still trapped in the nets of illusion? Actually, the lower mind itself can be thought of as a very unique sort of movie screen upon which is projected not only factual data but manufactured information as well, both of which subtly blend to offer you not only a distorted view of a particular singular event but, in fact, a completely distorted view of both life and the world.

The higher mind, on the other hand, is quite different. True, it also records all the events and sensory information, both internal and external, being presented to it, but with one great difference: it does not make judgments. It sees an event clearly and without bias and stores all incoming sensory information without the slightest embellishment. Fear, anger, and the emotions are not to be found dominant there. Since meditation quiets the lower mind, allowing the higher mind to come forward, it follows that if the higher mind was central and operational in a person's life, fear would itself disappear.

Just as one could dispel the fears generated by the illusions depicted in a movie by understanding the non-reality of what is actually taking place on the screen, so can one dispel the equally inordinate fears generated by the subtle illusions created by the world and projected onto the screen of one's lower mind. With the sword of meditation, you must cut through the web of illusion and be free—free to live a life devoid of fear and illusion.

Q: **What about the things that people carry with them, such as guilt, anger, and painful experiences? Could you address this?**

A: There is an old story:

> Zen monks in training at a monastery are not supposed to have any contact whatsoever with women. In fact, they are not even allowed to speak to them. One morning just before sunrise, a young monk and an old monk were on their way back to the monastery from the local village. Just after sunrise they came to a small stream. Standing by the stream was a beautiful geisha dressed in a bright red silken kimono. She was afraid of ruining her kimono in an attempt to ford the stream and did not know what to do.
>
> Noticing her dilemma, the old monk spoke to her for a few moments, then lifted her up and carried her across the stream. He gently placed her on the other side. The two monks then continued their journey to the monastery. They walked all day without a single word passing between them. Finally, just after sunset, they reached the monastery gate. The young monk could not keep silent any longer and, turning to the old monk, said, "How could you?"
>
> "How could I what?" replied the old monk.
>
> "You know that we are not allowed to have anything to do with women while we are in training," said the young monk. "How could you pick that woman up this morning and carry her across the stream?"

Smiling, the old monk remonstrated, "How could you!"

"How could I what?" answered the puzzled young monk.

"This morning, at sunrise, I picked the geisha up, carried her across the stream, and then I put her down. You have been carrying her all morning, all afternoon, and into the evening. When are you going to put her down?"

It is the nature of the naive, untrained lower mind to unknowingly collect and carry some of life's negative experiences to the point where they become ponderously burdensome. Often, these negative experiences interfere with one's ability to enjoy life and they can actually drive us like sheep recklessly down the narrow, dark, and serpentine road toward various stages of depression. How many geishas do you carry? And how often have these geishas of yours interfered with your enjoyment of life?

The beginning of "putting down the geisha" is to understand that all your life experiences are teachers. That's right! Even your seemingly most negative life experiences are teachers. In fact, more often than not, they turn out to be the very best teachers and are not to be avoided. They broaden you and teach you, if you are attentive, the truth about the nature of your lower mind and its relationship to the very matrix of existence. So, instead of fruitlessly fighting these experiences or running from them, one must learn to accept them. When accepted and properly understood, a person will find that all of his "geishas" will gradually disappear, leaving him unburdened, tranquil, and happy!

Q: Sometimes I do something that results in guilt, and my conscience bothers me. What is the cause of a guilty conscience? How can I rid myself of it?

A: The lower mind, in truth, only knows the difference between right and wrong if what is recorded on the lower mind tape contains that information. In a sense, it is quite beyond the average person's control to reason right and wrong when it lacks the basic programming that is required in order for it to do so. It is very much like a computer that has been negligently misprogrammed and, as a consequence, produces only erroneous results. If the computer is misprogrammed, how could it produce anything but mistakes?

It is true that what is recorded on the lower mind tape is also recorded on the higher mind tape, but there are two major factors that influence the higher mind tape that are ostensibly missing on the lower mind tape. The first is that, besides all the sundry information that has been recorded on the higher mind tape in a person's present incarnation, there exists the vast ocean of information and experiences that were recorded on that person's higher mind tape from countless past lives. All the good and the bad lessons from a person's previous lives are indelibly recorded there for all time. To have been a moral person in any or all of one's past lives would necessarily have been responsible, in part, for the recording of those principles of right and wrong on their higher mind tape. Secondly, as I had previously mentioned, the higher mind is a person's link with God and the universe, and information of a moral nature is certain to come to it from those sources.

Everyone makes mistakes. Everyone! Why? Because of the very frail and mistake-making nature intrinsic to the lower mind. Remember, the lower mind is invariably capricious and childlike, and often does what is expedient and in its own self-interest. It sometimes, for example, causes us to enter into actions that result in injury to others. Even though the lower mind believes that its actions were correct at the time, that rectitude, again, was based solely on the erroneous notions of right and wrong previously recorded on its tape. A guilty conscience will come to a person when the difference between right and wrong that was recorded on the higher mind tape bleeds through to the lower mind. You will find a guilty conscience occurring most often during those times when the lower mind is quieter than normal. Why? Because when the lower mind is quiescent, there is a great deal less interference with any messages or information coming to it from the higher mind.

Let me give you an example, one I am sure that you can readily identify with. It is very common. Think back to your youth. As a teenager, it was natural to go through little rebellions with your parents. When those arguments occurred, the lower minds of those involved were very tense and agitated and so were either partially or totally out of control. As the argument evolved, frustration invariably set in. Consequently, there was an ego-generated vying for control. As your anger increased, so did your lack of control until, out of frustration, you said or did something that you shouldn't have. You may have resorted to hurtful insults and offensive language. At the time of the fight, your lower mind was so agitated that you acted quite without thought. Later on, when your lower mind settled down and became quiet, it first allowed the messages and information coming from your higher mind to get through. However, because your lower mind was not totally quiescent, all you were able to receive was the mere sense of it, not the letter of it. That sense of it entering your lower mind was, in fact, responsible for your feelings of guilt. In other words, because of all the past understandings of right and wrong variously recorded on your higher mind tape, the higher mind tape acted in the capacity of an invisible but not so

187

quiet moral monitor and sent its sundry messages of morality to you from your own past, whether you liked it or not. The result is what is commonly called a guilty conscience.

Of course at times, more often than not, the lower mind, as soon as it feels the uncomfortable tremors of guilt, looks to immediately justify its capricious actions through the often manipulative machinations prompted by its own self-interest. It would, for example, justify its actions by firmly fixing the blame, in this case, on the parents. How? With such egocentric thoughts as, "They don't understand me," or, "They started it," or, "What do they know?" or, "They're too stupid to understand anything!" This is one of the handy devices that the lower mind uses to overcome guilt. I am sure that you have experienced it. Of course, another way that the lower mind deals with feelings of guilt is to apologize. By apologizing, the lower mind looks to make things right. It seeks to maintain an eternal balance, if you will, of the morality inherent within the principles that are ingrained on one's higher mind tape.

Of course, the lower mind, being self-serving, will often preempt the possibility of a guilty feeling by justifying its actions prior to an event. This, also, is really very common. For example, the lower mind might say, "Everyone is a thief and a liar, so I'm just doing what they would do," or, "If I don't do it to him, he will do it to me," or, "All my friends cheat on their wives, so why shouldn't I?" You get the idea. The lower mind justifies its actions so that guilt not only is assiduously avoided, but one can actually become a hero to oneself as the result of first justifying an action and then actually executing it. Naturally, when this occurs, even the vaguest possibility of a guilty conscience is totally out of the question. And since the execution of an immoral act brings not only a sense of sublime satisfaction in terms of personal achievement, it actually creates a very real sense of taking a giant leap forward in one's personal evolution and promotes the repeating of that act sans guilt.

People who are prone to committing violent acts, thefts, et cetera, almost always have prior justification for those acts. The lower mind simply looks to protect itself against the waves of guilt that it would ordinarily experience if it did not take that precaution. In an odd way, it is a sort of guilt insurance. This guilt insurance allows those individuals to loot, pillage, cheat, lie, commit acts of violence against their fellow man, et cetera, and is, in large part, responsible for the development of immoral principles that lead not only to personal immoral acts but to immoral acts committed on a much larger scale within and between nations.

Q: **What about the mind and the power of self-healing? Can you speak about it a little bit?**

A: Briefly, healing of one sort or another is taking place in the body all the time—germs are being combated, injuries are being repaired, dead cells are being replaced—it is a series of ongoing reparation processes, all of which are under the direction of the higher mind.

To begin to understand the healing process, you must realize that each and every cell of the body has a private life, as well as a life of function within the context of the total body. That is, it has a consciousness that allows it to simultaneously operate both as an individual cell and as a vital functioning constituent of the whole.

Moreover, every cell, without exception, has a *sey'chol keh'sher* or mind link with the higher mind of the body to which it is native. This ever present, ever functioning mind link is what facilitates the unparalleled ease with which the billions of individual cells of the human body act in concert with each other for the common good of the whole. It is because of the sey'chol keh'sher that any foreign cells or

189

organisms, disease-producing or benign, that invade the body are considered and subsequently dealt with as something alien. This is so because those cells and organisms lack the familial characteristics required for acceptance by the higher mind.

Whenever there is disease in the body, the information concerning the particulars of that disease, such as that of the nature and magnitude of the invading organisms, is rapidly disseminated to the higher mind which, in turn, directs the process of healing—including, but not limited to, the introduction of more M'retz Na'she to that area. It is the sey'chol keh'sher, for instance, that transmits the orders to the leukocytes or white blood cells to attack and destroy the alien interlopers.

In cases of trauma to the body, the higher mind, when possible, oversees the replacement of damaged cells according to the particular design of the sheath. This, of course, indicates why and how a lizard, having lost its tail, can grow a new one.

Naturally, the amount of M'retz Na'she that is available to the higher mind will determine, for the most part, its ability to effectively deal with disease or injury. It is for this reason that, depending on the nature of the disease or injury, the higher mind may very well divert M'retz Na'she from other areas of the body in an attempt to set things aright. This, of course, in certain circumstances explains the malaise so often associated with severe trauma and disease. To help in the effort of recovery, particular regimens of special meditative techniques should be followed in order to both conserve the already dwindling supply of M'retz Na'she contained within the body, as well as to promote the accumulation of as much M'retz Na'she as possible from sources on the outside.

What the special meditations do is basically dual in nature. First, they quiet the lower mind down to the point where its activities relevant to the dissipation of M'retz Na'she are reduced to a minimum. Secondly, with the lower mind quiescent, the higher mind can be directed to increase its efforts at healing through the introduction of special orders relevant to mandated sheath changes. The combination of the two can cause almost miraculous healings and cures, quite beyond the normal.

Q: Growing up, I seemed to always be fighting with my parents or my older sister. It seems to go on in almost every family. How does the lower mind enter into situations like that?

A: Believe it or not, the cause of the family conflicts that you are speaking of actually has its origin in the misty primordial regions of the higher mind and not, as supposed, in the murky, frivolous, and self-centered tracts of the lower mind, although the lower mind does pick up on it and carry it to its conclusion.

The sibling rivalry and child-parent dissension that you speak of really has very little to do with what a psychologist might call personality disorders, or personality conflicts, and has nothing whatsoever to do with how one views one's parents or siblings intellectually.

The simple truth of the matter is really easy to understand. From time immemorial, the higher mind tape has been recording every experience, every thought, every feeling, and every sensory input occurring in each of a person's many incarnations. Since man has always been a social animal—that is, has always lived in and around others of his kind—the social skills necessary for his individual survival are recorded there. To this end, as in the case of all other animals, there has always been the need to establish a pecking order within their particular group, not, as many suppose, because Mother Nature mandates it, but because of the real and ever-present need to eat, protect oneself, and propagate the species. These practical needs,

191

and the methods of achieving them, are all recorded on the higher mind tape. Remember, the higher mind is with you always, in every incarnation. It is important to note that this compulsion to establish a pecking order is quite unapparent to the lower mind because the instructions come to it subliminally from the higher mind. This behind-the-scenes process, of course, both confuses and frustrates not only those who are involved with the problem directly, but also those who are brought into the fray as counselors.

Simply, this is how it works: Suppose, for example, that a family is composed of a father, mother, daughter, and son, the son being the youngest. The young son will, as he ages, invariably begin to argue and cause dissension with his older sister. This occurs because he has reached the point where the experiences recorded on his higher mind tape mandate him to challenge her in order to usurp her place in the pecking order and move up himself. As he matures, and assuming that he has nothing that impedes that maturity such as may be the case with mental incompetence or a debilitating disease, he will reach the point when she will no longer be a deterrent to his ascension in the family pecking order and he quickly passes her by. With this first passage comes an era of relative peace between them. This is so because the yielding to her brother's natural right of passage is also ingrained on her higher mind tape. This will cause her to yield, not only because she may, as an individual, lack the ability to prevent it from happening, but mostly because there seems to be a naturalness to it, one that she accepts, even though she cannot quite explain it to herself. As they both mature, there will be a growing sense of dependency that she will feel toward her brother. She will feel safe with her brother and raise him, knowingly or unknowingly, to the status of one who would defend her and keep her from harm. In most of nature, this is the way of things.

Now, however, the next person the young son must face in the pecking order is his mother. This presents much more of a problem because his mother will be doing whatever she can to maintain her place in the pecking order, and she wields a little more power than did her daughter. So, as the son ages and grows in physical stature, any fear tactics that the mother may have employed successfully in the past to control him, such as threats of corporal punishment, no longer frighten him—he has outgrown the fear of her as a formidable disciplinarian. When it reaches this point, the real campaign against his mother begins. He will, for example, instinctively become as rebellious as the current circumstances permit, all in an attempt to weaken her psychologically. He will challenge her at each and every opportunity, even arrogantly questioning her right to issue him any orders or imposing any sort of restriction on his movements. It may take several years of disruptive confrontation, but you can be sure that, eventually, he will pass her by in the pecking order.

Naturally, throughout the warring years, in a vain and often desperate attempt to delay the inevitable, the mother would often issue appeals to his father in order to gain support for her deteriorating position in the pecking order, but in the final analysis, any support that she receives inevitably proves to be nothing but a delaying tactic predestined to failure. Naturally, if there is no father figure present in the house to support her, she would be hard-pressed to effectively defend her position, and would succumb all the more quickly to her son's pressures.

In the case of the single mother, if she refuses to yield to her son, there will develop a very unfortunate consequence, and that is that their relationship would be fraught with "eternal" in-fighting and they, in most cases, will develop a love/hate relationship that will last for decades, if not longer.

Now, once the son passes the mother in the pecking order, he really has a problem, one that takes the form of the father. This is his final challenge, one that will dictate his ultimate status in the family. If the father is strong enough, the son will never be able to pass him in the pecking order. This will have the son, prompted by the instincts presented to him by his higher mind, leave the nest and strike off on his own or, if he stays at home, forever be placed second in the pecking order.

If the father is weak, and should the son ever challenge and defeat him, then he will assume a post at the top of the family pecking order and in general you can be sure that he will be around the home for a long time, especially if he is weak in areas of his personal development such as pursuing personal financial independence. This, of course, will delay him in establishing his own family.

So, by and large, all the turmoil and dissension that occurs in a family is really nothing more than an evolutionary imperative relayed to an individual by his or her ancient memories recorded on the higher mind tape. Of course, what I just said is to be considered the basic drive that causes most of the problems in a family—there can also be rare instances involving extenuating circumstances. Even so, there is nothing unnatural about it and it is the way of things. If parents understood this, if they could comprehend the influence of the concept of a pecking order recording on the higher mind tapes of the various members of their family, they could, by making certain rights of passage easier and painless, save not only themselves but everyone

in their family a great deal of unnecessary grief.

Q: **Could you speak just a little more about pecking order?**

A: Yes, of course. The pecking order is, far and away, the most singular fundamental element responsible for our setting in place not only the rules of our relationships with everyone around us but, for the most part, determines our incompatibility or compatibility within those relationships, as well.

If you take the time to consider the various relationships that you and others are currently involved in (i.e., family, friends, marriage, work, et cetera), you will find that the pecking order of those relationships is genuinely of prime importance. In fact, you can consider the existence of a pecking order, historically, as humanity's collective key to survival. Think about it! The concept of a pecking order is so ingrained on a person's higher mind tape from time immemorial that it influences almost every aspect of his current relationship with others. What I am saying is that the rules and recollections of a pecking order are part of everyone's ancient memory system and are the chief culprits in determining the status of their present relationships.

The truth is that, with rare exceptions, the idea of equality among people simply does not exist, not only because of an individual's drive to ascend the pecking order but because of an individual's constant battle to prevent being forced by others to descend the pecking order. So? So we, as individuals, inevitably wind up hating those who berate us and make us look or feel small and inadequate; conversely, we have a great love, an enormous affinity, for those who make us feel good about ourselves and place us high in the pecking order of that particular relationship. In fact, this is the reason why so many of us are prone to be taken in by praise and flattery and are repulsed and greatly disheartened by blame and chastisement.

The reason that we open ourselves up to flattery is because it seems to move us up another rung or two on the ladder of relational success, another higher place in the pecking order, if not in fact, then at least in our own minds. This is why flattery so often makes us feel good about ourselves and creates in us an increased sense of security and self-worth. In this context, our sensitivity to both praise and blame is understandable. Of course, our reactions to being arbitrarily maneuvered around the pecking order by others through their uses of praise or blame varies from person to person and is dependent on factors such as time, place, activity, and our own particular self-image at the moment. Ask yourself these questions: How does receiving praise or blame make you feel? Does it seem to increase your sense of personal self-worth? Does it make you feel above others somehow? If you answer "yes" to one or more of these questions, then you should understand exactly what I am talking about.

In our seemingly constant striving to ascend the pecking order, we often develop ambitions that set in motion a great many plans and schemes through which we attempt to collect various symbols of power and authority, including, but not limited to, the arbitrary sundry material objects that in our minds, if not in fact, might raise us to higher status among our fellow man. So, we avidly seek to collect titles, honors, money, huge sprawling homes, fancy cars, beautiful women, handsome men, et cetera, all in an attempt to propel ourselves upward to a station of higher dominance in the ever-fragile societal scheme of things. It is a seemingly constant struggle for power and status through acquisition and display that we find ourselves in, and from which the spiritually unenlightened person finds it nearly impossible to divorce himself from.

Both the individual and collective need to not only survive, but survive well. Our origins, back in the dim, obscure, nebulous, prehistory of humanity, are etched indelibly on our higher mind tape and cause us to continue to be slaves to those memories. That is, until we finally learn to conquer those memories and free ourselves. This, of course, will happen to everyone as a natural result of our personal spiritual evolution.

Clearly, you have only to look around you to see the incredible influence of the pecking order at work in your everyday life. You will see it at home, at your place of employment, at social gatherings, everywhere. No one will go out of their way to show you their solidly built, inexpensive Timex watch, but they will turn handsprings if they had to in order to make sure that you catch a glimpse of their ten-thousand dollar Rolex beauty. You will see people living in dilapidated hovels but sporting solid gold chains around their necks and driving very expensive cars. You will see people lying, cheating, stealing, kowtowing, fighting, brow-beating, maiming, and murdering to get ahead and ascend the pecking order ladder, or committing those deeds just to maintain their present status. This is the insidiousness of this particular ancient memory. It is real, and it is at work!

Just one more thought on the subject. The concept of pecking order does not exist only between individuals and small groups, it also exists between nations. The idea of pecking order determines, to a great extent, the security of those nations. The wealthier, better armed, and more fundamentally sound a nation shows itself to be before the world, the safer that country believes it will be from international violation. Of course, as history has proven, when you show yourself to be high in the international pecking order, you incur the displeasure, jealousy, and hatred of those below you. When each of the conquering empires fell, no matter how much good they had contributed to the world, the only people to feel remorse were the elite of those empires, not the people subjugated by them.

Q: I have heard you use the term "secondary courage." What exactly is that?

A: Secondary courage is actually an artificial courage that a person experiences once he is safely removed from a perilous or potentially dangerous situation. It is really a quite common experience, one that I am sure you will be able to identify with. Let me explain.

One morning you take an appliance to a local repair shop to be fixed. For one reason or another, it really doesn't matter why, the repairman is very nasty to you. In fact, he is so arrogant and offensive to you that it makes you angry, very angry. You try to reason with him, but this only seems to make matters worse. His intractable attitude now makes you so angry that you want to hit him, but you don't. Why? Simply because you are afraid to. In fact, you are so frightened by this man that you are even afraid to speak up and verbally defend yourself. The result is that you leave his presence with your tail between your legs, greatly depleted, frazzled, and feeling less than a man. Later that evening, when you are nestled safe and warm in your bed, your mind begins to reflect on the events that took place with the repairman that morning. Suddenly, you find yourself wishing that you had struck him or, at least, stood up for yourself. You may even think that if you had it all to do over again you would have most certainly punched that man right in the nose, or at least stood up for yourself and argued him to the ground. This sudden change of heart is what I term secondary bravery. You can understand it to be an awkward attempt by the lower mind to salvage one's self-image. It is a controlled daydream with violent overtones that always has a safe and ego-satisfying outcome.

198

Q: **What is gender bravery?**

A: Gender bravery is really something quite common, and yet very interesting. Briefly, it's a type of bravery that only exists when one's adversary is of the opposite sex. Let me explain.

Members of the same sex will generally be very cautious when they are involved in an argument because the social taboos that are normally in place when dealing with members of the opposite sex are simply nonexistent. That is, no-no's such as a man striking a woman or a woman striking a man simply do not apply. When you are dealing with a person of the same gender in an argument, for example, should an escalation of emotion ensue there becomes a very real potential for violence. And so, this barbarous potential causes both parties to be cautious, very cautious, and they generally stop short of actually coming to blows.

Gender bravery comes about, for example, when a woman gets upset with a repairman. She may say things and do things to that repairman that the average man would never do. She will yell at him, curse at him, threaten him, and may even go so far as to strike him. Yet, the average woman would do none of those things to another woman because the possibility for violence is there. Why? Because she knows that the man would be reluctant to strike her and that affords her a wide latitude to maneuver about in. It is actually the physical disparity that exists between her and the repairman that allows her to do it and get away with it. If she had to confront a repairwoman, on the other hand, she would have a tendency to be much less demonstrative.

199

Similarly, a man would very often say things to a woman in an argument that he would never entertain saying to another man. His physical superiority over a woman makes him fearless of the consequences of his actions. He knows that the potential for violence resulting in his own injury is very low and so he can "bravely" yell, curse, and threaten a woman at will and with relative impunity.

Do any of my examples sound familiar to you? I am sure that they do. As I said, gender bravery is really quite common.

Q: **What are "convenient memories"? I've heard you use that term on several occasions.**

A: Convenient memories are just that, convenient memories. That is, the lower mind often conveniently alters the recollection of a particular past event when honor or safety is at stake. It could, for instance, choose not to remember exactly what transpired during a conversation, or may opt not to recall the precise elements that led up to a particular argument. In fact, when it comes to convenient memories, the lower mind can go to the extreme of actually fabricating the facts of a past event or conversation. The paradox is that when this happens, the lower mind truly believes the fabricated events to be true. It may even convince itself, as an instrument of rebuttal, that it has perfect recall. This, of course, makes it impossible to reconcile an argument with someone who has convenient memories because he cannot recollect the truth of the events that actually transpired. Instead, he can only recall the truth fabricated by his own lower mind.

Clearly, it can be an extremely frustrating experience to attempt a reconciliation when the other party cannot recall the actual truth of the event but believes, instead, in the lies presented to him by his lower mind. It places you in a position where there is nothing that you can do to convince the other person that his memory of the event is wrong. I am sure that you have experienced this, replete with all of its attendant frustrations. If you have had this experience, then you know firsthand just what convenient memories are.

Just a word of advice: When the lower mind creates convenient memories, those fabricated recollections are so real, so compelling, that it is very difficult to tell them apart from the actual event. To this end, it is very important that you take into consideration the possibility that you, yourself, have fallen prey to your own lower mind machinations. And so, discussion becomes paramount in an argument that seems to be irreconcilable if there is going to be any sort of peaceful resolution. It's something to think about.

Q: **How would you define "perfection"? I have always tried to be perfect in whatever I do. I have found that it has always caused me problems, even in my relationships with my spouse, parents, and friends. It is almost an obsession with me. What's wrong?**

A: "Perfection" is a term that I use without any particular concept in mind. This is so, because the term is really meaningless. Why? Because all things not only being surrounded by but actually being part of the perfection of existence render it meaningless. How could it have meaning if it describes, without exception, everything that exists? That is, everything in the manifest universe is perfect in and of itself. You, for example, are a perfect you and cannot be duplicated. Even the best mimics or impersonators cannot duplicate you exactly, so how can you be less than perfect?

A broken teacup is a perfectly broken teacup; a wilted rose is a perfectly wilted rose. Everything is perfect in and of itself. The idea of perfection takes on a reality of sorts and becomes a problem only when arbitrary standards of perfection are created and adhered to by the lower mind. Once, of course, standards of perfection are created and in place, it very quickly becomes a source of grief because the lower mind then finds it impossible to be able to meet those standards. This leads, often, to sporadic fits of

201

depression and a general sense of dissatisfaction with both oneself and life.

Whatever arbitrary standards of perfection are created by a person's lower mind he almost invariably and quite unfairly tends to impose on others. Moreover, he especially expects those whom he loves, those closest to him, unrealistically to be able to meet his particular criteria of perfection. He expects his children, for example, to be perfect children, his spouse to be a perfect spouse, his friends to be perfect friends, et cetera. This expectation of perfection naturally causes a great many problems in his personal relationships and can lead to tragic relational consequences if he doesn't relent. The irony is that he expects others to live up to the arbitrary standards of perfection that his lower mind created when he, himself, cannot even attain them.

In order to break this vicious cycle of interrelational mistreatment, you must come to understand what is actually taking place. You must understand that the problem is really inside of you and not, necessarily, inside of your friends or loved ones. It is all created, imposed, and monitored by the perfection police of your own lower mind. You must know that, just as you have created your own standards of perfection, all those around you have created theirs and that conflicts are inevitable when their list doesn't quite coincide with yours, when their aspirations and subsequent performances do not meet standards acceptable to you.

Relational problems stemming from arbitrary standards of perfection are really quite common. Parents, for instance, generally already have in place a set of normal standards that they expect their offspring to meet. They expect their children, for example, to be well behaved, to be good students in school, to cultivate nice friends, never to get into trouble, to have good careers when they grow up, to marry well, and to present them with beautiful grandchildren. This list, of course, is not a bad list and is, in fact, almost every parent's dream for their children. However, when the list is altered by one's arbitrary concepts of perfection, then the list sounds more like this: they expect their children to be angels, to be honor students, to become doctors or lawyers, to marry doctors or lawyers, and to present them with ideal grandchildren who are perfect clones of themselves. Naturally, when this list of perfection cannot be met, the parent, unrealistically, becomes disappointed and blames the child. If vocalized to the child, resentment and distancing occurs, and the child is made to feel inferior. This, of course, is unjust, not only to the child, but to the parent, as well.

When the perfection police of the lower mind come across something that they think is lacking in someone, something lacking in a friend, for instance, then that friendship is doomed to failure, strained under the weight of unrealistic expectations. How many potentially good friendships have you lost? How many have been irretrievably broken because of one participant's arbitrary and unyielding concepts of perfection?

Because of concepts of perfection, many people unrealistically expect their friendships to parallel or even surpass the glorious and storied friendship enjoyed by mythology's Damon and Pythias. This again is unfair to both parties of the relationship.

Understand that concepts of perfection are just that— concepts, ideas created by and perpetuated by the lower mind. The lower mind creates these standards and, thinking that they are tangible and realistically capable of being met, imposes them on not just their relationships but on all aspects of the world around them. Whenever standards of perfection are in place, the lower mind begins to discriminate both the outward and inward appearances, qualities, and worthiness of people, places, and things. This, of course, leads a person deeper and deeper into ignorance and darkness. For this reason, it is better to give up such notions and allow things to be what they are. What are they? They are perfect in their very own way.

Q: **You say that the higher mind has the ability to see the future. Could you explain?**

A: A very simple way to demonstrate the higher mind's ability to see the future is through the common experience of déjà vu, a familiar but sporadic phenomenon in a person's life, one that I am sure you have experienced. When déjà vu occurs, one second everything seems fine and normal and then, suddenly, you have the distinct feeling that you have been here and done this before. You feel certain, for example, that you know who is about to come through the door and what he is going to say and do.

The truth of the matter is that you have not been there before, nor have you done what it is you are doing before. What actually takes place in a déjà vu experience is that, at odd times, the higher mind and lower mind, in a sense, switch places. That is, the higher mind comes forward and dominates, while the lower mind is relegated, subtly, to a momentary passivity, a temporary obscurity. The process is, of course, spontaneous and short-lived, but when it does occur, one is privy to the higher mind's extraordinary ability to glimpse the future. So, in short, the higher mind suddenly switches places with the lower mind, quickly glimpses the future, and then rapidly switches back. It is not that you have done or experienced these things before but, having glimpsed the future, however briefly, you are now simply living the future that you have seen. This is déjà vu and an example of the higher mind's ability to see the future.

Those individuals who have passed into the higher stages of meditation have no trouble at all seeing the future. Since

204

their higher minds are normally forward and their lower minds are quiet and passive, glimpsing the future is not at all uncommon. In fact, for those individuals who are walking a true spiritual path, it is a very normal occurrence.

Parenthetically, let me say that phenomena such as clairvoyance, telepathy, psychokinesis, precognition, and psychometry all lie within the boundless and mysterious realm of the higher mind. This is why those who enter into deep and protracted meditation often develop what in Sanskrit is called the *Siddhis* or powers. Meditation is the key that unlocks those abilities. But I have to make it clear to you that the development of the Siddhis is not what meditation is all about. Although the Siddhis are interesting, one should never attach oneself to them. One should treat them merely as interesting natural phenomena and then go on. If one makes the grievous error of attaching too much importance to them, then one's spiritual progress will be stunted, if not stopped altogether.

Q: There are a number of people who claim to have the ability to see the future and some of them are fairly accurate. But the problem is that their accuracy is inconstant. Why is that?

A: When it comes to seeing the future, the problem with accuracy is really quite academic. Whenever a person glimpses the future, he is actually seeing the future based on the present circumstances and conditions. That is, whatever is taking place at the current moment will give the seer one vision of the future only. This, of course, is dicey and subject to change from moment to moment because variable factors, such as the exercising of human free will, can change from moment to moment. When this occurs, then naturally the future springing from those options changes.

205

Understand that there is a difference between a prediction and a prophesy. A prediction is really the result of a volitional peering into the future in an attempt to learn about some upcoming event. This is what psychics do. This sort of thing, of course, has the psychic seeing a future based on the present moment and so is often an event that will only come to pass if everything remains constant. This is why their percentage of accurately predicting the future suffers greatly.

A prophesy, on the other hand, is a prediction of a future event based on either information or an actual vision coming from God. Here, the accuracy is one hundred percent because of God's ability to see the future in all of its aspects, which has taken into consideration all possible human volitional intervention. Further, God has the ability to both prevent any interference with the future that He wants, and to put in place the elements necessary to assure that future. So, if you want unfailing accuracy, seek a prophet, not a psychic.

Part 3

Cabbages
and
Kings

Just a reminder: In Part 3, the questions that I answer
become more eclectic and deal with a wide range of
subjects. Although seeming to lie outside of the
parameters of the art of Torishimaru Aiki Jutsu
proper, the answers to the questions presented in this
section are, again, directly attributable to the deep
spiritual insights that I have gained over the years.

Q: **Could you explain how you believe the universe
    came into being?**

A: To understand how the physical universe came into being,
    you must first understand something about the nature of the
    infinity of God. Now, when I say that God is infinite, I
    mean just that—infinite. I do not mean, however, that God
    is just infinite in some respects, but that He is infinite in all
    respects. That is, God is infinitely good and infinitely bad;
    infinitely perfect and infinitely imperfect; infinitely this and
    infinitely that, in every possible degree and in every possible
    combination. Do you understand? God is all possibilities.

    God is also all things; not just some things, but
    everything that exists or does not exist, everything that
    has always existed, and everything that will never and
    can never exist.

    Moreover, God is omnipresent; that is, God is
    everywhere, not just some places, but everywhere. God is
    not just in your body, but in every single cell of your body—
    every molecule, every atom, every boson, meson, quark,
    every subatomic particle of your body. Nothing can exist
    outside of God.

    That having been said, you must next understand that
    God has both a manifest nature and an unmanifest nature.
    The unmanifest nature of God we call Ain Sof, the
    unmanifest universe, and the manifest nature of God we
    call Ain Sof Aur, the manifest universe.

209

Ain Sof Aur, the manifest universe, has its origin in the arcane depths of the unmanifest aspect of God. There, within Ain Sof, exists the potential for an infinite number of possibilities including, but not limited to, an infinite number of creative and non-creative eruptions called Netznutzot, or flashings. You can think of a flashing as a great spewing of God into God. These flashings are actually manifested as the spewing of the Great Indigo, which is composed of both the masculine and feminine energies of God. The masculine energy of God is called the M'retz Za'char and the feminine energy, the M'retz Na'she.

At first, the M'retz Za'char and M'retz Na'she are one and form the perfect emptiness of Ain Sof. When a flashing occurs, the M'retz Za'char and M'retz Na'she stream out from Ain Sof in the form of the Great Indigo or Divine Thought. There they split into two separate streams, the pure feminine and the pure masculine. Then, as quickly as they flashed out and divided, they flash back, coming together in perfect union, and resolving back into the unpredicable emptiness of Ain Sof.

The sequence for a perfect flashing is as follows:

$$\text{Ain Sof} = \text{Great Indigo} = \text{M'retz Za'char and}$$
$$\text{M'retz Na'she} = \text{Great Indigo} = \text{Ain Sof}$$

Throughout eternity, an infinite number of such flashings occur without incident. However, understanding that God is infinite in an infinite amount of ways, one must come to realize that endemic to that understanding is the truth that God is not just infinitely perfect but infinitely imperfect, as well. The flashing that I have just described is, of course, one of an infinite number of perfect flashings resulting in the original state. However, when a flashing is imperfect, a monumental problem results—there is a resultant imbalance that exists between the M'retz Za'char and M'retz Na'she that prevents them from reuniting and returning back into

Ain Sof. Instead, they reunite in odd combinations that result in the creation of matter.

For an imbalanced flashing the sequence is as follows:

$$\text{Ain Sof = Great Indigo = M'retz Za'char}$$
$$\text{and M'retz Na'she = matter}$$

This matter has been traveling outwardly from the source of the great flashing for many billions of years. Thus, we have the creation of the manifest universe with its atoms, molecules, elements, galaxies, nebulae, stars, planets, living beings, et cetera.

Q: You mentioned the "infinity of God." How do we as human beings fit into that infinity? Could you explain a little more?

A: Yes, certainly. Understand that for anyone to even remotely comprehend the majestic nature of God, one must first come to a reasonable understanding regarding the nature of infinity itself. That is, one must first apprehend all that the concept of infinity entails and be able to adapt that understanding to God. Of course, any intellectual understanding of the true nature of God would be, at best, incomplete without God's approval and assistance.

To begin your understanding, let me present you with an example. Suppose that you were standing on a road that was infinitely long. That is, when you look in one direction the road stretches out without end and when you turn around you notice the same thing—the road stretches out, also without stopping, toward the infinite. What this means is that with an infinitely long road in front of you and an infinitely long road behind you, no matter how far you walk along that road in either direction, you would always be exactly in the middle of its length. It is inescapable. Now, suppose that the same road that you are standing on were also infinitely wide. That is, infinitely wide throughout its infinite length. As you look to your left, you see the road

211

stretching out without end and when you look toward your right, you could see that it too stretches out without end. Just as you were in the center of the road when you dealt with only its length, you are, similarly, in the center of the road when you deal with its width. So what we have is a road that is both infinitely long and infinitely wide with you forever, inextricably, in the exact center of it. Now, however, no matter what direction you turn toward, all you would see is road, even if you choose to look diagonally. This, of course, is dealing with infinity in a plane or linear way.

We must now take the next step in our understanding and tackle infinity in a three-dimensional way. To understand it three-dimensionally, I must present a second example. Instead of standing on a road, I will submerge you in a great ocean. Here, no matter which way you look, no matter which direction you choose to face, all you see is water—water that stretches out infinitely, without beginning and without end. Here, no matter which direction you choose to swim, you will always be at the three-dimensional center of that vast eternal ocean. If you can understand this, if you can feel this, then you have only the merest insight into how you, I, and all things exist within God. But my explanation is not yet complete. Why? Because currently I have only taken you to the point where you find yourself centered within the corpus of God, but still not one with God. At this point you and God are still two.

For a more complete understanding, we also have to come to terms with the infinity of God's omnipresence. I will keep my explanation very brief.

212

To understand God's omnipresence, that is, existing everywhere, requires just a slight modification of the ocean example I just gave you. Simply stated: If God is omnipresent, if God exists everywhere, then, naturally, God must be that vast eternal ocean that you find yourself the center of. Likewise, if God exists everywhere, then God must

exist within every square centimeter of your body. In fact, if
He is omnipresent, then there is not a molecule, atom, or
subatomic particle of your body that God is not. Further,
logic dictates that if there is no place that God is not, then
everything, all of existence, must be one with God, for a
physical separation cannot exist by this definition. So, if the
water of that great eternal ocean is composed of God, and
you are likewise composed of God, then you must,
necessarily, also be at one with that infinite ocean.

Since the dimensional infinity of God cannot exclude the
quality of the omnipresent infinity of God, then all of
physical existence, including yourself, not being able to
separate from those composite infinities, must be an
inextricable part of those infinities, and so is eternally
part of God.

Q: I have always been confused when it came to understanding
the infinity of time. You've often spoken of the infinity of
God relative to time. Could you explain time to me?

A: Certainly, but I will be brief. Even so, I think that I can give
you some sense of it.

When one thinks of time, one generally thinks of it in a
very linear way—that is, as moving from the past into the
present and then from the present onward into the future.
When we speak of this sort of linear time in terms of
infinity, we find ourselves once again standing on an infinite
road, similar to the example I gave to you in the previous
question when you asked for an understanding concerning
physical infinities relative to God. The road of time being
infinite—that is, with an infinite past behind us and an
infinite future before us—we find ourselves, regardless of
where we arbitrarily journey along that infinite road, ever
relegated to the precise center of it. To escape from the
center of linear time would be like trying to escape from the
presence of your own shadow—an impossibility.

213

Time, however, is not merely unidirectional, it also moves sideways or laterally. To better understand this concept, you must visualize the infinite road of linear time as also being infinitely wide. That is, regardless of which way you turn, you are seeing time move off toward infinity. Can you see it? You may think it doesn't make sense that time could have these qualities but, in fact, it makes a great deal of sense. Let me explain.

Time itself exists only if there is an event taking place to mark it and an observer present to witness it. An event is defined as not only something that must be in motion with a beginning and an end, but can rightly be defined as something simply in existence. In fact, existence itself is an event.

Now, suppose that two events were taking place simultaneously in two different rooms of your house. And suppose that the two rooms were parallel to each other. Further, suppose that you are in one room and the door separating the rooms is closed, preventing you from seeing what, if anything, is taking place there. For you, only a witnessed event, that of your own existence, is real to you. Any event taking place in the other room, being totally unknown to you, is naturally unreal. In fact, if the very existence of the other room were unknown to you, it and the events taking place within it would be both unreal and nonexistent in your life. But, under those conditions, do they really exist? Yes, of course they do, even if you are unaware of them. They exist in what we may call two-dimensional time. That is, they exist as events that are occurring at the same time and existing on the same plane, but are parallel to each other on that plane.

Now, suppose that instead of having just one room parallel to the one you are in, there were an infinite number of rooms parallel to yours, lined up one after the other and stretching not only to the left or right of your room but in every direction, just as in the case of the infinitely wide road. Can you visualize these rooms? Can you see them lined up to infinity in every direction? If you can, you are well on your way to understanding two-dimensional time and parallel existence. Now, let me reiterate that an event does not have to be something cataclysmic. It can be as innocuous as something merely existing and not doing much of anything remarkable. This having been said, I am going to ask you now to remove the walls of the infinite number of rooms in your visualization. With the walls down, if you were able to move in any direction, you would encounter an infinite number of events taking place. It cannot be avoided. If you were to move to your left or right, you would be moving into areas of parallel time. However, if you moved forward or backward, you would be back to moving in the linear, one-dimensional time that you are familiar with. If you move diagonally, depending on your choice of direction you would be moving angularly forward or backward in two-dimension time. In fact, by altering the angle, you would be able to move angularly in two-dimensional time in an infinite number of directions, each resulting in an infinite number of possibilities.

Now, if we increase the location of the infinite number of wall-less rooms existing on that one plane to include an infinite number of directions (i.e., 360 degrees in every direction, up, down, et cetera, similar to a sphere), then an infinity of planes are created, and we are now moving into the area of three-dimensional time. Bear in mind that to move forward or backward, left or right, upward or downward, as well as angularly on the same plane, would still have one moving in a parallel way. However, what we would have then is a three-dimensional view of time. Just as we found ourselves inextricably centered in the corpus of God in the physical explanation of infinity, we now find

215

ourselves immersed in the precise center of an infinite ocean of time.

So what is it that ultimately marks time? What is the ultimate event? It has to be the omnipresence of God in all of existence—including, but not limited to, everything that exists within God either as a physical reality or as a great potential. Why even the potential? Because the potential of an event is in itself an event. In three-dimensional time, as with three-dimensional space, wherever you move, whatever direction you take, for however long you choose to take that direction, you are always, inextricably, bound to its center, bound within God. What I have described as three-dimensional time we commonly call eternity.

And so, there you sit, listening to me now, quietly centered in the infinity of time and space, within the infinite being of God . . . as are we all.

Q: **Can you speak a little bit about evolution?**

A: The theory of evolution has become not only accepted by the scientific community as an axiomatic truth but has gained enormous acceptance by the general population, as well. Still, as immutable as the theory seems, a number of fundamental problems remain unsolved for the scientist. One such problem is the enigma of adaptation. Yes, science accepts the fact that adaptation occurs, but clearly science does not understand the mechanics of that process. This is a very real problem for the proponents of evolution because, after all, the ability for a life form to institute physiological changes in itself forms the entire basis of the evolution theory, doesn't it? Scientists, for the most part, simply scratch their heads and admit that they are stumped. They understand why evolution happens but are at a loss to understand how it happens. This may be a good time for me to resolve this enigma.

As a matter of introduction, let me say that the scientific community, through the inroads that they have made into understanding evolution, is also, simultaneously, proving both the existence of the higher mind and the reality of ancient memories. I will explain.

First, as I have already mentioned, you must understand and accept the fact that the higher mind is not only one's link with the infinite but also one's personal link with one's own eternal past. Every experience that a living being has is recorded in the higher mind for all time. When I say "being," I mean every form of sentient life—from microbes to man, from amoebae to elephants, from grass to giant redwoods—all life, all without exception.

Everything is born, everything lives, everything dies, and everything reincarnates—man, monkey, virus, bacteria, clam, grass, tree, bird, snail, worm, amoebae—everything. Each of these innumerable individual sentient beings have higher mind tapes that survive death and reincarnate with them. If a living entity finds that there is a need for change, if it determines through its experiences in life that there is a need for an environmental adaptation to take place in order to assure its survival in subsequent incarnations, it is recorded there in its higher mind.

Understand that every sentient being, every life form that exists, has a sheath or ethereal form that is responsible for the final configuration of that being's physical body. You can think of it as a kind of ethereal mold that the growing physical body fills out. Whatever form the sheath possesses, the physical body will possess.

There is a special relationship existing between the higher mind and the sheath. The higher mind is to the sheath what the lower mind is to the physical body. At the time of incarnation, when the need for adaptation and change recorded on the higher mind tape plays back, it subtly

217

influences the structure of the sheath. That is, the higher mind has the enormous faculty of being able to alter the shape and characteristics of the sheath according to what is required to assure survival of that particular person or life form. So, if a snake, such as the king snake, has recorded on its higher mind tape the memory of its unfortunate encounter with a coral snake, and that encounter resulted in the king snake's unwanted demise, all that the higher mind of the king snake would have to do is alter its sheath in the correct way, creating the reincarnated king snake, suddenly, miraculously, resembling a coral snake. Every adaptation that has taken place since the beginning of life on earth has been made in the very same fashion. Whether those changes were made to help conceal it, to help it defend itself, to help it capture prey or, as in the case of man, help it to stand on two feet in order to not only free man's hands to facilitate the ability to carry things but to aid it in ambulation, it is all the workings of the higher mind and the influence that the higher mind has on the structure of the sheath and subsequent structures of the physical body. Naturally, some adaptations come about over an extended period of time, but still it is the higher mind that is responsible for the change.

A good rule of thumb to remember concerning adaptation is that the more intellectually developed the sentient being is, the more difficult it is for the higher mind of that being to bring about quick structural changes. This is due to the interference that the lower mind offers to the evolutionary process. Humankind has learned to manufacture those things that they require to assure their survival, thus wresting the responsibility out of the sphere of the higher mind. If humankind needed protection from the elements and from predators, they created the necessary shelters and implements of defense. Similarly, if they needed to change their hunting habits in order to secure more food, they simply invented better weapons and traps to bring that about.

As we descend down the evolutionary ladder, we find that the lower mind becomes less influential and the higher mind becomes more and more the master. The lower we descend, the more we find that the dominance of the higher mind's influence reaches the point where great physical changes can take place within only a few generations. Such is the case with infectious microorganisms that quickly adapt to our current antibiotics. In only a few decades' time, these infections may develop an amazing immunity to our wonder drugs; subsequently, new and hearty strains are developed, leaving us in an ever-constant struggle to overpower them. This is evolution at its best, doing what is needed to be done in order to assure the survival of the organism. It is what I call "crisis evolution," based solely on the need to make a lightning-quick adaptation or perish.

A virtual master of this higher mind-influenced adaptation technique is the chameleon, which can almost instantly alter its color to conform with its environment. The mechanism that allows the chameleon to do this is to be found within its higher mind, which has brought it to the evolutionary stage where its ability to change color is an automatic response to its environment. How? Simply stated, the chameleon's higher mind has ingrained on its tape all the necessary elements inherent for crisis evolution, and over the necessary passage of time, it created a sheath to produce a physical body that allows for that sort of quick change. It is now merely a matter of course for the chameleon to instantly change its color.

We, as human beings, have evolved from microscopic unicellular plants to unicellular animals and onward to our present state through the sheath-influencing machinations of our higher minds. Yes, a number of branches in our evolution have occurred during that time, but the foundation of those deviations have been the result of an individual's personal ancient memories (PAM) recorded indelibly on their higher mind tape. It's all there!

Again, all evolutionary changes occur in direct response to the personal ancient memories (PAM) recorded on that life form's higher mind tape, producing a mandated reaction of the higher mind to influence the nature of that being's sheath in accordance with the specific terms of that necessary change. This then, my friend, is the missing piece of the evolutionary puzzle confounding the scientific community today.

Q: What about people who don't believe in reincarnation?

A: Whether or not a person believes in reincarnation is ultimately unimportant. It would be like someone not believing in the existence of gravity. Believing or not believing does not alter the fact that it exists and affects them.

Anyone believing in any sort of life after death experience, whether they call it heaven, nirvana, paradise, sheol, or hell, believes in some form of reincarnation. They just may not believe that a person is reborn in this world, that's all. It may simply be that the word "reincarnation" is not found in their personally accepted description of what occurs after death. After all, to live even just one existence, anywhere at all, after this current life comes to an end is reincarnation, isn't it?

Trust me, the truth of the existence of reincarnation will eventually come to all of those who do not believe or understand it right now. It may take some time, but it will happen. Such knowledge inevitably dawns in a person as they mature spiritually. You must understand that coming to the realization of the existence of reincarnation is an evolutionary mandate; it is a necessary and unavoidable part of the learning process that will lead to humanity's spiritual emancipation required by God for His own redemption.

Q: **If reincarnation really exists, then why is it I can't remember any of my past lives?**

A: If you are not doing what you have to do to quiet your lower mind, there is no reason why you should or even could remember any of your past-life experiences. All your past-life experiences are recorded on your higher mind tape and do not exist on your lower mind tape.

Your past-life experiences not only exist but are actually with you now and are, in large part, responsible for whatever you are today. The problem is that your lower mind, born with your present body, which began at conception recording all of your present-life experiences, is naturally unaware of your past lives. The lower mind is ignorant of your past lives because none of those past-life experiences are recorded on its tape. It is much like playing a rock-and-roll tape and not believing in the existence of the classical works of Chopin, Grieg, or Beethoven, or country and western music, or grand opera, et cetera, because they are not to be found there. Of course, their existence is real—you are simply looking for them on the wrong tape.

Anyone seeking their past-life experiences must access their higher mind tape. In order to do this, the loud and talkative lower mind must be made quiet and the higher mind brought forward. This must be done through the process of correct meditation. Only when the higher mind is truly dominant will access to its tape be granted and your personal past be revealed to you.

221

Q: What exactly is the soul?

A: The soul is you and the soul is God. The soul that is you is that part of God that is separated and frozen in this dark and enigmatic world of matter.

After one of the infinite number of great flashings of God into manifest existence, God separated from God. This separation was caused by an imbalance that occurred between the M'retz Za'char and the M'retz Na'she at the time of the great flashing that resulted in the creation of physical matter. This physical matter was the manifestation of an infinite number of locked up or bound minute pieces of God. Physical matter is God!

To understand this better, I want to give you an analogy. In this analogy I want you to imagine an infinite ocean. This ocean is God. In the cold climes of the Void, a great sea spray was produced by the wind. This wind was also God, the breath of God. This great sea spray, composed of a myriad number of minute drops of ocean water, was blown from the surface of the ocean and came into contact with the frigid cold air of the Great Void. Coming into contact with the cold air, the sea spray was transformed into an infinite number of ice crystals, which settled on the surface of that vast ocean and combined to form a great sheet of ice. The sheet of ice, eventually, being continuously bombarded by the ongoing fall of ice crystals from the original sea spray, became an iceberg floating on the great eternal ocean of God. This iceberg is the manifest universe, and one of the myriad of very tiny ice crystals is you. The ice crystals were born of the sea spray, which itself was born of the great ocean of God. All are of the same material: God. The great ocean is the soul of God, the essence of God. Do you understand? You are made of the very essence of God, from the very soul of God. You and God are one!

The Redemption of God is the ultimate reuniting of God with God. That is, the iceberg or manifest universe must and will be melted—liquefied, if you will—so that it flows back into the sea and there is reunion. Remember, the iceberg is nothing but frozen sea. This concept, in fact, was the "Waters separating from the Waters" referred to in the Bible. As a constant reminder of the fact that every atom of the manifest universe is God, we affirm in our prayers that "God is One!"

The soul of man is the soul of God covered with ages of defilement. This defilement causes us to naively believe that we are separate and apart from God, just as the myriad tiny ice crystals that formed the huge iceberg believe, erroneously, that they are something different and apart from the great sea that gave birth to them. In order to see the truth of our original natures, the defilement must be cleared away, and this can only be accomplished through meditation and detachment from this world of illusion.

Q: I have often heard the terms "old soul" and "young soul." What exactly are old souls and young souls?

A: In point of fact, the terms "old soul" and "young soul" are misnomers, for all souls are eternal and therefore equally as ageless. The terms "experienced soul" and "inexperienced soul" are closer to the point and explain, on sight, a great deal more.

Back before the creation of the physical universe, before the Great Spewing and subsequent imbalance, all souls were at one with God and without defilement. That exalted state of immaculate existence will be achieved again when all physical matter is dissolved and returned back into the pristine unmanifest nature of God.

223

In the beginning, at the time that the physical universe first came into being, an inexpressible number of infinitesimal pristine pieces of God became enwrapped in gross matter and were subsequently bound by the finite limits of the manifest universe. Those minute unblemished portions of God are what we call the souls of living beings.

In their endeavor to unfetter themselves from the restrictive bonds imposed upon them by their encasement in physical matter, the souls of all sentient life utilized the creative power inherent in that composition to issue innumerable corrective mandates from which ensued eons of physical evolvement. Yes, from the very beginning, the souls of all living creatures began to assert their power in order to alter the matter in which they were encased. That willful determination produced the innumerable life forms that are extant in the world today, including that of humankind who, though even now are in their relatively early stages of spiritual evolution, are beginning to make more and more enlightening inroads into the deep and magnificent truth of their long-hidden spiritual nature. This innate drive toward spiritual enlightenment is in complete and perfect accord with the fulfillment of God's desire to correct the imbalance and subsequent separation.

From our beginnings as a simple life form to our present state, we have evolved to the point where we can, at last, partake of the spiritual processes that will eventually lead not only to our own emancipation but that of God's as well. Because we are bound to the physical universe and cannot hope to make our way out of it without treading the long and narrow spiritual path to freedom, we must continuously reincarnate in order to secure our spiritual education and fulfill God's numinous evolutionary mandates. And so, throughout each of our many incarnations, we have been assiduously collecting great amounts of information concerning our origins. Everything that we learn, everything that we experience along the way, is recorded indelibly on our higher mind tapes for our personal future use.

Each life that we spend in the pursuit of the Eternal, in that noble quest for the ultimate spiritual insight, is recorded on our higher mind tapes and causes us, in each

224

new incarnation, to reinvolve ourselves in the business of spiritual exploration. An experienced soul is simply one that has a long history of spiritual involvement, making sometimes slow but always steady spiritual improvement, life after life. An inexperienced soul is one that is just starting to spread its spiritual wings, a beginner, a tyro just setting out on an already well-traveled spiritual path.

There is, however, a third category, one that I call the naive soul. This soul, although as equally ageless and endowed as both the experienced and inexperienced souls, has not yet reached that point in its evolution where the call of the Eternal summoning them to spiritual pursuits has broken through the morass of lower mind obstructions. In time, even they will actively and ardently pursue the Eternal in fulfillment of their part in God's Redemption. This is the way of things.

Q: I've heard people talk about the soul but I've never found anyone who has actually *seen* a soul. Why is that? I mean, where did the idea that we have souls come from? Have you ever seen a soul? If so, do you know what it would mean to the world if you were to tell the rest of us how to see one? I think that it would change the entire world's view on life, death, and God. In fact, I think it would be the greatest discovery of all time. Please, if you know, tell us.

A: When I speak of the higher mind being humanity's link with the infinite, with God, I mean that it is that part of us that is in direct contact with our own souls, which is the purest source of God in us all. Therefore, it shouldn't surprise you to learn that the information we receive concerning the existence of the soul comes to us through that very link, through the subtle and mystical auspices of the higher mind.

Since the very beginning, humanity has been receiving enormous amounts of information via this mystical connection—but most were unable decipher and assimilate

225

that information due to the uncontrollable interference generated by their lower minds. What information? Information not only concerning the actual existence of the soul itself, but information from their soul, from God, that collectively constitute the very keys with which to unlock the most arcane and heretofore illusive secrets of existence.

The fact that no one has proven the existence of the soul before now rests squarely on the fact that they simply did not know where or how to look for it. Even so, intuitively, they knew that it existed. For your sake, and for the sake of the countless number of people around the world who would like to not only see their own souls but who would like to experience their own souls, I will explain the procedure and put the matter to rest once and for all. Then, your own experience will prove to you that your soul really does exist. It will be a journey of discovery that you will not soon forget and I haven't the slightest doubt that it will change your view of how you see yourself, others, and existence itself forever.

> **Author's Note:** I have never made these techniques public before and am doing so now not only to finally put this great mystery to rest, but in the sincere and fervent hope that such knowledge and experience so gained will contribute in no small part to humanity's quest for truth, wisdom, and freedom from the uncertainties that have plagued it throughout its existence. Furthermore, it is my sincere belief that, once the truth concerning the existence of the soul is experienced and information from the soul is assimilated, war, hatred, greed, and the ten thousand causes of man's inhumanity to man will finally come to an end. Please accept this as a gift in the same spirit with which I offer it—in humility and the hope for a better world.

I call the journey to the soul the *Ultimate Journey* and the merging with the soul the *Ultimate Union*. You will find that the Ultimate Journey is far and away the greatest of all possible journeys and that the Ultimate Union is without a doubt the supreme and irrefutable epitome of mystical experience. However, for both to be experienced, each and every step that I present below must be followed implicitly, without deviation or capricious experimentation. Do exactly as I instruct and I assure you that it will lead to the greatest mystical experience of your life.

Now, try this:

The Preparation

1. Do not eat for at least two hours prior to the journey. A feeling of fullness in the stomach will interfere with your ability to concentrate. You may, however, take in some liquids (i.e., water, soup, et cetera), but not to where it makes you feel full.
2. Make sure that you are free of bodily distractions such as annoying, painful areas that will destroy your ability to concentrate. Later, as you begin to master the technique, you will be able to make the journey whether you are in discomfort or not.
3. Choose a quiet place, free from noise and distraction. It may be a quiet room of your home or some quiet area outdoors where you can be alone, away from people and distracting noises. If you choose to do it in your home, the room should be candle-lit and well ventilated, especially if you choose to burn incense.
4. Wear loose clothing or, if you prefer, no clothing at all. Tight-fitting clothing will interfere with your journey by bringing unwanted physical sensations to the attention of your lower mind senses.

The Journey

1. Seat yourself in a comfortable position. It may be a meditative cross-legged position or a kneeling position similar to the Zen seiza position. Or you may, if you like, sit in a chair.

2. Calm your lower mind by doing the following simple breathing exercise: Close your eyes and follow your breath. That is, with your mind's eye, follow your breath as it enters through your nose and observe it as it fills your hollow body from the very tip of your toes to the top of your head. When you exhale, reverse the procedure as you follow your breath up from the tips of your toes and out of your nose. Your inhalations should be slow and even and your exhalations should be even slower. After a few minutes, your lower mind should be nice and calm. You may, if necessary, continue this technique until you feel that your lower mind is at peace.

3. Just below the sternum or breastbone, in the area known as the solar plexus, is a mystical gate called the Sha'ar Nefesh, the Gate of the Soul. With your eyes gently closed, enter through that gate by directing your mind and willing yourself through that point in the body. Once inside, you will see an infinite expanse of darkness, like infinite space without stars. This great expanse is called the Great Sea of the Soul.

4. Begin to travel deeper and deeper into the Great Sea of the Soul by directing your mind out deeper and deeper into the Void. In time, you will see a small black dot suspended within the Great Sea. At first, it may be difficult to see, but it is there. Once you have located it, will yourself toward it. As you approach it, you will notice that it is actually a large black sphere

with blackness appearing to be radiating outwardly from the center. Although that radiated blackness seems to be somewhat diaphanous, you will find that you cannot see through it. This darkness is called the Tza'eef A'fel, the Dark Veil. It is a protective shield surrounding the object of your quest, for within the spherical Tza'eef A'fel is your soul. The Tza'eef A'fel should part automatically as you stand before it. When it does, you will see your soul, a brilliantly white, almost plasmic entity. You will find that the light of your soul, though appearing to be very bright, is not the least bit blinding. If you have followed every step described above, you will find yourself looking at your very own soul.

The Great Union

1. To merge with your soul, you must enter the light. Care must be taken not to harbor any self-conscious thoughts or thoughts that relate to mundane matters or you will find that as soon as you enter the light you will be immediately expelled and once again facing the Tza'eef A'fel. Understand that the soul is pure and so you must be free from impure thoughts. Do not become discouraged if it takes you several attempts to enter. You must keep trying.

    Once inside, you will find yourself automatically and totally engulfed by that light. Then, after a moment or two, something miraculous will happen and you will find yourself entirely dissolved in that great light where suddenly, miraculously, there is no you, and then, at the same time, there *is* you. This is the Great Union. When this happens, you are in your original state—the state that you were in prior to Creation. You are now at one with God, for the light

229

within your soul is God. Having become one with your own soul, with God, you are now privy to the greatest source of information available to humanity, an endless treasure trove of great mystical knowledge. You will experience your own infinity and learn the truth of your own immortality. You will experience God and the great matter of both God's existence, and the truth of the existence of your soul will at last be settled for you.

2. When you wish to return, just think "return" and you will find yourself automatically expelled and standing in front of the Tza'eef A'fel, the Dark Veil. Once you are in front of the Veil, then you may slowly open your eyes. You have just returned from the greatest journey and the most unique experience that a person could have.

Q: **What does a person actually experience during the death process?**

A: The death process has actually been experienced by everyone, including yourself, many, many times in past incarnations and is not as frightening as one may imagine. In fact, the actual process itself is rather serenely pleasant.

The death process commences with a gradual withdrawal of the senses, beginning with the withdrawal of the sense of touch. This withdrawal of the sense of touch starts in the extremities, that is, in the fingers of the hands and toes of the feet, then slowly moves up the legs and down the arms toward the torso. It then proceeds up the torso to areas of the neck and head. This loss of sensitivity sweeps over the body like the gentlest of waves. At this point all pain ceases to exist, even if there was a great deal of pain caused by the disease or injury prior to the onset of this process. As the wave of desensitization reaches the head, there begins a withdrawal of the sense of vision. At this time, a period of swooning or passing out begins and the consciousness associated with the lower mind ceases to function along with the various organs of the body, including the heart. Of course, when the heart stops, the person is ostensibly dead. I say ostensibly dead because the higher mind still continues to operate and the sheath containing the soul continues to exist.

Because the lower mind is now no longer functioning, it has stopped interfering with or blocking out the functioning higher mind. It is at this time that the higher mind is free to take over that person's consciousness. I must point out that even though the person has entered into the swooning or unconscious stage of the death process he can still hear, and what he hears will still be recorded on his higher mind tape. The faculty of hearing is the very last physical sense to shut down.

At this point, death is complete, and the sheath that contains both the soul and functioning higher mind tape rises serenely from the body. There may be, of course, just the slightest sense of disorientation, but it is a temporary condition and soon passes. Because the higher mind is now functioning without the interference normally generated by the lower mind, a different sort of consciousness sensation is now experienced by the deceased. The deceased can now both hear and see and, as a result, is totally aware of what is taking place in the room or place of his death.

It should be noted that, with rare exceptions, the sheath of the deceased is bound to this plane of existence for a period ranging from forty-nine days to one year. It normally takes that long to achieve total separation. That is, from the time of death, it takes approximately that long for the silver cord to disintegrate, thus totally freeing the sheath from the physical body. Until this occurs, you may say that the deceased is still around and accessible.

Q: **When other masters speak of balance in the universe, you speak of imbalance. Why?**

A: Of course, I cannot speak for others who claim that balance exists, but currently the truth of the matter is that there is no balance in the universe. What we have, however, is a manifest universe that is seeking balance. You must understand that if there were balance, there would not be movement. Only when the feminine and masculine energies of God responsible for the creation of the manifest universe separate from the matter that their imbalance created will there be what one could call true balance. The problem, of course, is that when this does occur and the masculine and feminine do combine, nothingness is created.

If we take the time to look at nature, we see a magnificent and incessant striving for balance. We see not only the world, but the entire manifest universe constantly writhing in the throes of change. It is those changes that are indicative of an unbalanced universe. In fact, that is what evolution is: a relentless striving within the living world for balance. It is the perpetual search for balance that causes and promotes amazingly new and innovative evolutionary changes among creatures of the world. Don't be misled, we are part of the universe's imbalance. We, ourselves, throughout the course of our individual existences are caught in the middle of a defective, imbalanced world. So, if I speak of imbalance, it is only because it is true.

Q: **If everything in the universe is one, why is that oneness hidden?**

232

A: The oneness inherent in the universe is not hidden at all. Far from it—it is more than plain to those who have the eyes to see it. If it is, in fact, as hidden as you think it is, then it is hidden in a very unusual way. It is hidden in plain sight.

What makes the oneness of all things difficult to see are the impediments to that vision offered by the lower mind.

The lower mind, in its attempt to understand the universe, is really moving in the wrong direction . . . it is moving backwards. That is, it is looking at the macrocosm in its attempt to understand the microcosm. If you cannot see the oneness in the universe, it is because your lower mind is too busy making deep and protracted explorations outside of yourself, when it should be seeking the truth of the nature of existence on the inside.

In a very real sense, it is almost a fool's errand to explore the nature of the universe externally when the information you are seeking is already in your possession. That is, your higher mind already has access to the information you are searching for, and yet you turn all the investigatory responsibilities over to the limited faculties of the lower mind. It is like trying to measure the seemingly endless expanse of the manifest universe with nothing but a tiny six-inch ruler. Doing this, you should not expect to have any meaningful results any time soon.

Quiet the lower mind through the discipline of meditation and the higher mind will reign. Then the "mysterious" oneness will not only become apparent but will, in fact, manifest itself everywhere you look. You will not be able to avoid seeing it.

Q: **When I think of peace, I have certain ideas in mind, but when you speak of peace, I have the distinct feeling that your definition is different. Can you explain?**

A: When the average person thinks of peace, he thinks of it merely as the absence of war or external conflict. Yes, that is one definition of peace, but it is not mine. If there exists any conflict at all, any vestige of struggle, either internally or externally in a person's life, how can that person be said to have peace, true peace?

Let us suppose, for the moment, that there are no external conflicts occurring at the present time in your life.

233

You are experiencing no wars, no disputes, and no conflicts of any kind with anyone or anything. Do you still have peace? Yes? But are you at peace within yourself? If you say that there are absolutely no internal conflicts taking place within you, then you are, indeed, a rarity. But if there are internal conflicts either constantly or sporadically taking place within you, then there simply is no peace for you regardless of how serene the external circumstances of your life seem to be. To have peace, true peace, you must have oneness and harmony, both internally and externally, with all existence.

Q: **Do you have any thoughts about world peace?**

A: Yes. World peace can never and will never start at the United Nations. As well-intentioned as the United Nations is, its members are faced with a verifiably impossible task. You cannot have peace within nations and between nations until the people who comprise the populations of those nations are themselves, as individuals, peaceful people. World peace must begin deep within the psyche of the individual. It is foolish to think that it can happen any other way. To the people of the world who prayed, wished, or hoped for world peace, I ask you to look deep within yourself. Are you or are you not, yourself, a peaceful person? If you are not, then you, and people like you, are collectively responsible for the enormous lack of peace in the world today.

Unfortunately, the seeds of violence are sown and nurtured in the fertile fields of the lower mind. What are these seeds? They are the seeds of anger, greed, jealousy, hatred, et cetera, which are born out of one's attachments to things and ideas. These attachments that have been recorded on our higher mind tapes since time immemorial are reintroduced each incarnation. As long as we fall prey to our own personal attachments, there will never be peace—

234

not in our personal lives, not in our countries, not anywhere in the world. It is the very existence of the attachments one has to things and ideas that motivates one to act in one's own self-interest, thoughtlessly and without regard to consequences.

To have world peace, true and abiding world peace, all the inhabitants of the earth must free themselves from the nets of attachment. They must, as individuals, take the necessary steps that will place them on a spiritual path that will bring this about. They will have no other choice. The things and ideas that they are attached to are, in reality, no-things and will only lead them further into darkness.

However, if you are truly a man or woman of peace and are free from the insidious attachments to no-things, then find others like yourself and join with them and teach those who are not peaceful within themselves how to find that freedom. Soon, your ranks will grow, mature, and widen, but take care that you maintain your own personal peace. If you lose that, you lose it all, and all hope of world peace will remain forever just that . . . a hope and nothing more.

Q: What would you consider to be the perfect form of government?

A: Currently, there are no perfect forms of government in the world, nor were there any perfect forms of government in the past. Why? Because there have never been any perfect leaders. In order to have a perfect form of government, the leaders would have to be perfect themselves. That is, they would have to be completely devoid of self-interest and not govern over the people, but govern *for* the people.

235

The perfect form of government would have to rest on the broad and powerful shoulders of a philosopher-king. And that philosopher-king would have to be raised, from birth, by a group of men and women who would groom that child in the ways of detachment and wisdom. Of course, the royal tutors would themselves have to be detached from the world. Their detachment is of prime importance, because it would make them incorruptible; they could not be bribed by money, fame, or power, and would raise the philosopher-king in the same manner and with the very same ideals. The philosopher-king would then, for all intents and purposes, live in the world but not be *of* the world. Since he would be unattached to things, he would be given absolute authority to rule. Why? Because his decisions would not be based on self-interest and so he would rule always with the interest of the people in mind. His decisions would be pure and he would govern with wisdom. He would have no personal ambitions and would own nothing.

There would exist no principle of primogeniture because without that principle there would be no motivation for him to become devious and corrupt in his attempts to secure the throne for his son. In fact, there would be no need for primogeniture because his replacement would not come from his loins but from the ranks of the infants of others, infants who themselves would be groomed for positions of leadership. Moreover, governors, law enforcement officers, judges, and local representatives of the people would also be raised just as the philosopher-king is raised: that is, to be detached from the things of the world and to be morally incorruptible.

The only leaders who are fit to lead are leaders who act without the slightest trace of self-interest, people who are detached from the ideas of selfness and the pursuit of personal acquisition.

So, as things stand now, a perfect form of government can and will remain only an idea, a dream. There are too many people currently entrenched in positions of power in the world who are too caught up in the web of illusion and attachment to ever permit it to happen.

Q: What is karma? Does it really exist?

A: Karma is an ancient Sanskrit word that stands for the immutable workings of repayment that one accrues according to one's actions, a law of cause and effect. That is, if you commit a good act, you will receive a good reward or blessing. If you commit an evil act, you will be punished. It does exist!

Karma has its origin in the multitudinous attachments that people have toward ideas of birth, death, and abiding. It is these attachments toward things that bind a person, through karma, to the Wheel of Rebirth. Until all of a person's karma, good or bad, is expiated, he will be bound to an endless cycle of rebirth. In order to free oneself from the bonds of karma, one must relinquish all one's attachments to the things of this world. Even though a person commits nothing but good deeds that bear good fruit, so long as that person is still bound by his attachments, that person will return over and over again. Good karma, bad karma . . . it really doesn't matter. What difference does it make if you are bound by gold chains or iron chains? You are still bound, you are still in captivity.

Sometimes karmic repayment comes quickly; sometimes it is delayed. Nevertheless, you can be assured that repayment is coming. This is an undebatable truth. Just as milk takes time to curdle, so does a person's karma, good or bad, take time to catch up to him. It is nature seeking a balance.

Although I do not generally use the term, karma is in operation all the time and is inescapable. You can think of it as divine recompense. Remember, nothing is hidden from God, nothing at all.

237

Q: **Which came first, the chicken or the egg? I'm sorry, I just couldn't resist asking.**

A: That's all right! I'll answer it anyway. I will put the matter to rest for you. It is really not that difficult to understand. The truth of the matter is that it was the egg that came first. Why? Because, if you understand the mechanics of evolution, then you should understand that whatever gave birth to the first chicken was not quite a chicken herself, she was something very close to a chicken but not quite a chicken. Since chickens develop within shelled eggs, then it stands to reason that the mother of the first chicken laid the egg that contained the first chicken embryo. And so, it was the egg that saw the first light of day, and not the chicken maturing inside of it.

Q: **I've heard you mention the terms "feminine vampire" and "feminine donor." What are they?**

A: A "feminine vampire" is a term I coined to describe a person who draws feminine energy (M'retz Na'she) from those around them. Because they, themselves, have a lack of a certain amount of M'retz Na'she in their shields, they often unwittingly siphon off the M'retz Na'she from the shields or magen of other people.

If you have ever experienced a drain of energy after being around a certain person, then you have experienced the workings of a feminine vampire. In other words, having contact with this person leaves you tired, both physically and mentally. In fact, because of this, you may even find yourself avoiding them as much as possible without even knowing why.

On the other hand, there are people who are actually so full of M'retz Na'she that they are energy donors and have the tendency to draw a great many people to them. They always seem to be social ringleaders. Wherever they go, those around them go. For example, think back to the time of your youth and the friends you had. Was there one particular friend of yours within that group who seemed to be the central figure or driving force within that group; one who always seemed to have all the others following his lead? I am sure there was, there always is. This person, who I call a feminine donor, issued feminine energy to everyone else within his sphere of influence. Of course, receiving the bonus or gift of extra M'retz Na'she made everyone feel good and so, wherever the feminine donor went, they went; whatever he wanted to do, they did. If he wanted to go to the movies, for example, everyone would wind up going to the movies with him. The members of that group found themselves always wanting to be around him even without really knowing why, and at those times when he was not present, everyone felt as if something was oddly missing. For some strange reason, unknown to them, everyone did not feel as good as they felt when he was around. Feminine vampires and feminine donors are really very common. I wouldn't be surprised if you could name the feminine vampires and feminine donors who existed in your life back then. In fact, I wouldn't be surprised if you could name the feminine vampires and feminine donors who are part of your life now. Think about it.

Q: What is your view on psychology and psychiatry?

A: I believe that psychology and psychiatry are both useful practices and do help a great many people. However, the practitioners in these fields understand the nature of the mind differently than I do. As a result, their therapies often take a great deal of time in order to be effective. This is not good, of course. Clearly, when a person is suffering, time is an enormously important factor.

239

Not too long ago, I received a phone call from a woman who told me that she had read an article about me in one of the martial arts magazines and wondered if I would be able to help her husband. She explained that her husband was a commodities broker and, for some reason that no one could understand, he suddenly developed a fear that prevented him from being able to use the telephone. As a result, he was literally out of work for over a year. I told her that I could help him, but he would have to travel across the country to come and see me. She asked how long it would take and I told her that he should be cured the very same day. She said that she was desperate and would try it, but that she had her doubts because her husband had been in therapy for some nine months without noticeable results.

I met with her husband two weeks later. We met at 9 A.M. and by 1 P.M. he was cured of his affliction. They thought that it was miraculous. But, no, it wasn't a miracle. It was really very easy. The difficulties he was having had nothing to do with how he related to his parents when he was a child, or how he related to friends or siblings. It had absolutely nothing to do with what a therapist generally looks to stir up. After hearing his story, I understood right away that his inability to use the telephone stemmed from the fact that, in business, his telephone was used to gamble. That is, to gamble with other peoples' money. This put him under enormous stress because he cared a great deal for his clients. It was so stressful that his lower mind, rather than suffer that potential for guilt, opted to avoid it by keeping him from using the phone. There was nothing complicated at all about the cause of his problem.

The cure contained only two basic elements. First, I had to appeal to his lower mind to come to an understanding as to the reason for his dilemma. This required that I approach the subject in a logical way, and he readily accepted my explanation as to the cause of his inability to use the

240

telephone. Yes, my explanation made him feel better, but he was not cured yet. There was something else that I had to do—I had to now make an appeal to his higher mind. Why? Because whatever was recorded on his lower mind tape was also recorded on his higher mind tape, too.

To effectively access his higher mind tape, I had to introduce him to a very special type of meditation. Once this was done, I was then able to override the relevant negative information recorded on his higher mind tape by installing new information concerning the basis of his affliction. This I did and it resulted in his cure. It was neither hypnosis nor any sort of conventional therapy. His cure was based, primarily, on the understanding that the higher mind and the lower mind both exist and are operational, and that in order to effectively bring about a cure both the lower mind and the higher mind must be brought into agreement. That is, both his lower mind and his higher mind must understand and accept the explanation of the basis of his fears. Moreover, since the lower mind does not have the innate ability to retain and perpetually use the logical explanation concerning his disorder, the higher mind must assume the responsibility and, since his higher mind was continuously operating behind the scenes, it did what it had to do to bring about the cure. How? By allaying his lower mind's fears through continually issuing the necessary support information required by his lower mind. He returned home that day and went back to work. He has been functioning without fear since that time.

What the practitioners of psychology and psychiatry need to do is to open themselves up to new understandings of the nature of the mind. When treating patients, they should take into consideration the entire patient. That is, besides exploring the possible causes of an infliction in a patient's present life, they should also consider that a person's suffering may possibly be the result of some salient traumatic event that was recorded on his higher mind tape in a previous life.

Suppose, for example, that a patient was suffering from claustrophobia (fear of closed-in places). Spending years in therapy may prove totally fruitless if the traumatic event that brought on the fear-ridden claustrophobic reaction had its genesis in one of the patient's past lives. In fact, if this was the case, that patient would never be cured by conventional methods of treatment and would suffer needlessly from claustrophobia the rest of this present incarnation. To quickly and effectively cure such a patient, the practitioner must address the malady at both the lower mind and the higher mind levels. First, the lower mind must be made aware of the particulars of the traumatic event as it is recorded on the higher mind tape. Second, the traumatic event recorded on the higher mind tape must be accessed and either ameliorated or bypassed so that the particulars of that event do not bleed into the patient's lower mind any longer. When this is done, the cure is at hand.

Psychological terms such as ego, id, subconscious, et cetera, must be assiduously put aside. In fact, it may be better if they were thrown away completely and replaced by terms eminently more relevant to an understanding of the workings of both the lower and higher minds. The new formula for understanding a person's current psychological problems should be:

lower mind + higher mind +
past lives = present circumstances

Psychologists and psychiatrists should selflessly lay aside their institutional, provincial views of the mind so that they may free themselves to soar to greater heights in their quest for understanding.

Q: **You spoke of fear. Could you explain a little more about fear and phobias and how they may relate to one's past?**

A: Fear is the commonest of all primal emotions but not necessarily the most destructive, as many might think. Fear, for example, can cause us to remove ourselves from a potentially dangerous situation or it can prevent us from creating a potentially dangerous situation. Fear is, in part, also responsible for a great number of the evolutionary changes that all creatures, including man, have undergone in order to keep them safe and inviolable from predation. If you look at the numerous members of the animal and plant kingdoms, you see the result of countless evolutionary changes that they have undergone in order to maintain their existence—the chameleon's ability to change color, the mouse's development of an acute sense of hearing, the prairie dog's excellent eyesight, et cetera. There are many examples of this kind of change and they are all based on a fear reaction recorded on the higher mind tape and carried down into subsequent incarnations.

Most fears fall under two basic categories relevant to the higher mind: as common ancient memories or as personal ancient memories. Fears based on personal ancient memories are just that—fears that are peculiar to a person based on that individual's past experiences. Examples of fear-based personal ancient memories could be the result of past traumatic events such as fires, wars, personal conflicts, and deaths. Fears based on common ancient memories are those fears shared by all the members of a particular species. An example of fear as a common ancient memory is exhibited by a herd of zebras when smelling the presence of a lion. Due to their common ancient memories, as well as some current memories, no doubt, the zebras react in a communal panic to a lion's scent and bolt en masse for safety. Of course, fear-based common ancient memories

243

often become muddled when an individual, in this case a zebra, has embedded on its higher mind tape the personal experience of being attacked and killed by a lion in some past incarnation.

With humans, fear predominately falls into the category of personal ancient memories, memories that often seem to predetermine an individual's reaction to certain events in their present lives. For example, a girl named Jayne, for as far back as she can remember, has always been afraid to go swimming. She feared the water. Going back into one of her former lives gives us the reason. It seems that in the early part of the sixteenth century, she was a passenger on a small ship, a caravel, which sank in the Adriatic Sea not far from Venice. Her watery death left a lasting impression on her higher mind tape, which bled into her current life and produced a fear reaction to water that even she couldn't understand. Of course, now she understands it. I'm not saying that because she finally understood the reason for her fear that she suddenly, miraculously, turned into a water-lover. All that I am saying is that she now understands the reason for her fear of water and can now deal with it. Understand that her fear of water had nothing to do with how she related to her father or mother or how she got along with her older brother when they were kids. Her fear of water was based on an actual traumatic incident that happened to her almost five hundred years ago.

There are innumerable documented cases similar to Jayne's that have been recorded by countless hypnotherapists who have hypnotically aged-regressed their subjects back into former lives, so in this there is nothing new. I'm sure that you've read many books on the subject and so it is not my intention to entertain you with a thousand more such stories. The point is that Jayne's fear was a personal experience and, as such, influenced her current life.

Q: **What is your explanation for the existence of homosexuality?**

A: Homosexuality is really a naturally occurring phenomenon. To understand it, one must look at it in the context of both evolution and reincarnation. First, you must understand that what we are today, human beings, is the result of billions of years of evolution. There was a time in the dim, misty regions of the past when our spirits incarnated as unicellular creatures that reproduced asexually. That is, we would reproduce ourselves through a rather simple process of self-division. Each of us in that form had both male and female attributes. In time, through the evolutionary process, we developed from these unicellular animals into specialized microscopic multicellular animals that required the aid of another of their species in order to reproduce. This was the humble beginnings of partner-oriented sexuality, the beginning of the sexes. You must remember that even as unicellular microscopic animals, the higher mind tape was recording all of our experiences, and those numerous experiences were destined to influence all of our subsequent incarnations as we ascended the evolutionary ladder. Believe it or not, those ancient memories still influence us today!

Secondly, you must understand that each of us has been reborn into this world many, many times. Males, generally, reincarnate as males, and females as females. This is due to a higher mind sexual predisposition that has its genesis back at the time when we, for the first time, incarnated as a very simple male or female organism. However, sometimes a chemical imbalance occurs at conception that causes the creation of the "wrong" type of body. When this occurs, a male soul may find himself confined to a female body, or a female soul finds itself occupying a male body. It is not a genetic problem, it is simply a chemical mishap that has

245

nothing whatsoever to do with the actual person—merely the physical body that he or she may temporarily inhabit.

Bearing in mind that throughout all of a person's many reincarnations the higher mind tape survives, it is easy to understand that when a male-programmed soul finds itself in a female body that they may be attracted to others who are, on the surface, of the same sex. The same, of course, applies to a soul that is predominantly female and finds itself encased in a male body. Do you understand? It is neither a mental disorder nor a genetic abnormality as labeled by some, and although it affects only a small portion of the world's population at any one time, it is really quite normal and consistent with the deviations presented by numerous reincarnations.

Parenthetically, let me say that souls in their original pristine state are amorphous, that is, both male and female simultaneously, with neither sex playing a dominant role. Masculine-feminine existences did not begin until evolution brought them into being long after the creation of life in Ain Sof Aur. When it did occur, the female aspect and the male aspect separated from each other, and the need for sexual union began.

Q: Why is it that a person's view of the physical world is so limited? Why is it that they miss so much concerning the truth of the world around them?

A: It is not so very difficult to understand, especially when you realize that the physical sense organs that are supplying the data to the lower mind about the world are, at best, inferior instruments. The average person relying solely on his physical sense organs to describe the world to him is at an extreme disadvantage. Whatever his physical senses tell him about the physical world around him, however incorrect that information may be, dictates what his physical world becomes. To the average person, if he cannot see it, hear it, smell it, taste it, or touch it, it simply does not exist.

Of course, numerous members of the animal kingdom would adamantly disagree with man's physical view of the world in a number of ways. An eagle, for instance, who can detect the movement of a mouse in the grass, can do so at a distance of one mile. Man would see nothing at such a distance and would either argue that the mouse did not exist, or at best be very skeptical. A dog, whose sense of hearing is so acute that it can hear the slightest sound outside and across the street from one's home, would respond to that sound with barking and great suspicion, while his master would hear nothing and so consider it nothing to be concerned about. A shark has such an acute sense of smell that it could detect blood in water to the ratio of one part in one million. Do you understand? To animals, the physical world that they come into contact with lies well beyond the reach of the inferior physical senses of man to detect. In comparison to the rest of the animal world, man is basically blind, deaf, and insensitive to the realities existing around him.

It is the inadequate data that man's senses feed to his lower mind that his lower mind uses to determine the nature of his physical world. In his ignorance, man pompously and foolishly says to himself, "I know what the physical world is like. I can see it, touch it, hear it, taste it, and smell it! How can anything else exist?" It is for this reason that man misses so much of the truth concerning the world around him.

247

Q: Everyone says that a person should sleep eight hours a night. How much sleep does a person really need?

A: How much sleep a person requires nightly really depends on how much M'retz Na'she that person spends during the course of their day. Let me explain. Each human being comes equipped with two batteries. The first battery is non-rechargeable and is connected to the person's sheath. It contains X amount of M'retz Na'she and, as that energy depletes during the course of a person's life, the body goes through the various stages of aging until, finally, there is not enough M'retz Na'she remaining to support life and that person dies. It is this non-rechargeable battery that supplies the necessary energy to maintain the various organs of the body.

The second battery is a rechargeable one and needs to be recharged on a daily basis. This is the battery that supplies the daily power necessary to allow the various systems of the body to function at a certain level. We receive the daily M'retz Na'she we need from various sources: from the food that we eat, from the air that we breathe, and, in fact, even from the people we associate with. When we sleep at night, the various mechanisms of the body, such as that of digestion, are extracting the required M'retz Na'she, in this case, from the food that we ingested and is resupplying our rechargeable battery with it. You can say, in a way, that we are topping off our batteries. Since what we are doing is simply replacing the M'retz Na'she that is missing from our rechargeable battery, it follows that the amount of energy one needs in order to do this is determined by the amount spent during the course of one's day. It also follows that the less M'retz Na'she spent, the less time is required for the completion of the topping off process.

During the course of the day, when the body is active, all the systems of the body are utilizing the M'retz Na'she from the rechargeable battery. The more active we are, the more energy we spend. In order to make the recharging more efficient, the mind starts placing various bodily systems on standby and has them functioning at minimal capacity. Without this standby mode, it would be like pouring water into a barrel that has a large hole in the bottom; the more you pour in, the more would pour out, and so filling the barrel would become a lengthy, cumbersome, and inefficient process.

The lower mind, in fact, looks not only to reduce the drain of M'retz Na'she caused by the various systems of the body by placing them in a standby mode but must, and does, even place itself in a standby mode. When the lower mind places both itself and the body into this standby mode, we call it sleep.

As a person ages, a couple of naturally occurring phenomena take place within the body. In the first, as the amount of M'retz Na'she contained in the non-rechargeable battery depletes, the energy that it supplies to the various organs of the body is markedly decreased. This decrease of the sustaining M'retz Na'she causes an appropriate reduction in the rate and proficiency at which those organs operate. This lower rate of activity, in turn, results in a much lower energy requirement, which means that there is less of a drain on the rechargeable battery. This, in turn, translates into less sleep being required in order to top off the battery. The less energy one spends during the course of one's day, the less sleep is required in order to replace it. It is that simple.

So, does a person really require eight hours of sleep? It depends on their particular energy requirements. Some people require eight hours, some only five hours. I, for example, do very well with only four hours of sleep daily. It's all very personal.

249

Q: There have been times in my life when I slept a full eight hours or more but have woken up tired. Could you explain why this happens and how to correct this problem?

A: People who are fixated on the idea that a person must get eight hours of sleep in order to be healthy are misinformed.

The problem is that, when a person believes that they need eight hours of sleep, they construct their lives around that idea. That is, a person who must get up at seven o'clock in the morning in order to go to work would look at the clock the night before and say, "It's eleven o'clock . . . I have to get to bed or I will be tired in the morning." A person who thinks that way will almost always be tired when he gets up in the morning. Why? Because he will climb into bed when he is not really tired enough to fall asleep, and so will just lie there in a vain attempt to force sleep upon himself. Does this sound the least bit familiar to you? If it does, you must understand that the very fact that you are not tired enough to sleep right away should tell you that you have too much M'retz Na'she left in your rechargeable battery for your lower mind to be triggered into entering the sleep or standby mode. If you force yourself to sleep, you will toss and turn all night because that excess M'retz Na'she will keep your lower mind in the active mode all night. The ongoing nocturnal activity of your lower mind is a great drain on your energy supply—it is an energy leak. So, on the one hand, you are sleeping in order to increase your energy level while simultaneously spending a great deal of energy thinking all night. What would be the logical result? That's right, a lower energy level in the morning. This sort of thing is like not driving your car in order to save gas, yet leaving the engine running all night while you are not using it. If the car is running all night, don't expect to have a full tank of gas in the morning.

250

To remedy this situation is really very simple. First, you must get rid of any notions of how many hours of sleep you need. Simply get rid of it. Secondly, you must learn to trust your body. It will tell you when you are tired enough to go to sleep. Learn to listen to it. If you are not tired enough to sleep . . . don't go to bed.

If you want to sleep and you are not quite tired enough, then what you have to do is find a way of depleting your M'retz Na'she levels to the point where the lower mind begins the shutdown or enters the sleep or standby mode. One suggestion, if you do have trouble sleeping, is to try this: do what I call "puzzling out." That is, do crossword puzzles in bed or read or do mind work. Doing these things causes the lower mind to expend a great deal of M'retz Na'she quickly and this expenditure will then allow the lower mind to enter the sleep mode gently and naturally. You will find that it will not be a restless inefficient sleep and you will wake up refreshed and full of vigor in the morning.

Q: **What about the use of affirmations to overcome depression? Can they help?**

A: The constant reciting of affirmations, such as "Every day in every way I am getting better and better" or "I am a great guy, a good person," et cetera, often can help certain individuals suffering from occasional lows. But when there is a real problem existing within that person, such as chronic depression, it has to be addressed and not just covered up with an affirmation.

The use of an affirmation often is very much like putting a bandage on a limb that has been torn from the body—in the final analysis, it is simply not going to do the job. When a person reaches the point where he is reduced to using affirmations, then it is clear that he needs some sort of professional outside help. And so, instead of trying to cover up the problem with affirmations, he should be spending his time going directly to the underlying problem and getting rid of it.

Q: What are your feelings about vegetarianism?

A: Vegetarianism is neither good nor bad, necessarily. People turn to vegetarianism for many different reasons. Some people do it for health reasons, some do it for religious reasons, and some people do it for what they call humanitarian reasons. It is all really very personal.

Those who do it for health reasons do it to avoid not only the toxins introduced into the body by certain meats during the digestive process but to avoid the cholesterol inherent in certain meats, especially beef. Their idea is, basically, that an once of prevention is worth a pound of cure. There is something to that.

Those people who turn to vegetarianism for religious reasons might consider this: both Gautama Buddha and Jesus of Nazareth ate meat. Vegetarianism in Buddhism, in fact, did not occur until a little later, after Gautama, while the practice of vegetarianism in Christianity, Judaism, and Islam, as a religious ethic, was never even a remote consideration.

Now, there are, of course, practitioners of vegetarianism who do it for strictly humanitarian reasons and believe that the eating of animals is a cruel and inhumane practice. This, in certain circles, is highly commendable, but if this is your reason for considering vegetarianism, then don't be a hypocrite and run out to buy or use leather products. How would it fit in with your ethics to be opposed to the slaughtering of an animal for food but also be turning a blind eye to the slaughtering of an animal for clothing?

252

As I said, vegetarianism is a very personal choice, one based on very personal reasons. Still, there is this caveat. A strict vegetarian—that is, one who will not eat anything that is "animal"—will find out that, sooner or later, they will become deficient in certain necessary proteins that cannot be found in the botanical world. This protein deficiency could lead to some very serious health problems. So, with this in mind, one might imagine that if the purpose of vegetarianism is to live a longer, healthier lifestyle, then it might be, in the final analysis, actually counterproductive.

Just in passing, let me say that Adolf Hitler and Benito Mussolini were both vegetarians. Adolf Hitler, paradoxically, thought that the eating of animal flesh was a very cruel and disgusting thing to do. Strange!

Q: **I understand that you see the body differently than do most western doctors and scientists. Do you have any insights into any diseases that may help them in their search for cures?**

A: Yes, I have a number of them, but too many to go into just now. I will, however, address one: the common cold. Over the years western science has successfully developed cures for a great many diseases, but with all their modern technology and determination they have not come close to discovering the cure for the common cold. Why is that? The fact is, the common cold is not a disease. Yes, of course, there are microbes that can produce similar symptoms but, even so, the common cold is not a disease. Let me explain. As you know, there was a time early in man's evolution when he did not have the means to control his environment. There were no air conditioners, no central heating units, no clothing, no planes to fly him to a warmer climate, et cetera. In those days, primitive man, just like any other mammal, would go through a physiological alteration at the change of seasons. That is, when the weather would change, say, from summer to fall, or from winter to spring, primitive man's body would adapt accordingly—hair would thicken, fat content of the body would change, et cetera. If you take the time to observe what occurs to dogs when the seasons change, then you will understand exactly what I am talking about. When the seasons change, a dog's coat will either thicken, as it does at the onset of cold weather, or thin,

253

when the weather warms. This is a natural and necessary event in the life of all mammals.

As man evolved to the point where he learned to control his environment he, in a sense, began to fool the thermostatic mechanism of his body responsible for such environmental adaptations. Interestingly, if you look at the statistics, you will immediately recognize the fact that most people come down with the common cold at the time of the change of seasons. Why? Why are people more susceptible to the common cold then, than at other times? That's right! Because it is a natural physiological response to a change of seasons.

To understand this a little better, consider a person stepping out of a hot shower into a cold room. This sort of thing is setting the stage for that person to come down with a cold. What happens is that the body, experiencing the sudden chill, relays that sensory information to the higher mind which, in turn, triggers the body's thermostat into believing that it is actually late in entering the winter mode. So, instead of a normal easing into the winter mode, it attempts to compress the winterization of the body into a very short period of time. This rushing to winterize is what is responsible for production of the symptoms of what we call the common cold—sneezing, runny nose, congestion, et cetera.

If people were to ease into the change of seasons by gradually adapting their clothing, for example, or avoiding situations where they subject their bodies to sudden drops or risings in temperature, they could, for all intents and purposes, avoid colds completely. Clearly, western science, though meaning well, is wasting time and money by running around trying to cure something that is not even a disease. No wonder they haven't arrived at a cure for it. How could they?

254

Q: Could you please speak a little about cancer?

A: I will make it brief. The human body has a marvelous propensity toward overcompensating for trauma. When a bone is traumatized through fracture, for example, the higher mind finds itself in the "I must repair the damage" mode. Often, the higher mind repairs the break by over-calcification of the damaged bone. That is, it actually supplies more calcium to the fractured area than is actually needed. As a result, the site of the fracture becomes stronger than the undamaged bone surrounding it. It is the higher mind's way of protecting the injury site from future damage.

Similarly, when there is a steady, systematic destruction of cells in a particular area of the body spanning a protracted period of time, such as in the case of skin cancer due to overexposure to inordinate amounts of solar radiation, the higher mind seeks to compensate for the damage by oversupplying that area with replacement cells. The higher mind, knowing of the ongoing (daily) damage, causes a speeding-up of cell division in the affected area in order to maintain the necessary living cell count. That is, the higher mind anticipates what has become the normal destroyed cell count ahead of time and supplies the battleground with more and faster growing cells. Since cell division is accelerated and because of the propensity of the higher mind toward overcompensation, tumors form. This is exactly what occurs in certain cases of cancer.

What can be done? What should be done? Well, if operable, the tumor could, in certain cases, be surgically excised or the errant cells could be irradiated or chemical treatment might be of help, but these processes treat the symptoms and not the cause. In fact, these treatments often exacerbate the malady by supporting or reinforcing the information concerning cell destruction that the higher mind is initially responding to. This, of course, more often

255

than not, precipitates an unfortunate reoccurrence of tumor growth.

Since the lower mind supplies M'retz Na'she to the various bodily systems according to a definite hierarchical order (i.e., it will shut down the renal system before it shuts down the heart, the digestive system before the renal system, et cetera), it will most certainly stop empowering the tumor if other life-sustaining organs are in immanent peril. If a pseudo-malevolent condition could be artificially induced in the patient so as to cause the body to shunt M'retz Na'she away from the tumorous cell producing process, the runaway cell-producing process would necessarily be impeded or even totally shut down.

In a sense, the body would no longer consider the original area of cell destruction as being an immediate threat to the survival of the body as a whole, and would redirect its attention to the affected area higher up its hierarchical ladder. The result would be a slowing-up or complete cessation of tumor growth, and remission would ensue.

A controlled interference with the more important systems of the body over a protracted period of time would cause the higher mind to reprogram itself, and this reprogramming would necessarily result in the cessation of the root cause of the cancer.

Another way of interfering with the cancer process is to address the higher mind directly. In certain cases, by installing new information on the higher mind tape, it would be possible to reprogram it to relent in supporting the rapid cell division in the affected area of the body. This would cause remission and the body would normalize. It is a re-educative mind/body process.

Q: **What makes a master?**

A: A master is only a title and helps to establish a pecking order, that's all. In truth, I cannot see how anyone can master anything, especially in the martial arts. In the martial arts, as in music, mathematics, and poetry, there exists an infinite number of potentials and possibilities and naturally, when you are dealing with infinities, to claim that one has mastered an infinite number of techniques is utterly absurd. I am learning all the time. Through my meditations, new principles are unveiled to me constantly that consequently open up many new avenues of esoteric exploration with an unnameable number of possible practicable applications. With this in mind, I can only define a master, at best, as a very advanced student walking a spiritual path.

Q: **What are your feelings about forgiveness?**

A: No one is exempt from the need for forgiveness, no one! And no one is immune from the commission of foolish acts which, intentionally or accidentally, injure others. To be able to forgive someone for injuries that you have sustained at their hands is a great power to possess. It is a power that will help to free you from the bonds of attachment, one that will send your spirit soaring above that of the common man. The alternative, of course, is to condemn yourself to carry grief and anger with you all the days of your life. This is foolishness.

Those who seek forgiveness from God for a sin or an act of foolishness that they have committed must be willing to forgive others their sins and acts of foolishness. Why should God grant you forgiveness when you are not willing to forgive others? God will not forgive you if you do not forgive others. In fact, whatever you seek from God you must, if it is within your power, be willing to extend to other people.

257

Q: **Is it possible to communicate with animals so that they actually understand what you are saying?**

A: Yes, communication with animals can be done, but it must be performed on their level. You cannot expect an animal to communicate on a human level.

Suppose, for example, that you wanted to communicate with a cat. To bring this about you must first have an understanding of a cat's nature. That is, you must first understand how cats normally communicate with each other. Purring, of course, indicates friendliness and affection, hair standing up on a cat's back is indicative of fear, a cat's ears lowered indicates aggression, et cetera. This lets you know a cat's present attitude. Other cats recognize these signals, so must you. Recognizing a cat's state of mind will indicate to you what you must do in order to facilitate communication. If a cat is in an agitated state, then you know that you must first calm the cat down. Once calm, the cat's higher mind gates will be open and receptive. You can bring this about by sending a mental picture to the cat of you petting it or even one of you yielding to it in a docile way.

Like man, animals, having lower minds, think in pictures, not words. This makes interaction relatively easy. To communicate with an animal, one must send it a mental picture of what it is that you want to say. For example, if you want a cat to approach you, you must send the cat a positive reward-oriented mental picture of what the cat should expect when it comes to you. That is, you could picture an image of you petting or caressing it, feeding it, et cetera. This communication, of course, must be done on a higher mind level—that is, from your higher mind to the cat's higher mind. In order to do this effectively, your lower mind must be made quiet so that your higher mind will come forward and dominate. It is at this point that the

258

mental image should be willed to the cat. If the image that the cat receives is clear enough, the cat will respond and come to you.

It is easier to communicate with animals this way than it is with other humans because it is higher mind communication. A human's higher mind is generally too recessive to make unimpeded telepathic communication possible. Animals, however, having less interference coming from their lower minds, are more receptive to extrasensory communication. Remember, if you want to communicate with an animal, you must deal with the animal in a way that it will understand. You must deal with a dog in a dog way and any mental pictures that you send must be characteristically dog-oriented images. Try it. Experiment with it. You may be very pleasantly surprised at the results.

Q: There is a strange phenomenon that takes place whenever I take a trip. It seems that whenever I drive to a new destination, it takes longer to get there than it does to drive home. Could you explain what is actually taking place?

A: Whenever a person travels to a new place or even a very familiar place, if there is a sense of looking forward to arriving, there are several things that will take place within his lower mind. First, since it is a destination that one is looking forward to, the lower mind enters into a state of excited anticipation. This state of mind is typified by thoughts and statements such as, "I can't wait until we get there," or "Mom, are we there yet?" Second, this sense of excited anticipation causes the lower mind to attach itself to arbitrary ideas of time and distance. This means that the lower mind, in a sense, is almost literally counting off the miles and keeping track of the time. This preoccupation with time and distance (vis-à-vis the counting off of the miles) causes, in effect, time to drag. It is, of course, nothing but an illusion.

Coming home, on the contrary, seems much faster because one's preoccupation with arbitrary concepts of time and distance do not exist. Unless one is in a hurry to get home, one now has the opportunity to engage the lower mind with other things, such as pleasant conversation, a peaceful nap, looking out the window and seeing the sights, et cetera. When the lower mind is diverted in this way, it is no longer marking time and before one knows it, one is home. In reality, unless the route home is different than the route that one took to get there or traffic or weather conditions change, the time and distance must be just about the same.

Q: **Will science and mysticism eventually merge together?**

A: There was a time, during the Dark and Middle Ages, when mysticism and science were already merged together. It was called alchemy. Unfortunately, there were too many charlatans around at that time. Too many mystics were charlatans at science, and too many scientists were charlatans at mysticism. Because of this, it was better that mysticism and science parted and became two separate entities.

Now, of course, with so many advances in science, there exists a definite trend for the two disciplines to merge once again. However, this time I think that it will be different. Those modern mystics who believe that modern science is rapidly chipping away at the basis of their beliefs are wrong. They should understand that modern science is actually proving the existence of the mystical nature of the universe without even realizing it. That's right! Modern science, as it evolves, is actually proving the mystic's case.

It has always been clear to me that the scientist who has not probed his science deeply enough is the one who is adamantly opposed to the mystical interpretations of the matrix of existence. They are the ones who, like blind men positioned at different parts of an elephant, try in vain to describe the elephant's totality based on very little information. On the other hand, some scientists—and there are currently very few, unfortunately, who have penetrated the mysteries of their science deep enough—are not only very open to the mystical understandings of nature but very often have reached those self-same understandings on their own.

The major problem with science is that the scientists are trying to take the universe apart, much like a child would take apart a small radio, in an attempt to understand just how it works. They will, undoubtedly, continue taking things apart until they reach the indivisible essence of God, which is, ironically, what the true mystic has already discovered.

In 1906, when Albert Einstein published his Special Theory of Relativity, he was interviewed by a reporter from Chicago and was asked by that reporter if he believed in God. Einstein replied with a definitive "No!" Two decades later, in 1926, when Einstein published his General Theory of Relativity, he happened to be interviewed by that very same reporter again. Once again, the reporter asked him if he believed in God, but this time, Einstein replied with a definitive "Yes!"

What changed in Albert Einstein is quite easy to understand. Between the years 1906 and 1926, Einstein had the opportunity to probe his science deep enough to reach the mystical, and in so doing came to the realization that God did, in fact, exist. Not only that, but Einstein realized that true science and true mysticism are not, as previously supposed, opposed to one another.

Although seemingly traveling in diametrically opposite directions, science and mysticism not only will meet, they *must* meet. Why? Because truth is truth! The ultimate truth of the mystical experience must be the same as the ultimate truth realized through the deepest of scientific explorations. In reality, they are the same—if not in technique or philosophy, then in attempting to reach the true source of all existence: God.

Part 4

How the Principles
Apply to Life
and
Business

The White Crane Stands in the Water, That's All!

Principle: Just Doing/No Opponent

Martial Action: Four assailants surround me, their katanas
(swords) already drawn, lingering in the middle chamber
(between the waist and shoulder) and glistening in the sun.
They are preparing to attack.

I stand in silence, centered in the Eternal Void, my sword
drawn and resting quietly in the lower chamber (below the
waist). My attackers have much to do—it shows in their
stances and radiates from their faces—I can sense it in their
breathing. Their lower minds are full of ideas and their
shields press awkwardly against my own. Their lower
minds, laden with plans, will drive them to their demise.

My higher mind is merged with the Great Indigo . . .
there is nothing to do, and so everything gets done. Not
stopping at their physical forms, my mind passes through
them and they are encompassed. They and I are one within
the Eternal Void of God and in that endless oneness all
things are dissolved. Their hope for victory and their desire
for conquest will be the foundation of their undoing. In an
instant, they set their attack in motion. I respond. In less
than a heartbeat, my blade passes through the Void . . .
that's all.

Life Application: Things are what they are. When the lower
mind arbitrarily labels a person, object, or an action as
something threatening, it moves toward that object and
pushes against it. This pushing creates more and more
opposition to that object and the lower mind becomes more
and more enmeshed in the machinations that create more
and greater negative labels. In so doing, it strengthens that
object by adding to it false and misleading characteristics.
This only further increases the idea of threat and mires us

265

deeper and deeper in illusion. Once set in motion, it rapidly develops into a cycle of discrimination that will eventually lead to self-destruction. The lower mind, caught in that delusion, becomes a hunger-crazed serpent that believes erroneously that its own tail is another snake. In both fear and jealousy, with fangs bared, it strikes often and hard at that other snake in order to subdue it. Then it begins to eat, not realizing that the more it swallows, the more it diminishes itself.

The idea of No Opponent has as its basis the principle of Just Doing. In Just Doing, the mind is allowed to flow toward the object of its concentration unimpeded by that object. No thoughts are developed, and nothing about that object is predicated. By so doing, the essence of the object is seen unfettered by the subtle influences of the lower mind and so remains pristine in its appearance and impotent in its ability to disturb one's serenity. In the art of Torishimaru Aiki Jutsu, I teach the novice student from the very beginning that an opponent is what he is and his actions are what they are—that's all. Do not exacerbate your opponent's talents by adding abilities dreamed up by the inconstant workings of the lower mind. He is what he is, that's all.

In life, people are what people are, objects are what objects are, and events are what events are. Labels only cloud your view of them. When you are caught up in the active process of labeling people, objects, and events as opponents, for example, then you ignorantly empower them as opponents, and opponents they become. Suddenly, your world is turned into a perpetual nightmare filled with dark and foreboding enemies. In a fighting situation, if I were to think of my attacker as an opponent, then I would be forced to think in terms of him against me. This way of thinking only leads to thoughts and actions created and sustained by the demons of the emotions. It causes one to act rashly and imprudently out of desperation and fear. If I were to make that grievous mistake and treat my attackers as opponents, then how would I ever be able to see the oneness in all of the action that is taking place? How would I be able to see and experience the peace and serenity underlying all of the chaos? So, to remind my students of the oneness, I use the expression "Not Two" and they learn to let go of the idea that an opponent exists when they train. "Not Two" means just that, not two. It means that it is not you against him or them, but that their actions are an intricate part of what you are doing. How can there be "two" to someone with that understanding?

How we think is how we make our world. As soon as one thinks of the attacker as something separate and apart from himself, then suddenly other concepts arise, concepts that only further the illusion. Once one entertains the idea of an opponent, it leads to such concepts as life and death, winning and losing, pain and no pain, et cetera. Should this sort of thinking occur to a martial artist, then all is lost and one must fight a desperate fight, a grim and frightening fight for life. This is not the way of the true martial artist and not the way that anyone should live one's life.

When I use the term "opponent," you must understand that I have to immediately withdraw that term, for I do not mean that an opponent actually exists—I simply use that term as an expression to convey an idea, that's all. It is a term that is ultimately as empty and illusory as the object or person it is supposed to represent. In truth, the concept of an opponent is created and perpetuated by the whims and subtle workings of the lower mind. In the course of your life, how many people, places, objects, and events have you come across that you have arbitrarily labeled as opponents? How many negative labels have you employed to describe them when, if you had taken the time to view them without your personal prejudices, they would have been

267

miraculously reduced to nothing more than innocuous objects, places, events, or persons of fleeting impact and importance to you, at best? One who arbitrarily paints the world according to personal prejudices becomes like a pigeon soaring haphazardly among a sky full of kites—everywhere it turns, it faces attack. You will find that if you assiduously put away your prejudices, put your paint brushes down and see things as they truly are, that suddenly, wondrously, all your self-created opponents in life will disappear and you will be left blessed by a peace that you have never experienced before. So I say to you, people are just people and they do what people do; objects are objects, and events are events—that's all.

Business Application: In business, one may have the tendency to assume that your competition is your opponent, someone that you have to best at every turn or he will destroy you financially. Rubbish! In reality, your survival in business does not depend on what your competition does, it depends on what *you* do. Your task is to create the best product that you can or offer the best service to the public that you can devise. Spending a lot of time, money, and energy to investigate the sundry activities of your competition will only take away from the time, effort, and funds that you can put into your business. This, of course, would be what your competition wants you to do. He would be very happy if you dissipated your assets on such foolishness. In the martial arts, when one's life hangs in the balance, one cannot afford to give up control of the encounter to those who would do us in. In life and in business, you too must not give up that control. Instead, you must be the trendsetter, the one great light shining in the darkness of financial uncertainty, and let the others spend their time, money, and energy trying to keep up with you.

In business, you must be fearless in the face of adversity. But that fearlessness must be tempered with keen insight and flawless action. You must learn in business, as in life, what you can swallow and what can swallow you. When your lower mind has you grappling with problems and you feel inundated and swamped, it is time to take a step back and quiet yourself. In the stillness, in the serenity, all things will be seen in their essence, devoid of predication. When this occurs, the answers will flow to you unimpeded by the lower mind. Moreover, as a business person, you must understand and be completely at ease with the fact that problems are as natural in business as they are in life, in general. You must be able to accept them as axiomatic but be able to deal with them in a very natural way. This is how your character as a business person is developed. You must remain constant in that understanding and accept the vicissitudes, good or bad, negative or positive, as part of your business life.

The tiger restlessly prowls the jungle in search of prey; the monkey ceaselessly chatters and leaps about aimlessly in the trees; the white crane stands silently in the water.

The Panther Walks the Forest Unafraid

Principle: The Gauntlet

Martial Action: When walking between two lines of potential assailants, knowing that each has the option to attack or let me pass unharmed, I keep my eyes forward and walk slowly. I am the panther astir in the night, at one with the clear embracing darkness within the Void of God.

To worry about which opponent will attack is a regrettable error that will lead to indecision. It will cause tsukis, gaps in the flow that is me, and delay my response.

So, unencumbered by thoughts of self, life, death, pain, victory, defeat, and opponents, I expand my shield, touching them all. None can escape. Those who plan to attack must have the thought of that action and that thought produces a gentle pressure on my shield. Nothing is hidden, nothing is missing, everything is known to me. The panther knows these things . . . it is his nature to know. Though my assailants try to be subtle, covert, and clever, their secret is revealed by their thoughts and my response is sure, effortless, and finalizing.

Life Application: Sadly, the world is, as it has always been, an orbiting cage filled with tigers and mice. The tigers, forever plotting, scheming, and conniving, ply their furtive efforts in order to accede to greater and greater status while the mice, scurrying around in the darkness, hope to survive just one more night.

In life, each of us walks the gauntlet daily, slowly making our way among the tigers, those who are potentially dangerous not only to our peace of mind, our finances, and our happiness, but often to our physical health, as well. To allow the mere existence of the tigers to dictate the boundaries of our happiness and limit our potential in any area whatsoever is a grievous error, for then, out of fear and ignorance, we find ourselves abjectly turning over the reins of our lives to them without the faintest hope of redemption. When we allow our present and future happiness to be determined by the self-centered, self-motivated, self-styled whims and connivings of others, then we are condemning ourselves to a life of perpetual fasting and finding no rest from them, even in our sleep. To truly be free, we must boldly walk the path of life aware of the existence of the tigers and prepared to deal with each tiger in turn. But we must be neither paranoid about them nor surprised if and when their paths cross our own.

We, ourselves, must make every effort to be neither a tiger nor a mouse; neither the aggressor nor the prey. We must maintain a philosophy producing a standard of conduct typifying our true spiritual natures, one in union with God and all of creation. To yield to the ephemeral and assume the base, violent, aggressive, grasping, and ultimately unrewarding nature of the tiger is not what is in our best self-interests. Neither is it in our interest to assume the mantle of the mouse, cowering in abject fear over the particulars of our survival. It is better to find our own true natures and assume our proper role in the play of creation, that of a truly spiritual being exempt from fear and unsullied by the urge to aggress and possess. In the end, all of the tigers and mice will perish, and only the truly spiritual person will be left to inherit the earth. Of this, I have no doubt.

Business Application: In business, as in our everyday lives, tigers and mice also exist. Of course, the mice are really not a problem when it comes to business unless they are found within our own houses. That is, unless we find that we are in partnership with them and their mouse-like frailties interfere with our concepts and plans of expansion. In business, chance-taking is an intricate part of the process of growth. When we are in league with one who is too cautious, too frightened, and too indecisive to take responsible chances, then we are doomed to evolutionary stagnation and eventual dissolution. To prevent this, the mice must either be educated in the ways of business, relegated to a powerless position, or gotten rid of altogether.

271

The business tigers are encountered not only out in the open, but are also found insidiously lurking, hidden in the dark and foreboding places along our paths, waiting to spring out of that darkness and destroy us. Some of the tigers in your business life you may already be aware of, others are more subtle. Using their stealth to remain hidden, they work their deviousness in the deceitful covert of anonymity. They are the most vicious and potentially the most devastating of all, and so one must make every effort to flush them out of their hiding places and deal with them. But how can this be done without jeopardizing ourselves?

One way of driving them out into the open is to apply a subtle pressure on them. You can think of it as much the same pressure exerted on a tiger by the drum beaters of India, slowly and methodically driving the tiger out into the open. In business, exerting a gentle pressure on the tigers will often do exactly the same thing. It will cause them to make both their presence and intentions known. The precise procedure to bring them to the foreground really depends on the nature of the business that you are in, but generally the tigers expose themselves when the following conditions come to their attention:

1. Actual or potential financial difficulties
2. Word of product unreliability
3. Staff or employee unrest
4. General negative press

Of course, there are other possibilities, but in general, any one of the four listed above will bring out the tigers. They will be quick to seize the opportunity to advance themselves at your expense. To flush them out into the open, all you would have to do is to let it be known that one of those conditions exists. Naturally, it isn't something that you would want to make known to the public. To prevent this, you have to carefully control both the amount and direction of that information. It will work.

In business, it is important to know who the tigers are. Once known, they can be controlled, avoided, or even used, if you have the means, in order to further your business enterprises. You must be the panther, at one with the darkness of night, aware of the tigers but unafraid of their wiles.

The Panther's Claw, the Dragon's Talon, the Serpent's Venom

Principle: The Proper Weapon

Martial Action: My opponent stands confidently in front of me. His stance and demeanor tell me that he is well trained in the arts. He waits for the proper moment and then attacks. I drop my stance, moving toward the nethermost region of the lower chamber as I point an extended index finger toward the ground. I capture his lower mind, redirecting him toward the ground, and pin him in place. He cannot move; I have sealed off the ten directions. Raising my right hand, I project a pulse of feminine energy, which strikes his shield and captures his higher mind. Now, he has no offense or defense and all of his targets are bared and vulnerable to me. Without thought, without hesitation, I glide forward, entering his sphere. Still, he cannot move but must submit as the slightly curved fingers of my needle-hand strike flick out and penetrate his eyes. He drops to his knees, covering his eyes with his hands—the defense is done, there is no need to go further.

Clearly, to have attacked his eyes with a vertical fist strike, top-fist strike, an elbow strike, a kick, or some other improper weapon would have been a wasted effort and the result of the effort would have been unrewarding. With my fingers I can attack the eyes, throat, liver, spleen, et cetera. Through the use of *osae dores* (special holds) I can incapacitate an opponent with little effort and no harm. With projections I can harm or not harm. And with a sword, I can dismember and cause death. Many options present themselves, but only to one who has mastered the various weapons and is skilled in their application.

Once the weapons are mastered and the proper targets for each weapon are learned, success will follow. The

273

panther has its claws, the dragon has its talons, the serpent has its venom.

Life Application: In life, the tools available to us that can facilitate our individual survival are varied and many. Some are innate and natural to us. They are skills that we bring into the present life from our past lives. Other skills are acquired, the fortuitous result of our numerous negative and positive present-life experiences. Together, they form each of our present skill arsenals.

There are many, many skills to be found in our personal arsenals; no one is without them. You have only to take an inventory to find out just what your particular skills are. Naturally, this requires a great deal of introspection, but you will come to learn that it is time well spent. Skills come in all sizes and shapes and vary in depth, strength, and clarity from individual to individual. There are skills, for example, such as the ability to reason, to feel, to assimilate knowledge, to deal with misfortune, pain, suffering, and to adapt to the numerous and often sudden vicissitudes of life. Are you a great communicator? That is a skill. Are you level-headed when others are prone to be panicky and out of control? That too is a skill. Are you a good provider? A good and nurturing mother? They are skills. In short, skills are the tools of our lives that help make us strong and viable human beings. In fact, we couldn't survive without them.

As I mentioned, skills exist in order to help facilitate our journey through life, but they can only be employed to our advantage when they are used correctly and are drawn on at the proper time. Bearing this in mind, it should be no great surprise to learn that, although everyone has a large number of skills in their arsenals, many people lack the ability to use their skills to their best advantage.

In the martial arts, for example, the higher in rank you go, the more skills you acquire that you find have more and more relevance to everyday life. One such skill is that of patience. We learn that when negative situations arise in life, patience is one of our best tools. Patience teaches us not to overreact and use too much force to correct a situation. Do you have such a tool? If so, do you use it? When? What other tools do you have?

Understand, it isn't just the random "out of our control" situations in life that require proper skill and timing. Often, our own lower minds will take a minor situation, one that does not require much to correct it, and magnify it until it appears to be only rectifiable by the most enormous, most drastic, and most dramatic of superhuman efforts. Often, this magnification causes a person to overreact and overextend himself in ways that deplete his strength and have him give up before ever bringing the situation to resolution. In fact, sometimes the lower mind will take a minor situation and magnify it to the point where one actually gives up without even trying. This is the nature of the lower mind.

To properly react to life's negative situations, you must have an understanding of the general nature of life, the specifics of your particular difficulty, a mastery over the survival tools that you have available to you, and the right timing. Without all four elements, you will find it nearly impossible to escape negative situations unscathed.

When you are cold, even to the point of shivering, it is an overreaction to curse the cold and set yourself on fire. The proper reaction, based on correct timing, use of personal tools, and patience will reduce everything to manageable proportions. Remain cool and collected. Face each difficulty and deal with it unopposed by your own prejudices, and everything will remain in proportion and the pieces of the puzzle you are faced with will naturally fall into place. Know your strengths and strengthen your weaknesses . . . build your arsenal.

275

Business Application: One of the greatest impediments to success in business is to overreact to the tribulations that are known to occur and are natural to business in general and your business in particular. Sales go up and down, clients are gained and lost, subordinates make mistakes and better procedures are discovered—this is the way of business.

An excellent business person, knowledgeable in his craft, just like an excellent martial artist knowledgeable in his, learns to utilize the proper weapon to effectively take care of each and every situation. If, for example, your sales figures are going down, it would be better to consider not just the competency of your sales staff but the timing, distribution, quality, and advertising of your product, as well. Also, it may be wise to consider the present needs of the buying public. Is your product still a currently viable entity? Can it be improved? Can it be presented to the public in a new way, a way that will stimulate sales? There are so many questions that have to be answered before you start ranting, raving, and capriciously firing your sales staff. Know your business! Know your products! Know your clients!

The panther exercises patience in order to capture its prey, for it knows that this is the natural way of things. For this noble cat to act rashly, impatiently, and angrily would mean that it would not eat that day nor any other day and would ultimately perish as a result of its unchecked enthusiasm. The business person acting in this same manner, caught up in the dire throes of his own passion, greed, and impatience, would be facing his own financial destruction. This would be a grievous error. The panther's claw, the dragon's talon, the serpent's venom—all are effective in the hands of those who best know how to use them.

Outnumbered, the Elephant Charges the Lions

Principle: When Outnumbered . . . Attack!

Martial Action: A dozen armed attackers surround me, each slowly maneuvering within the Great Void for the best possible attack position. Clearly, they want to take my life. They voice their threats sporadically in loud and angry tones, but I am at peace, secure within the sea of Indigo. They grow impatient and are waiting for their moment to arrive. Their demeanors indicate that no quarter is to be given. If I am to survive, then I must act quickly, for there will be no victory in delay, no honor in an undefended death. Any hesitation, any further tarrying, and I will loose a vital and stalwart ally, the element of surprise. Outnumbering me, and although seeing my sword drawn and resting in the middle chamber, they expect the barest resistance and an easy victory—that is their weakness. So, I do what they expect the least, what they fear the most—I move first. Catching them off guard, they fall beneath my sword. The victory is mine.

Life Application: At times in life we find ourselves beset by seemingly innumerable problems that, if not bravely confronted, will most certainly mean our ruin. Some people opt to do nothing and in so doing hope to forestall the inevitable through their sloth. They abjectly resign themselves to an inescapable defeat right from the beginning without putting up any sort of defense. This is not condonable. It is like an ostrich burying its head in the sand, thinking that if it can't see the predator, that the predator can't see it. Many an ostrich has lost its life that way.

Others spend too much time and effort just sitting around thinking about the problems. They neither run from them nor do they do anything to take care of them, they just mope around the house with long, worried expressions on their faces, bending under the weight that their dilemma is placing on them. These are the people who are most prone to fits of depression. To them, their problems simply won't go away. But, then again, how could their problems go away if all they do is sit around and think about them? They are like people with a freezer full of food starving to death because they are too caught up in their reveries about eating to actually get up and cook themselves a meal. Why? Because they are caught up in a lower mind-created loop of depressive self-pity. That is, the more they think about their problems, the more energy they spend; the more energy they spend, the more overpowering their problems seem, which causes them in turn to spend more time thinking about them. They become weaker and weaker without reaching a resolution to their problems. This unfortunate situation is more common than you might suspect. In fact, I would venture to say that it is the predominant factor in the advancement of depressive episodes in America today, if not in the entire western world.

In both cases cited above, the cure is actually very simple, but it requires a little effort. First, it demands that you break away from your depressive stupor by committing yourself to the fray. This means that you must stir yourself to action and boldly pick up the gauntlet thrown down on the ground by circumstance. It is life, daring you to fight or continue suffering. It is life telling you that the choice is yours—accept or decline. The only choice that a wise and noble person has, of course, is to accept the challenge—but with the understanding that there is nothing that cannot be done, nothing that you cannot do.

278

Once you have accepted the challenge, you must then make every effort not to allow your lower mind to paint grim, foreboding pictures of the problems you are facing. The lower mind must not be given the power to predicate anything concerning them. To prevent the lower mind from doing that, I recommend meditation, for under its aegis the lower mind can be made quiet and free you from the sundry bonds and illusions of its capricious picture painting. Once this freedom is felt, you will be able to view your problems in their true nature, unsullied and unmagnified. Suddenly, they won't seem so insurmountable, so beyond your control, and the proper method of dealing with them will come to you. In fact, I wouldn't be surprised if you already know what you have to do to clear each of your problems up, you just haven't done it. Once you understand what has to be done, you must advance, attacking each problem one at a time, without fear, without despair, without anger, and without hesitation. In so doing, you will be elated to find that it won't be long before you gain victory over them all. It is the noble way of dealing with life. In battle, victory is gained by destroying the opposing army, but that can only occur through the conquest of individual soldiers who comprise that army. This is what you must do in order to free yourself from the army of problems that presently confronts you. This is the way of things.

Business Application: It is common among people in the business world to be beset by problems, sometimes appearing as singular situations and sometimes as part of a great deluge, an enormous ranging wall of financial, logistical, and labor-related issues. For all our liking or disliking, it is simply the nature of the beast. Problems are an unavoidable part of occupational existence, a fact of business life.

The experienced business person, one used to the numerous slings and arrows of the business world, will automatically attack the problems without the slightest hesitation and almost always emerge victorious, but the inexperienced business person, one lacking the necessary insights, will either panic and run from the problems or panic and overreact to them. Either way, the person of inexperience will ultimately succumb to the pressures of those problems and, besides anguishing at their hands, could possibly lose their business in the bargain. This, of course, is not good.

If you are the inexperienced business person, then the very first step to take if you are beset by a multitude of business problems is to take a step back and look at the problems individually and with an attitude of detachment. That is, you must look at your problems as dispassionately as would an outside expert that you would hire to come in and troubleshoot your business and make qualified suggestions. If you were to do this, you would discover that one particular problem is often the parent of many, if not all, of the others. Once the parent problem is identified, then you must proceed by attacking it first. Remember, many times taking care of the parent problem will automatically take care of all of the others. Then, everything falls like dominoes. This will leave you free to attack the singular, unrelated problems one at a time, until everything is resolved.

In the martial arts, we understand that in order to properly handle multiple attackers, one must not submit oneself to the idea that collectively they are invulnerable and beyond our ability to handle effectively. This way of thinking would be the harbinger of our own destruction. An accomplished martial artist understands that each attacker is an individual and has the same weaknesses and vulnerabilities that he has always been subject to. In fact, he

knows that there are some attackers who would not dare to attack as individuals but only as members of an insidious pack. The accomplished martial artist knows that the fears that haunt his attackers as individuals are still with them as members of the group. Moreover, the well-trained martial artist knows that by preemptively attacking them, the surprise will automatically cause their lower minds to move backward and impel them to take a defensive attitude. When this happens, the effectiveness of their offense is destroyed and one can relatively select and defeat each of them, practically at one's leisure.

So it is in the business world, when one is beset by multiple problems where attacking them will reveal each of their weaknesses and automatically present to you the proper method of their destruction. The tallest mountain can be torn down one stone at a time; a mountain of business problems can be dismantled one problem at a time. Outnumbered, the elephant charges the lions and survives.

The Water Buffalo's Strength Is In His Size; His Weakness Is Found There Also

Principle: Using Your Opponent's Strength Against Him

Martial Action: My opponent stands before me, silent and motionless, clearly gathering courage for his offensive. His thought is of victory, his lower mind is filled with the need to win. The rising pressure he exerts on my shield tells me that he is about to set his aggression in motion. Subtly, I expand my shield and encompass him; he cannot escape. His mind is wavering. Feeling the pressure of time and not yet in oneness with the Great Void, he attacks nevertheless, but his movements are stilted, half-hearted, and lacking in both power and conviction. At the critical moment, I project him in a small arc to the ground. He quickly regains himself, stands, and then attacks me a second time. This time, his anger is stirred up. He is out of control and launches a second attack with all the strength, speed, and ferocity that he can muster—a fatal mistake. Now, with more ease, I project him in a large, high, sweeping arc and he crashes to the ground with devastating force. He is undone and cannot regain himself to launch a third attack but must suffer the injuries caused by the employment of his own strength and recklessness.

It was the increased magnitude of his strength, generated by his anger and his need to win attitude, which defeated him in his second attack. That increased strength allowed me to send him higher and further than I did in defending his first attack. In the art of Torishimaru Aiki Jutsu, the more strength that an attacker uses, the more we have to use against him. Always, the attacker's own uncontrolled strength is his undoing when facing one skilled in the art of control and rooted in the deepest realms of the Great Void.

Life Application: Armed with the proper knowledge and trained in the proper technique, there is nothing that we cannot do in life, there is nothing that cannot be done, there is nothing that cannot be achieved. Too often, however, facing even a little adversity, some people buckle, fold, fall apart, and give up without even making the slightest attempt at trying to deal with the problem. They refrain from action because, in their minds, it is easier to sacrifice themselves on the altar of failure than to endure the pressures bearing down on them on the sometimes trouble-laden and generally uncertain road to success. This inferior way of thinking, this ignoble manner of behavior, is not our way in Torishimaru Aiki Jutsu. To us, it is the act of doing that is important and not the final outcome. To us, success and failure are not two different things.

Unfortunately, most people place too much importance on the ideas of success and failure. To them, failure is to be assiduously avoided and success is to be vigorously sought after. Moreover, they consider the achievement of success not only of paramount importance in their own life but is, when achieved, something to be admired in others. To them, success or failure in whatever they endeavor to do are treated as diametric opposites. Paradoxically, it is just this way of thinking that creates the foundation for their inability to achieve the success that they are looking for. This manner of reasoning has them giving up when they think that the road they are traveling may get too difficult to traverse; they want to achieve success, yes, but they want to have it on their own terms, unopposed and right now. If they can't have it their way, they become perplexed and depressed and refuse to make any effort to procure accomplishment at all. Sadly, they never realize that it is the journey and not the destination that is important. If you are one of their number, then you have it in your power to change your life—to rid yourself, once and for all, from the chains that bind you to failure. All you have to do is to have your goal firmly set in your mind, understand the steps necessary to achieve that goal, and then, regardless of the problems that arise along the way to that success, hold onto your luggage, take one step at a time, and enjoy the journey. Do that and, before you know it, you will arrive at your chosen destination and be all the better for it. To give up in fear of the potential perils of a journey, especially when those dangers are, for the most part, mind-created, is a foolish and unproductive thing to do. It is not my way, and not what I teach.

You must boldly embark on the journey unafraid of failure, unintimidated by the mind-created presence of any negative thoughts. You must understand and accept as fact that when and if you do come across adversities along the path, you can learn to use them to your advantage, you can learn to use the strength of that adversity to further your journey down the road. You must understand and patiently accept the idea that when one's strength in life is limited and one is faced with a seemingly omnipotent adversary, with the proper technique and the proper understanding, the opposition you are facing can be used to great advantage and hasten you to your goal. In the art of Torishimaru Aiki Jutsu, such an understanding is axiomatic among its practitioners. We know that by understanding the direction and magnitude of the attacker's strength, coupled with proper technique, victory is assured. It is assured, not by opposing the attacker's strength, but by flowing with it and adding the attacker's strength to our own. We know when all the elements are in place that it will culminate in the attacker's destruction, his self-destruction.

Several years ago, a student came to me and told me that he was going to quit college and go to work for his uncle. The reason he gave me was that he simply wasn't up to the challenges that college presented to him. He couldn't tolerate what he believed was an inordinate amount of pressure exerted on him by the instructors in many of his courses. Knowing that this was the easy way out, he was distraught and a little ashamed.

It was clear to me that he had absolutely no understanding as to why his professors were so stringent. If he had, he could have figured a way out of his dilemma all by himself. I explained to him that his instructor's strengths lay in the knowledge of the subjects that they taught and that instead of opposing those strengths, he should yield and move with them in order to utilize them to his advantage. "How," he asked timidly, "could I do that?" "It's simple," I replied. "All you have to do is to take advantage of their classes and to pursue the subject further than the classes allow by speaking to your instructors and getting each of them to donate time away from class to further you in your studies. Trust me."

284

My student, believing in the principle, took my advice and proceeded to press each of his instructors relentlessly for a deeper and deeper understanding of their subject. Some gave him more of their time, others didn't, but all of them immediately eased their pressure on him. Why? Because their pressure was primarily intended to motivate their student to learn as much of what they had to teach as possible. When my student moved with that pressure and took it to the point where his college professors had no misconceptions concerning his motivation, they relented, satisfied that they need not worry about him. Of course, once my student felt the release of their pressure, he immediately settled down and began to master each of his subjects tension-free. So it was that by using his professors' strengths, he was able to turn a voluntary, abject, ignoble defeat into a satisfying and rewarding victory.

Business Application: In recent years, great strides have been made in the field of personal home computers. The reason for those advances is that the competition for market share has all the companies involved in a fierce rivalry with each other to produce faster, more efficient, memory-laden machines. The companies that dominate the computer industry are those companies that have learned to use their competitor's strength against them. Without mentioning any names, it is easy to see how the smaller, less financially endowed companies have been able to use the strength of the technology developed by the larger firms to make for themselves an honorable place in the ever-growing circle of successful computer manufacturers. In their wisdom, they cleverly stood on the shoulders of industry giants and used the considerable strength of those giants in the field to benefit themselves. This is a wise way of growing.

Of course, it isn't one-sided. Even the giants of the computer industry keep their eyes out for any advances made by their lesser competition. They, more than anyone, are aware of how to use their opponent's strength to their own best advantage. They do this in order to maintain their success and assure themselves of the constant ability to outdistance the competition. Their leaders have great business acumen and experience in such matters.

Naturally, the computer industry is just one example of this train of thought. Understand that, regardless of the nature of your business, you can do the same thing. A wise businessman never looks to oppose the strength of his competition; instead, he learns to benefit from his competition's strength by learning the techniques that led to their particular success. Then, by applying that very same formula, often with only slight variations, he is able to achieve his own success.

The hyena and the wild dog are successful and flourish, not because of their own hunting acumen, but because they know the way of the lion. How do they know the way of the lion? Because from the very beginning of time, they patiently observed and assimilated what the lion had to teach.

The Panther Bides Its Time, Springing Neither Too Early Nor Too Late

Principle: Proper Timing

Martial Action: I stand motionless, with my sword still sheathed, at one with the Great Void and dissolved in the peace of the Indigo. My attacker, his sword drawn and hovering in the lower chamber, moves slowly to my left and then to my right. My still-sheathed sword presents him with questions. It is a riddle I have presented to his lower mind to solve. This makes him unsure of himself and causes him to look for a suitable point of entry, a weakness in my defense. If I unsheathe my sword, then he will be in his element, an arrangement that he is used to, and a great advantage will be lost.

If I draw my weapon and move too soon, he will retreat, gliding safely out of reach; if I move too late, the advantage is his and all will be lost. Like a skilled panther, I wait and patiently bide my time. Quietly, I follow his breathing. The questions I have planted in his mind are coming to fruition and are quickly being replaced by a growing impatience. This will be the cause of his undoing. His ever-burgeoning impatience will lead him to make a fatal mistake. The sudden increase in pressure against my shield tells me that the time is approaching. Still, I remain motionless. Then, suddenly, his impatience has won out and he attacks, trying to stun me with his great ki-ai (spiritual shout). The instant that he crosses the boundary of my sphere, I draw my sword and, executing a lateral cut, sever his hara, the source of his spiritual strength. It is done. It was all in the timing.

Life Application: In life, while understanding your circumstances and knowing that you will have to make a move, one should always watch one's timing. It is often the difference between victory and defeat, between gaining your objective quickly and easily or losing it forever. In love, business investments, asking for a raise, making the right choice of vacations, in all things, timing is not only one of the most important factors, it is ultimately an essential factor for success. To rely merely on chance in decision making could very well result in causing you to suffer a perpetual fast throughout your entire existence. In fact, it will have you convinced that you are simply unlucky in anything that you attempt to do in life. This, of course, will ultimately have you stop trying to succeed and will therefore relegate you to a world of abject misery with no chance for personal redemption.

For a martial artist to rely on luck, or for him to depend solely on one's opponent making a mistake, would be an unfortunate circumstance with invariably unfortunate results. Yes, luck could occur and opponents have been known to make mistakes, but for a martial artist to rely on those two occurrences actually taking place would most likely lead to his demise. A noble man, as a truly spiritual man, must not rely on such factors as would make him dependent on things outside of himself; it detracts from his reliance on his own prowess, his own expertise. The accomplished martial artist has learned to depend on his own innate qualities, his own mastered skills. Just like the masterful martial artist, you should learn to sharpen your skills to the point where any action taken in life becomes effortless and free from the entanglements created and offered by the lower mind. With your skills honed to a fine edge, you must watch your timing. Do this, and you will find that there is nothing that cannot be done, nothing that you cannot achieve in your life.

Not too long ago, during *dokusan*, a private conversation between master and student, a young man explained to me that he had asked his employer for a raise three times over the past year and was turned down all three times. He went on to explain that even though he loved his job, he was seriously thinking of quitting. He thought that his employer simply didn't appreciate all the hard work that he had put into his job. This not only annoyed him, but he felt somewhat frustrated with himself. When I had him explain to me the precise circumstances that were current each time he had asked for a raise, the reasons for his failure became more and more apparent. "I guess I have bad luck in bosses," he said to me, looking a little out of sorts. "Not at all," I said, smiling. "You simply have a consistently poor sense of timing."

It seemed that each time he had asked his employer for a raise, something negative happened to be taking place in his employer's life. The first time he asked, for example, the business was undergoing a renovation that plagued his boss with a series of financial as well as serious practical problems. The second time he had asked for a raise, his boss was going through marital problems. The last time he had asked, his boss was suffering a painful gum disorder and was short-tempered and down on the world as a result. Clearly, all three requests were summarily rejected, not for a lack of merit, but merely for lack of proper timing.

I convinced my student to try one more time to get his raise, and if what I told him to do didn't work, then I would agree he would be justified in quitting. He agreed to try again. I asked him if he knew of any happy event coming up in his employer's life, anything at all. It could be a fortunate business situation, for instance, or a joyous personal event, it didn't matter which. My student told me that he only knew of one, the upcoming birth of his employer's first grandchild. It was to take place in about four or five weeks. I advised the student to be patient and wait until the child was born and then to ask for the raise on the third day. He did what I advised him to do and was rewarded for his patience with a raise larger than the one he had anticipated. This, of course, not only made my student very happy but further increased both his diligence and allegiance to his work. That made his boss happy. Everybody won. It was not luck at all, it was all in the timing.

Business Application: Those who know the stock market best will tell you that the secret of successful investing lies in the timing. They patiently bide their time and never make rash and capricious investments. They know that those who act on whims or out of impatience are more likely to lose in the market than win.

In business, you must always watch your timing; it is often the sole factor between success and failure. Even when you open a business, timing is everything. My wife, Sandy, for example, back in the late sixties, opened one of the first health food stores in the country. Everything in the store was natural and health-oriented. All the food items were organically grown, free from pesticides, and fresh from the farm. She was a stalwart pioneer in the then unheard-of idea of consuming non-pesticide-ridden food. The problem was that the idea was so novel, so unheard of, that demand for her goods was very low, too low, and she was eventually forced to close her store. My wife's idea was brilliant, the products were first-rate, and even her choice of location, New York City, was an excellent decision. All the right elements for success were there except one: timing. Back in those days, people were unaware of the benefits of organically grown food and so her clientele was too sparse to support the store and afford her a living. Today, of course, the health-consciousness of the consumer has risen to the point where such businesses flourish. Her success wasn't limited by her innovative thinking, nor by her products—it was doomed by her timing.

Even Leonardo da Vinci, the archetypal Renaissance Man, was stilted in a great many of his endeavors due to poor timing. Of course, in this case, the timing factor was completely out of his hands, but still it was the main reason for his inability to make practical a great number of his scientific discoveries. Inventions such as the helicopter, airplane, submarine, bicycle, and others certainly would have greatly changed the world for the better back in the Middle Ages, but the problem was that the technologies of the day couldn't possibly produce them. Back then, many of his scientific ideas, although novel and ingenious, were in many respects a great source of frustration for him. If he were alive today, however, with the tremendous technologies currently available, Leonardo would have been in his element, sated by the experience of witnessing many of his scientific ideas come to life. This is what proper timing can do.

In the business world, just as it is in the martial arts world, appropriate timing is an all-important factor and may make the difference between success and failure. Knowing this, you must learn to be patient in all your business ventures and trust in the idea that the opportunity for success will invariably present itself. Like a panther poised, waiting for its prey to pass beneath him, be wise, be patient, be alert. To achieve success, you must know the subject of your endeavor, create the best product or service that is within your power to create, and wait patiently for the best time to act. In the martial arts, when your life hangs in the balance, moving too soon or too late would be disastrous. The monkey who misses his branch, and the man who misses his opportunity, are both lost.

The Birch Stands Motionless In the Snow; The Owl Observes In Silence

Principle: No Wasted Effort/Just Doing

Martial Action: I stand quiet, motionless, and centered in the peace of the Great Void of God. The blade of my sword is primed in the rear of the lower chamber. With vigilance and patience, I watch my attacker as he moves left and right, forward and backward, and then left and right again in an effort to find a favorable position and gain the advantage. I remain calm and centered and wait, knowing that there is no benefit for him to achieve in all his movements, for I am the birch tree among the snowflakes, the owl upon the barren limb—a silent witness to all of his useless actions.

Impatiently, he wastes his feminine energy to no avail. He is weakening and loses concentration, quivering like the final leaf clinging hopelessly to a tree bough in the dead of a grim winter. His blade wavers within the middle chamber. He charges and I defend. With a single stroke of my blade, the leaf is severed from the bough and falls silently to the earth.

Life Application: The crowning glory of a panther is its economy of action. That is, it wisely wastes no action or energy in the pursuit and capture of its prey; it does what it has to do, nothing more, nothing less. It neither adds to the difficulty by doing too much nor increases that difficulty by doing too little. Wasting no time in action that is not required in order to achieve its goals nor in the delays inherent in fruitless speculation concerning those goals, the panther simply does what is needed to be done—that's all.

A great many people, on the other hand, have a tendency to be less direct in the pursuit of their objectives. Wasting too much time and effort in unnecessary preparation and execution, they become easily frustrated and voluntarily give up before their goals are realized. This is a tragedy, not only because it curtails a person's opportunity for self-fulfillment but because it is a situation that, in most cases, is completely and painlessly avoidable.

In order to understand the principle of No Wasted Effort, one need only look into one's own past and locate a particular action that was a truly selfless action. That is, an action that you committed to in which you had no thought of the ease or difficulty of the action, no thought of clinging or revulsion to the elements inherent in that action, and no thoughts of success or failure.

Do you remember what it was like going swimming and, instead of just diving into the pool right away, you walked over to the side and cautiously dipped your hand or foot into the water to see how cold it was? If the water was agreeably warm, then there was no difficulty at all in coming to the decision to dive in. But if the water felt cold, then you were faced with a big dilemma and you found yourself hesitating and standing by the side of the pool, trying to build up the courage to take the plunge. Of course, if you were with friends who had already entered the pool, then besides the fact that you really wanted to join them, you had to listen to their jeers and tauntings. Well, did you go in? Of course you did, but it wasn't until you reached the point where you said to yourself, "What the hell, I'll just do it!" Then, taking a deep breath, you just did it. If you can remember going through something like this, then you can also remember how truly easy the actual physical act of entering the pool really was. If you think about it, it was nothing but the mental reservations you had that made it all so difficult. Look at all the time you wasted standing there trying to drum up the courage to take the plunge. What were you thinking? Did you think that you were going to freeze to death? No, of course not. It was merely the idea of being temporarily uncomfortable that made you reluctant to enter the pool. It was only when you bypassed the intervention of the lower mind that you were finally able to consummate the action. If you had done that from the very start, then there would have been no wasted effort on your part and you could have begun enjoying the pool all the sooner.

Naturally, the situation at the pool is only one example of how the lower mind interferes with our lives by painting pictures and having us procrastinate in doing not only things that we have to do but things that we really want to do. Think about it. Take a moment to consider all the things that you delayed doing over the years, things that in your mind are repugnant or boring. Maybe there are things that you are delaying doing now? In the martial arts, such lower mind interference could cause our injury or death; in life it could cause missing out on a great many of the things that will bring you fulfillment.

The principle of Just Doing is not difficult to understand and can be mastered in three easy steps. All one has to do to apply this principle is as follows:

293

1. Take the time to understand all the steps necessary to successfully complete the action.
2. Quiet the lower mind to the point where it does not interfere with the action through its notorious ability of complicating an issue with speculations as to the ease, difficulty, and result of the action. This can be done through a brief period of meditation and/or breath control just before you have to engage in the action. (See Part 2)
3. Then, just do it. That's right . . . just do it!

It sounds simple, doesn't it? Well, it really is simple. Remember, the culprit in wasted effort is not the action itself but the lower mind and its interference. Even though logic dictates the need to make things easier, it is the nature of the lower mind to do just the opposite. It is the nature of the lower mind to take what in truth is a simple and direct course of action and complicate it to the point where one is left with a seemingly impossible task. Apply the three steps above when it comes time for you to act and a whole new world of success will open up to you.

Business Application: One evening, a businessman came to me for advice. He had wanted to expand his business for some years but was afraid to do it. It seemed that each time the notion to expand crossed his mind, he came up with a thousand reasons why that expansion would not work—too time consuming, too much of a commitment, too costly, too this, too that—a thousand excuses. In truth, it was none of these things. It was nothing but complications created and perpetuated by the vile machinations of his own lower mind. In short, he was thinking too much.

I had him enter a short period of meditation before we proceeded any further with our conversation. With his lower mind nice and serene, we continued to speak and he was able to understand how really simple it was to be successful in not only his dream of expansion, but in everything else that he wanted to achieve in life. He came to realize that to achieve success in any endeavor was nothing more than taking one positive step at a time and executing that step as cleanly and directly as possible—just doing. He came to understand that his lower mind had him thinking of all ten steps of his expansion all at once. This translated to him as an intenuous jumble of confusing images, unnerving thoughts, and seemingly unachievable goals, all frightening him into inaction. However, once he realized how truly simple his dream of expansion actually was, nothing was able to keep him from that success. In fact, the very next day he set his expansion plans in motion—he went out and did it. Not only did he achieve the expansion that he was looking for, but he was able to improve his business in ways that he had never considered possible before.

A barrel fills up drop by drop; success is achieved step by step. The rule is, therefore, to simplify your plans by breaking those plans down into a series of steps, making sure that each step is reduced to a simple, straightforward action. Then, simply proceed without fear, without attachment to the results of what you are doing, executing each step as your reach it—No Wasted Effort. Just do it! Never skip steps or avoid the proper execution of steps in order to attempt to achieve success more quickly. All that's important is the step that is front of you. The man who keeps his eyes fixed on the horizon and walks too quickly will trip over even the most easily avoidable things lying in plain sight at his feet.

The Bear Seeks the Honey But Acquires the Bees

Principle: Target Replacement

Martial Action: My attacker attempts to strike me with a straight punch. Centered in the Great Void, I raise my left hand, palm outward, and sweep it in front of me, feeling the pulse of feminine energy generated by his strike. My hand, crossing his intended target, captures that pulse and moves it off to the side, while I turn and lean in the direction that I want his strike to take. Within the Void I create a path through the unpartable Indigo. His strike moves along that path and is now beyond his control. His strike has missed his intended target and leaves him vulnerable to my counterattack. He is lost. His attack was his undoing. His intended target gave me the means.

Life Application: Often, life offers us viable alternatives that cede us the ability to avoid collision with a very large percentage of its many negative aggressions. The problem is that most people are totally unaware that these options exist and so find themselves in the unfortunate position of having to deal with most of them head-on.

Of course, there are some problems in life that can be avoided simply by shunting them to the side for awhile and allowing them to dissipate quietly over the course of time. This manner of dealing with certain problems is not an act of denial, but simply an understanding that they will disappear of their own accord, like bubbles rising to the surface of a stream and bursting without any outside help. In some instances, this would be the wise way of handling them. However, the number of such problems is limited and the rest cannot be walked away from so easily.

Listen! One afternoon, a young student told me that he was having trouble with one of his fellow workers. He told me how this man would constantly be playing mindless pranks that interfered with his ability to work properly and that he was afraid that he was going to get fired because of it. He wanted to tell his employer about this person but I advised him not to. Instead, I told him to place himself in a position where his employer had an easier opportunity to observe him at work. "What?" he asked, a little confused. "Because of this other guy, I want to hide from my boss. Besides, I don't want my boss standing over me all day. But if you think that it will end my problem, I'll do it. It won't be very difficult to move to another work bench in front of the boss's open door."

I smiled and told him, once the arrangements are made, to quietly dare the man to do these things again. Challenge him, but not loud enough for the boss to hear. I told him to trust me, have patience, and wait. He did what I suggested. It wasn't long, only a week or so, before my student told me that the prankster had been fired. He explained that because he did what I suggested and placed himself in a position where his boss had an easy view of him, that his boss couldn't help but observe the actions of the prankster and so angrily fired him right there on the spot.

When my student quietly challenged the prankster into doing his mischief, the prankster's ego immediately surfaced and he told my student all the things that he had done since he'd been working there and that the boss didn't suspect a thing. In fact, the prankster had a few choice words for his boss that his boss also witnessed.

This is an example of Target Replacement. Here, my student was the prankster's intended target, but with just a little ingenuity, coupled with trust in the method, he had transferred the prankster's attention away from himself and directed it toward his employer. The result clearly speaks for itself.

Business Application: In business, there are many uses for this principle. Attention, for instance, can often be shunted away from our business secrets through the employment of the principle of Target Replacement by emphasizing the importance of something else in their stead. For example, if I were involved in the sort of business where I wanted to keep my competitors from stealing my ideas, I would create a diversion that would place a great deal of emphasis on another one of my products or processes. They would be decoys, of course, but would be so natural, so lifelike that they couldn't be distinguished from the real thing. This, when properly executed, would have my competitors concentrating on what I wanted them to concentrate on and would afford me the luxury to develop my idea in peace. It may even cause my competition to spend a lot of time and effort in the process and that would be fine, too.

To bring this off, you must first be aware of what it is that your competitors are actually looking for—what product, process, information. Once you know, all you would have to do is to leak certain key pieces of information (about your decoy) to the right person, organization, or even the news media.

If I were in the computer software field, for example, and had the idea for a new type of business program, I would know that there are a thousand or more software developers who would work day and night on developing such a program if only they knew what I was trying to develop. Knowing how really competitive the computer software industry is, what I would do is to appeal to my competitors' greed and, in some cases, underhandedness, by placing a great deal of emphasis on my decoy—another lesser program, something that I would label and treat as something very special. The competition would then be facing one of two choices. They could opt to dismiss my endeavor as nothing special or, driven by greed, actively place all their efforts into finding out all the details and reproducing it. In fact, they would probably make every effort to come out with the program first. I know that some of you think that it is rather melodramatic to go through this sort of thing, but those of you in big business know that things such as industrial espionage do exist. You may even have been hurt by the nefarious practices of your competition and so the creation of a decoy may not seem so far-fetched to you. Clearly, the greedy fish is already caught as soon as it sees the hook and opens its mouth.

This was only an example of Target Replacement in the world of business—there are, of course, many other ways of using it, but you have the idea. Remember, the bear who seeks to steal the honey must also be able to cope with the bees.

The Gazelle Leads the Lion Further Than the Lion Can Endure

Principle: Yielding To Strength: When Pushed, I Turn; When Pulled, I Enter

Martial Action: My opponent reaches out to attack me with a push. With both hands he reaches toward my chest. Just as his shield touches mine, I turn my body, pivoting smoothly to my left, and he loses his balance to the corner. As he passes, with a gentle tap I send him crashing to the floor, deep in the lower chamber. Then, attacking me a second time, he secures my shirt with both of his hands and pulls me toward him. I enter, moving in the direction of that pull. Suddenly adding my strength to his, he loses his balance to his rear and again with a light tap I send him quickly to the ground.

In both instances, my victory was assured by yielding to my opponent's strength rather than opposing that strength. By adding only a small measure of my own strength to his, I am able to defeat him easily.

Life Application: Not every situation in life has to be met head-on. In fact, there are some situations that really shouldn't be, because sometimes, realistically, we simply lack the necessary strength required to achieve victory. In these cases, we can change disaster to triumph if we use the strength of the situation to our advantage by adding only a little bit of our own strength to it. In this way, we are often bringing the predicament to a rapid and often satisfying conclusion much faster then it would normally resolve itself if confronted head-on.

For example, I had a young student who on one particular occasion was afraid to go home, knowing that when his father got there he would discover a brand-new dent on the family car. He anticipated his father's anger and knew that he would be severely punished for it. He was distraught and beside himself with fear. My advice to the student was for him to yield to his father's impending response and to dissipate his father's anger before he arrived home. "How can I do that?" he asked anxiously. "It's easy," I replied. "But you must trust me."

I had the student yield to his father's strength by having him call his father at work and explain to him the nature of the circumstances that led up to the dent on the family car. Also, I had him explain to his father how truly sorry he was and that he would submit, without argument, to any punishment that his father thought suitable. This is yielding to strength. My student's contrite attitude, display of maturity, and sense of responsibility so pleased his father that it dissipated most of his anger almost immediately. By the time his father came home, his anger had turned to an understandable and controlled annoyance.

Here, my student was able to reduce his father's anger by yielding to it. That is, he preemptively gave his father the news about the dent rather than having his father discover the dent on his own. News of the accident, of course, fired up his father's anger, but anger, like a strong wind, does not last all day. As the hours passed, tempered with my student's contrition, his father's anger abated. By the time his father came home, he was able to flow quite easily with his father's reaction. In fact, he let his father know that he felt so guilty, so badly at having been involved in the accident, that he couldn't even go meet with his friends that afternoon. The genuineness of his remorse surprised his father so much that his father completely let go of any thought of punishment. In his father's eyes, he was punished enough.

Nature made the gazelle quick and taught it how to lead the lion to exhaustion. In so doing, the gazelle survives though it lacks the lion's strength. This is yielding.

Business Application: In business, whether you are offering products or services, there are times when you have to deal with dissatisfied customers. It's unavoidable. The worst course of action to take is one that opposes them. Any opposition to their complaints will only increase their desire for satisfaction and that can, and often does, translate into bad public relations and a decrease in consumer confidence in your product or service. This, of course, can mean lower sales and disappointing profits. No one in business wants that. Instead of attempting to rebut the customer's complaint, you can flow with his strength by politely listening to his complaint with all the sympathy, patience, and understanding that you can muster. Never, never, never make a customer's complaint a point of honor that has to be defended to the bitter end. To do so may mean, if not the bitter end of your business and your livelihood, at least, possibly, the beginning of a slow decline in sales if the word gets out.

By yielding to a customer's complaint right away, several important things are accomplished. First, you immediately take away the strength of his argument. Remember, the average person is coming to you already anticipating a great deal of resistance to his complaint. He is battle-ready and has built up a great deal of aggressiveness in anticipation of your negative response. This can lead to embarrassing scenes, complaints with the Better Business Bureau, negatives spread by word of mouth, and in some cases even violence. Who would want any of those events to occur?

Second, by yielding to him, you are placing yourself in a position that will allow you to lead him in the direction that you want him to go. When a dissatisfied customer earnestly believes that you understand his plight, it will pleasantly surprise him and not only will he be more civil but he will be open to any reasonable suggestions that you have to make in the matter.

Third, you must understand that accepting the return of an item will not break you, or at least shouldn't break you, and may very well prove to be to your benefit. Product returns and customer dissatisfaction are a natural part of any business. P.T. Barnum was correct when he said, "You can please some of the people all of the time, all of the people some of the time, but you can't please all the people all of the time." This is the way of things in business.

Even so, through application of the principle of Yielding, the customer unsatisfied with your product or service will be so pleased with your response to his complaint that not

302

only may he actually increase his business with you but he will be sure to tell his friends and relatives about your attitude and response. Then word of mouth will spread and ultimately increase your business beyond any newspaper, radio, or television advertising. By Yielding, you create a situation where everyone wins.

Never think for a second that Yielding is weakness. It is a strength that will, if properly employed, ultimately culminate in victory. The gazelle has two options when it comes to yielding to the strength of the lion. The first is to stand there and quietly submit—this is weakness; the second is to flee with dignity. The first leads to an inevitable death; the second to life. Yield and win, or oppose and lose. Remember that no store, no business, regardless of its assets, can withstand the displeasure of the consumer for long.

The Panther Leaps, the Eagle Soars, the Deer Flees; They Cannot Hide Their Natures

Principle: The Heart And Not The Eyes

Martial Action: Centered in the eternal peace of the Great Void, I stand motionless with my sword resting in the lower chamber. My opponent stares into my eyes but I do not return his gaze. I do so not out of fear but out of mistrust, for the eyes are known to deceive. Instead, I rest my eyes on the center of his chest, for hearts are not eyes and cannot lie, they cannot deceive. I wait patiently. In an instant, his heart forewarns me of his intention and declares his attack. In a single motion I parry his blade and my blade finds its mark. It is done.

Life Application: The eyes can tell us a great deal about a person, it's true. They can indicate, for example, a person's attitude, state of mind, intention to deceive, and even the current state of that person's health. However, there are those who, after a reasonable amount of practice, can use their eyes as a tool of deception, to beguile and convince others that their intentions are good and their motives pure when, in truth, they harbor nefarious schemes and champion ignoble causes.

In the martial arts, to be taken in by an opponent's eyes can be disastrous, leading to serious injury or even death. If your opponent looks to the left, it may be a ruse and he may move right; if he looks right, he may move left. The wise are not taken in by such actions.

To really know the truth of a person's intentions, we must know what lies in that person's heart, for hearts are impervious to even the most vile intentions, the cleverest treacheries, dictated to them by their lower minds. When there is a struggle for dominance between the dictates of a person's lower mind and the dictates of a person's heart, that person's actions can be seen as faltering and unclear, and their speech is filled with myriad contradictions. Such people are avoided by the wise, for the wise know that they are not to be trusted and that any association with them will only lead to great grief. To this end, the wise know that a crust of bread eaten in peace is better than a banquet partaken in anxiety.

The simplest and surest way to know what is in a person's heart is to judge them by their actions, not their words. Even a thousand declarations of love are effaced forever by a single act of betrayal; a hundred peace treaties are rendered worthless by a single act of aggression.

304

Business Application: Clearly, in business, action too speaks louder than words. In business, as in life, one is confronted by a large variety of people that one has to deal with. Some are honest and sincere while others are clever and devious, each following their own nature. The problem is that in life, we generally have more latitude when it comes to who we want to associate with. In business, very often, we are forced to have to deal with just about everyone.

In business, for example, the use of guile and flattery in order to consummate a deal is very common. It is part of the wooing process mastered by so many and fallen for by even a larger number. It is a major component of the smoke and mirror techniques used to facilitate an action on behalf of an avaricious go-getter. Is it wrong? No, not necessarily. It really depends on the quality of the goods or services being offered. Really, if the product or services are excellent, they will speak for themselves, and all the flattery, cajoling, and other inducements are nothing but a waste of time. Unfortunately, however, too many people can't see what those product or service qualities are until the smoke clears and the mirrors are taken away. Then, it's too late.

The world of business and the world of love are really very similar in a great many respects.

1. Boy sees girl and finds her attractive—salesman sees clients and finds them attractive
2. Boy approaches girl—salesman approaches client
3. Boy woos girl with flattery and flowers—salesman woos client with flattery and rhetoric
4. Girl yields and, good or bad, long- or short-term, a relationship begins—client yields and, good or bad, long- or short-term, a deal is made

In both situations, there is the possibility for happiness or grief. Too many hearts are broken and too many unfortunate business deals are made to be incautious when it comes to either. A wise person must look past the words, beyond the flattery. One truly wise in business, like one truly wise in love, looks to the heart of the person who he is dealing with and then proceeds from there. The wise businessman will always look past the rhetoric and get immediately to the point, to the heart of the matter at hand. Wisely, he will be direct in his actions and equally direct in his speech. In direct action and plain speaking there can be no place for deceit to hide.

In the art of Torishimaru Aiki Jutsu, we learn to neutralize our attacker's weapons right from the beginning. In business, plain talking and direct action will thwart the person of deceit by destroying the very foundation of his plans to deceive and beguile. It will unbalance him by taking his weapon away and forcing him to have to deal with you on your own terms. Suddenly, he is taken out of his element. This, of course, gives you the upper hand, the power and control to direct the course of business. Conduct business this way, from heart to heart, and you will have the power to do well and prosper. You will also develop the reputation of one who is straightforward and trustworthy.

A wise man knows when the wife flatters and embraces her husband without love that she has some other reason for it. A person wise in the affairs of business must keep this in mind. The panther leaps, the eagle soars, the deer flees . . . they cannot hide their natures.

A Strong Wind Does Not Last All Day

Principle: Facing The Wind

Martial Action: Centered in the Great Void, my soul merged with the Great Indigo, I stand poised before three attackers. They unsheathe their swords and voice their intentions to do me great harm. Like the great cackling din of frightened chickens at the approach of a fox, they raise their voices high and create a wind that cannot stir a leaf. But I am an old fox, learned in the way of such theatrical attempts at intimidation. Their words are as vain as rain pelting the surface of the ocean. I face that wind, immovable in my silence, unshakable in the bosom of the great emptiness within the Void of God.

Life Application: Language is a marvelously powerful tool. It not only facilitates our ability to communicate and establish an honest and loving rapport with another person, but it can also be used to beguile, cajole, insult, intimidate, and deceive. How language is used rests solely in the hands of the individual who uses it.

Some people, well versed in the use of language, use it to induce the listener into painting pictures in their lower minds, pictures that serve their own purposes, their own ends. One must be very careful when dealing with such people, for they are the Huns of the aural world, ravaging and pillaging innocents through their command over language and its uses.

A person of wisdom understands the difference between speech backed by honesty and sincerity and speech designed to cover up an impending nefarious intention. The wise are leery of the flatterer, one who knows how to use language to appeal to the unsuspecting lower minds of those he would influence. The wise know that flatterers are skilled in the art of ingratiation for their own benefit and for their own aims. A serpent wags his tongue to taste the air for prey and predators; the devious man wags his tongue only for prey.

One evening I was invited to a dinner party at a student's home. After dinner, some of us gathered in his den to play pool. The house rule was simple: If you win, you continue to play; if you lose, you have to wait until your turn comes up again.

There was a fellow there who seemed to dominate the game, and appeared by most to be unbeatable. Yes, he was fairly good at the game, but that wasn't his real forte. I watched him defeat players who were as skilled, or in one particular case, more skilled at the game than he was. His truly great expertise lay in his ability to rattle his opponents with a lot of inane chatter. While his opponants were preparing to shoot, for example, he would sing, whistle, and pass comments to them incessantly, resulting in his haggard opponents blundering even the easiest shots. When my turn came to play him, he tried to do to me what he had so successfully done to the others. He talked and talked, whistled, sang—all in an effort to unnerve me and break my concentration. He was really quite good at it but I knew two things that he didn't know. First, having had little opportunity to play the game, I knew that he had more skill than I did. Second, I knew that all his vocal theatrics, all his attempts to interfere with my ability to concentrate, were a total waste of his time and wouldn't work on me.

Just as we began and he started to chatter, I took my handkerchief out of my pocket and held it above my head. A moment later I dropped it to the floor. This caught his attention and temporarily created a tsuki or gap in his thought processes, causing him suddenly to go silent. When he recovered and began to chatter once again, I repeated myself and dropped the handkerchief a second time. After the third time, a little annoyed, he asked me what I was doing. I told him that I wanted to see how far my handkerchief would travel in the presence of all of this wind. A little embarrassed, he remained as silent as he could throughout the rest of our game. This took his edge away because over the years he had learned to make that chatter part of his game. Now, suddenly, he was forced to rely solely on his skill, something that made him nervous and uncomfortable. He became rattled by his own silence and as a result missed shots, simple shots, that he ordinarily wouldn't have missed. Yes, I won, but it was a combination of my marginal skill at the game, his inability to break my concentration, and his inability to maintain his own.

Understand that those who use the power of speech to intimidate you are those who are actually attempting to do three things. First, they are trying to demoralize and control you. That is, they are trying to beat you before any action takes place. Second, it is their way of occupying their own lower minds so that it doesn't paint pictures of their own possible injuries and sufferings. Third, it is their way to keep their weaknesses and insecurities inviolable from detection by others who may be present.

People who are prone to vocal intimidation create a great wind but, in the final analysis, it is only wind after all. A person of wisdom remains unshakable in his understanding of such people, and faces the wind they create without fear.

A noble man acts and then speaks; an ignoble man speaks and rarely acts. Such is the way of things. The wise know that a strong wind does not last all day.

Business Application: In the business world, one may have to deal, depending on your position, with irate customers, angry bosses, or disgruntled employees. Anger has a tendency to loosen most tongues and so there is every chance that when you have to deal with someone who is angry, you will have to endure their rantings and ravings. Understand that anything short of actual physical violence is nothing but wind. Armed with this knowledge, you should not allow your lower mind to augment that wind by summoning up images that will lead to your own loss of control, your own fear or anger. When faced with the wind generated by those you have to deal with, it would serve no useful purpose arguing back with them, trying to drive a point across to someone who is in no position to hear it.

Anger is a temporary madness that blinds and deafens a person, wrenching reason from their hands and making them absolutely impervious to any form of civil conversation. Knowing this, it would not be in your

309

best interest to push back at them verbally and anger them further. Instead, you should make every effort to reduce their anger to a level that would facilitate a quick and amicable solution. This can be accomplished by showing the irate customer, for example, that you understand the nature of their grievance, commiserate with their plight, and will do everything possible to see to it that they walk away satisfied. This should immediately settle them down to the point where you can deal with them. The idea that "the customer is always right" may not be true in every case, but it does make good business sense and in the long run will be good for profits.

With an angry boss, you must show him by your actions that you not only understand the nature of the problem but that you are genuinely contrite as a result. Arguing back or making unacceptable excuses will only result in getting you fired. When your employer sees that you are genuinely sorry and is under the impression that the incident will not happen again, he will relent.

Dealing with disgruntled employees is a little different. They are more likely to vent their complaints to each other and their spouses than they are to air them in front of their employer. Still, when an employer senses that the employees may have grievances, he should strike preemptively and begin a round of discussions with them that will address the causes of their anger. Doing this will save an employer a great amount of grief later on. Remember, unhappy employees will not only affect an employer's peace of mind now and in the future, but in many ways they may

310   ultimately affect their profits too. A forest fire can begin with the lighting of a single match; it is easier to extinguish the match properly now than to have to go through the effort and expense of having to extinguish a blazing, out of control forest fire later on.

In all of the cases that I mentioned above, you must face the wind with confidence and understanding, bearing in mind that strong winds do not last all day.

Stealth Is Not the Cat's Greatest Skill; His Greatest Skill Is Found In the Art of Patience

Principle: Facing The Panther

Martial Action: My attacker stands with his sword poised and ready in the upper chamber. He angrily glances left, then right, waiting for me to respond and acknowledge his challenge. I keep my sword sheathed and make no gesture for or against the fight. He wants the engagement to begin and is growing more and more impatient with the delay. His impatience is his weakness and will be the vehicle of his undoing.

I watch as his sword drops to the middle chamber and rises again. He bellows a verbal challenge in order to prod me into action. Instead, I assume seiza (a kneeling position) and wait quietly. Letting go of time and duality in the great expanse of the Void, I am prepared to bide motionless for twice an eternity.

His once-calm demeanor quickly erodes, passing through all of the stages of anger. His facial expression suddenly changes as his patience drives him to commit a desperate act. Unable to contain himself any longer, he lunges forward, his blade splitting the air for a downward head cut. With a single motion, I draw my sword. It is done.

311

Life Application: In the art of Torishimaru Aiki Jutsu, the panther symbolizes the visible forces of the earth, the material hazards each of us face as we journey through life.

To say that life is a perilous journey is something that everyone already recognizes, but the fact is that many of the dangers inherent in life are made even more hazardous by one's own lack of patience and ability to face them without fear. To run from the perilous elements of life would be to take them with you. By facing them, by Facing The Panther, there is a way to end their hold on you forever.

The operational word here is "accept." Accept! Accept! Accept! When perils and negative circumstances appear before you, you must accept them and then face them with a new understanding, a renewed vigor. You must accept them as an intricate part of both your life and your spiritual evolution. By doing so you will not only be able to use them to test your understanding of the world, but they will be a yardstick with which to measure the depth of your personal spiritual growth.

How strange it is that people are quick to accept the positive events in their lives and yet deny the negatives, when it is the ignoring of negative events that is in a great part responsible for many of the psychological problems that people are prone to suffer from. Denial is repression and suppression of problems that should have been faced and dissipated at their inception. Instead, the average person tries to ignore them, hoping that they'll just go away. The fact is that they don't go away, but are recorded in every detail on both the higher and lower mind tapes.

The wise are unchanged when experiencing both the negative and positive circumstances in life. Why? Because they understand that how they view an experience is what that experience becomes. The wise patiently accept negative experiences as learning experiences, experiences that only further them along their spiritual path. This, of course, changes a negative experience into a very positive experience and this is how it is recorded on both their higher and lower mind tapes, precluding the chance for any deep-rooted psychological problems later on.

Still, when negative events occur in your life, it doesn't mean that you should not rectify them if it is within your power to do so. Change what you can and accept what you can't. This is the way of the noble person. To patiently accept the often dire machinations of life's panthers undaunted, unshaken, and unsullied by their influence is the sign of a superior person and an enormous step on the path toward freedom, serenity, and true spiritual wisdom.

Business Application: The wise businessperson is patient and understanding, facing each new business challenge with the courage and vigor of one scaling a great mountain, one undaunted by the perils of the journey.

For those whose vocation or avocation it is to climb mountains, it is their great fortune to patiently accept the understanding that it is the journey itself that is the reward and the excitement and not just the planting of the flag on the mountain's icy summit. So it must be for the businessperson. If you want a stress-free and rewarding business life, you must approach it in exactly the same manner—enjoying the excitement and rewards of the climb but detached from any idea of a final victory. If you don't, you may find yourself bound hand and foot to a business life riddled with frustration and misery. How truly sad it would be to find, at the close of your life, that all the frustration and misery was for nothing and not only could have been avoided but, regretfully, *should* have been avoided.

Life, in the final analysis, is a series of choices; how you choose to live your business life may bring you either happiness or misery. You must choose wisely. No amount of wanting can quicken the growing of an apple tree. To break open an apple seed in order to extract an apple will leave you wanting for both the apple and the seed. Therefore, the

313

fruits of your labor will materialize only if the seed is properly planted and lovingly nurtured. Patience tempered with good business sense will bring you what you want.

When there is nothing to do, then everything gets done; once everything is done, then there is nothing to do. Stealth is a cat's asset, but patience is its greatest virtue.

The Panther Follows the Ancient Ways, the Calling of the Ancient Mind. There Is No Argument!

Principle: Freezing The Attacker and Offering No Choice

Martial Action: My opponent is preparing to attack. To move, his mind must issue the order. With the appearance of the thought that will precipitate his physical motion, I raise my left hand and project from my palm a wide shaft of feminine energy. Neither too little nor too much, neither too soon nor too late, the shaft of feminine energy strikes his shield. Alerting his higher mind, he freezes in his attack. He is neutralized and cannot move. I press inward and present my counterattack. He cannot defend himself and succumbs without a struggle.

Life Application: Anger, hatred, fear, and greed are the froward children of the lower mind and the unwitting parents of aggression. Appealing to the naive and disorderly offices of the lower mind to desist in clinging to these things is as useless as appealing to lightning in order to dissuade it from striking the surface of the ocean. The man or woman of wisdom knows that any appeal, if it is to be truly effective, must be made through the all-knowing offices of the higher mind, the link with the Eternal. The wise know that to appeal to the lower mind to monitor itself would be like asking the fox to watch over the chickens—and that would be a grievous error.

The higher mind will override the lower mind in all matters of defense, but only if the higher mind is stirred to action. A word, a gesture, a smile, a thought, anything at all that will affect the shield of the aggressor, can transcend the aegis of the lower mind and excite his higher mind to an action beyond his control. When this is done, all the faculties of the higher mind are brought to the fore, including an overpowering sense of right action and wrong action.

Know that within each of us lies a strong, unseverable bond with the Eternal, with God. It is always with us but the loud, self-centered lower mind, thinking itself separate and apart from God, creates its own concepts of the world and places itself solely on the seat of authority. But it is an uneasy crown that it bears, for it lacks the knowledge and experience to rule with wisdom. Instead it is a frightened master, ultimately cowering in the face of the world that it created for itself. Knowing this, the man of wisdom appeals to the higher mind of those with whom he comes into contact. He establishes mystical gates that transcend the common. He establishes bonds framed within the structure of the Eternal. When this happens, all the stalwart barriers separating people are dissolved and a blissful lasting interpersonal connection is achieved.

When dealing with aggressive people, you must understand that their aggression is sparked by insecurity defects that they have recorded on their lower mind tapes. Aggressiveness is their way of exercising control and safeguarding themselves. To bypass the aggressor's lower mind, you must be able to communicate higher mind to higher mind. To do this means that you first have to quiet your own lower mind and allow your higher mind to come forward. Once this happens, the communication between your higher minds will take place automatically and you will affect him in ways that will reduce his aggression.

In other words, you will find yourself communicating and stirring his higher mind to override his lower mind. Once done, he will be directed to right action regardless of what his lower mind is telling him to do. The effect is that he will decrease his aggressive behavior and not only not know why he is doing it but very often not even realize that his aggressiveness is leaving him.

Business Application: In business, as a matter of course, an employer is often called upon to establish many links. One such link that must be created and maintained is the one that exists between an employer and his employees. Of course, you could argue that you, as an employer, already have that link, but do you really? The sort of link that I am talking about is one that allows an employer to exercise a great amount of power and influence over his employees while simultaneously avoiding alienating them.

If you are an employer, then take a moment to think about the image that you believe your employees have concerning you. Be honest! Is it the image of a kind and gentle employer whom everyone obeys out of love and respect, or is it one of a grueling taskmaster cracking a whip and frightening everyone around him into obeisance? If the image that you come up with is anywhere near the second, then there are several things that you have to understand right away. The first is that you are placing yourself in a self-imposed isolation that ultimately undermines any hope of creating the unity that breeds the sort of esprit de corps that could make a business truly successful. Understand that, if this is the case, your subordinates submit to your will not out of their own free will but because they are too powerless and frightened to resist. It is the human condition to respond to tyranny with contempt and defiance. Is that what you want from your employees? Is this sort of control truly in your best interest and the best interest of your business? Do you want obedience to your will coupled with a quiet unrest seething under the surface among them? I hope not. If this is what is currently occurring in your business and you want to change it so that you not only have absolute control but happy employees at the same time, you can make those changes by understanding the following:

1. You are the boss and everyone knows that already. Moreover, your employees understand all the power and possibilities that come along with that position. They know that you can hire, fire, give raises, bestow bonuses, and move everyone around in the pecking order at will. This is one of those axiomatic understandings that all employees have of their bosses. That's a tremendous power to have over people, so why attempt to superimpose on that power the image of a cold, aloof, indifferent boss whose only interest is the furthering of his own financial empire? This sort of attitude makes trouble where there should be no trouble and will only alienate the very people responsible for your success—your employees.

2. The rule of thumb is this: "Happy employees mean happy bosses." To understand this, take a moment and put yourself in their place. Suppose that your employer was the sort of man who made life very unpleasant for his employees. What would you be looking to do? That's right! You'd be looking to change jobs! Well, while you're looking for a new job, what would your attitude be about your present job? Right! Since you would be looking for a better job, you couldn't care less about the quality of your work on this job. Suppose that fifty percent of the employees in the same company felt this way. This

would mean that there would be such an employee turnover in the business that it would be nearly impossible to maintain a staff of experienced workers and the workers who did stay wouldn't be very happy. This translates into poor product quality, poor sales, a constant flow of customer complaints, and a business that is doomed to failure. Do you understand?

3. You must understand that your employees are not your enemies and are in part responsible for the very success of your business. A wise employer knows this. A wise employer knows how to have the best of all possible worlds when it comes to his business. A wise employer knows that when his employees are happy, everyone wins. He knows that happy employees are loyal, honest, and hard-working.

Moreover, suppose that you were an employee of a business where the boss was lighthearted, affable, and took good care of his employees—making sure that the pay was adequate to meet the current standard of living, that health benefits were freely given, that holidays were paid holidays, and that good work was rewarded with raises and bonuses. With these benefits, would you want to work anywhere else? Would you be looking for another job? I don't think so. In fact, I think that you would find yourself working twice as hard, twice as carefully, and twice as efficiently, not only in order to reap the liberal benefits offered you by that employer but to ensure yourself a position with that company until you are ready to retire.

318

Imagine if your employees felt this way about your company! Yes, on the surface you may be spending more than you care to spend, but the benefits that your company would enjoy from such an investment would ultimately translate into better products and services for your clients, which naturally translates into more sales, more growth, and more profits. Think of it as the type of investment that pays for itself, the sort of investment that benefits everyone.

Never be greedy. In business, you often have to give up something in order to gain something. The lion takes his share of the kill first, but then allows the other members of the pride to eat their fill. Since the lionesses (your employees) do the hunting (the work), the lion (you) knows, with all his power, with all his authority, with all of his inherent majesty, that if because of his greed they starve to death, he will shortly thereafter starve to death with them. The panther follows the ancient ways, the subtle calling of the ancient mind . . . there is no argument.

The Lion Stalks, The Eland Runs

Principle: Weakening The Opponent

Martial Action: The attacker grabs my left wrist with his right hand. Knowing that he uses only as much strength in his grip that will allow him to exercise control over my movements, I dissolve myself in the Great Void, relaxing all the muscles of my arm and allowing it to go limp. He responds in kind by lessening his strength. Reducing my resistance, I have weakened his grip and lessened his strength. I perform a *hakko dore,* an escape technique, and step back to a safe and defensible position. I am free, with little effort. The weak controls the strong.

Life Application: Sadly, aggressive behavior is an intricate part of the human condition. It is a prominent part of humanity's ancient memories, those memories recorded indelibly on the higher mind tape. Stemming from the need to aggress in order to survive, as well as the need to find a suitable placement within the local pecking order, humankind has taken on a pattern of behavior that has

319

been reinforced constantly throughout an individual's many incarnations. Bearing this in mind, it is no small wonder that whenever we find ourselves among people for any length of time, we are bound to enter into strife situations fomented by those ancient behaviors. It can be said that humankind is aggressive as a matter of course and that all non-aggressive people are the exception rather than the mean example. Whether they are aware of it or not, those who practice non-aggression, being in the minority, are actually the trendsetters for those seeking to overturn and erase that portion of their own ancient memories responsible for wars and bloodshed. Unfortunately, even should they succeed in their own higher mind cleansing, they still live in a world where the majority—with all of their violent, aggressive, behaviors—rule.

Although belligerent and aggressive people cannot be changed overnight, they can easily be brought under temporary control, which is certainly a strongly needed ability to have when one is faced with so many of them on a daily basis. The rule is this: When sugar will kill, why feed someone poison? What this means is that control of an aggressive person can take place by yielding to their aggression, not by opposing it with aggression of your own. Understand that countering aggression with aggression will set you back in your spiritual development and relegate you back into one of their number. This would be a grievous error.

Yielding normally weakens their aggressive behavior because the basis of aggressive behavior is an attempt to enforce control over a particular situation. The aggressor looks to press his influence over others and establish a quick, often temporary, pecking order. Once he sets that pecking order and establishes himself, his aggression normally abates.

The rear wheels of a car are rigid and limited. Yes, they supply the power propelling the car forward, but it is the yielding, easily controlled front wheels that determine the direction that the entire vehicle, including the powerful rear wheels, will take. This is what yielding to aggression is all about: control. It is not abjectly ceding to the aggressor the power and opportunity to destroy you. It is simply about using your ability to yield in order to weaken the aggressor. It means that, at times, you may have to control your need to win and agree with the other person just to reduce his strength. Then, once weakened, many possibilities exist for you to use his minimized state to your advantage.

In an argument situation, for example, there is a verbal vying for control where the use of verbal resistance serves to only increase the strength of the other person. This, of course, just makes matters worse. By remaining calm and yielding temporary control of the argument to the other person, that person's strength will be reduced because the aggressor will have nothing to push back against. When there is nothing to push back against, the argument will die quietly of causes that you've created. It takes two to make an argument—no one could argue with only themselves present.

Remember, no one ever wins an argument. Understand that an argument is not a discussion. It is not a civil conversation or benign discourse where there is room to maneuver, where there is an exchange of speaking and listening. In an argument, the combatants are speaking and listening not to each other, but only to themselves. Because of this, no one is ever dissuaded and no minds are ever changed. It really makes arguing a complete waste of time, something that a person of wisdom chooses to avoid whenever possible.

Often, silence is the best argument to present to the other party. In that silence, ten thousand things are expressed that the other person will be unequipped to refute. A king, a wise person, both speak only once. The lion lies quietly in the shade; even so, who would ever dare argue with him?

Business Application: If you are the owner of a company, then the only opponent that you could possibly have is yourself. Certainly, your employees aren't opponents, nor are your competitors, unless of course you arbitrarily raise them to that status.

Here though, yielding to your own strength, your own impulses, may be just what you need to do in order to reduce the amount of stress in your life. Even so, you must be discriminating in what you yield to. That is, yield only to those strengths you possess that will further you in life and business, and not those strengths that will hinder your growth. This, of course, means that you have to know yourself, and to do that requires a great deal of introspection, free from the personal biases that we all have a tendency to ignore in ourselves. Here, yielding to your own strength means to allow a spiritual evolution to take place inside of you that will automatically root out and destroy your negative qualities, those things that will impede the fulfillment of everything that you are trying to do for yourself and your business. For example, it is very common for an employer to be so worried about the success of his business that he applies too much pressure on his subordinates to get them to produce. Yes, this is a strength of sorts, but it is the type of strength that if applied in excess will alienate the workers and hurt the employer in the long run. It will affect the employees in a negative way by wearing them down to the point where their craftsmanship and productivity deteriorates, translating into inferior products and lessening sales. You would have to agree that the employment of this type of strength would be counterproductive, at best, and so it would be better to

322

reduce that particular strength. In fact, it would be better, as a rule, to reduce any of your strengths that, in the final analysis, will stand in the way of your success. But to do that, you would have to step back a moment and take an honest inventory to see exactly where your strengths are actually weakening your prospects for success. You may be surprised to learn that you, and not your employees, clients, suppliers, et cetera, may be responsible for a large number of your business problems.

Another example of inner strength interfering with one's success would be that of the struggling artist caught up in the suffocating morass of egocentric artistic temperament. An artist, musician, sculptor, composer—anyone creative who is looking to achieve financial and creative success within their lifetime but whose strength of character has them ignoring the current artistic appetites of the general population—is going to suffer at his own hands. Someone who creates for his own pleasure and uses expressions such as "I create for myself and if the world doesn't like it, tough" is going to be a very poor and ultimately unfulfilled artist. The fact is that every creative person, even one with the "I don't give a damn what people think" attitude, is plying his creative skills in the hope that his efforts will be recognized, accepted, and rewarded by an adulating and grateful world.

Even the impressionist painter Van Gogh, as Bohemian and offbeat as he was, wanted to sell his paintings and be recognized by the world. The strength that he exhibited is seen in his unswerving devotion to his craft, his unwavering adherence to his style. The problem was that his strength happened to interfere with his ability to earn a living as an artist and, as a result, he died a pauper and an unrecognized talent. Of course, it could be argued that his paintings are worth a fortune today and that he is considered one of the greatest artists of that particular genre, but how had that recognition benefited him while he was alive? I cannot imagine anyone—artist, composer, anyone—who would rather be more successful dead than alive. So attitudes, however noble they may appear, are sometimes strengths that will ultimately lead one down the ebony-dark and vertical path to failure.

Now, if you are an employee, you have to understand that yielding to your employer's strength doesn't necessarily mean that you are voluntarily turning yourself into a spineless sycophant, toady, or yes-man sacrificing your self-respect on the fire of your employer's ambition. It simply means that you should be yielding to all legitimate wishes of your employer on the job because it is really in your best interest to do that. When executed in the right way, your self-respect will still remain intact. By acquiescing to your employer's legitimate needs without debate, you will actually be weakening the strength that he will normally apply in order to get you to do something. This is to your advantage. After all, you know that you are going to have to do it anyway, so why resist and suffer not only at your employer's hand, but at your own? Mumbling and grumbling about something that your boss wants you to do will not only make you miserable but cause unnecessary strife between the two of you. Should that happen, then of course you can kiss your promotion and/or raise good-bye, if you're lucky. If you aren't so fortunate, then you can say good-bye to your job. What is the sense in causing that to happen? So, when everyone around you mumbles and grumbles and incurs the employer's displeasure, you will appear as a loyal, trustworthy, hard-working employee. And

never assume that your boss is stupid. Never assume for a moment that your employer does not know who the grumblers are. Yielding selflessly to your employer's orders is like being a noble horse who obeys without the rider having to resort to the whip. This obeisance is what working for an employer is all about, isn't it? What would you want and expect from your employees? There is nothing demeaning in it, it is just the way of business. The lions stalks, the eland runs; do what is natural and fitting for your survival.

Important: The fact of the matter is that, in all of this, everyone is really self-employed. Regardless of your job description, regardless of where you happen to be on the company totem pole, you are truly in business for yourself. You put in your hours and are paid for your work. Just as you chose to be employed in your present position, you have the ability and the option, regardless of what your current financial circumstances are, to quit at any time. Think about it. Isn't everyone really self-employed?

The Tiger Moving Upwind Turns To Find the Water Buffalo Has Followed

Principle: Strengthening Your Opponent

Martial Action: The attacker secures my left wrist loosely with his right hand, using only that much strength as is required to bind me. His weakness has left me at a disadvantage, for it limits the variety of techniques that I have at my disposal. In order to execute a breath throw, I must get him to tighten his grip. To bring this about, I offer resistance by suddenly moving my captured arm toward him. This causes him to push back toward me and to use more strength in order to control me. His grip tightens. The trap is sprung as I merge with that strength within the Great Indigo. He, I, and that Great Ocean of the Eternal are one and inseparable. Flowing like a current within the motionless yet ever-moving Indigo, I lead his strength up and forward in a large, smooth arc. He is lost in that flow and I project him easily. He crashes to the ground, a victim of his own desire to control, his own increase in strength.

Life Application: In life, the application of the principle of Strengthening Your Opponent is very much akin to the generally accepted psychological principle of reverse psychology. That is, that one can motivate a person to move in a certain direction by offering an opposition to that movement. For example, suppose that you wanted your child to want to play the piano. Of course, you could impose piano lessons on the child but, as so often happens, the child sooner or later rebels against those lessons and looks to end his studies. No, clearly, the imposition of piano lessons is very rarely successful unless the child has a driving innate ambition to study, one devoid of the need for outside stimuli. In many areas, the development of the desire to learn has to be instilled in the child long before lessons in almost anything are offered. If you play the piano yourself, for example, then you can expose the child to the joy of playing the piano by allowing the child see how much enjoyment you are receiving by playing. This by itself could be enough of an inducement to begin the process. However, the association is still tenuous and must be made stronger. To do this, you must gently but firmly put off any request by the child regarding piano lessons. To gently deny the request will make the child, in most cases, desire to play the piano all the more. When you reach the point where you feel that the child's desire is at its maximum, then you can safely offer him the piano lessons without any fear of the child growing bored and quitting before achieving competency. This happens because you have intentionally created on the lower mind tape of the child a need to bring this ambition to fruition. It becomes a void in the child's life that he needs to fill.

There are other instances where we might need to increase strength in another person in order to successfully bring about positive results. Very often, for example, when dealing with order-resistant individuals, one can get them to take direction and accomplish the particular task you want them to do by offering instructions that have them moving in the opposite direction. This is very common among adolescents who have reached that stage in their development where they are looking to move up in the family pecking order and are resistant to orders given by those whom they are challenging. A son, for instance, will reach the point in his natural development where he will challenge the authority of his mother. Even if he believes that what his mother is telling him to do is correct and proper, he will resist as a result of an evolutionary imperative subtly dictated to him by his ancient memories. He resents any suggestion that even resembles an order and has not only his mother, but everyone else in the family, walking around on tip-toes, careful not to stir him up and start a war. He is order-resistant and a real problem. When his mother says "black," he says "white." When she says "stay," he is out the door.

With order-resistant people, what we need to do is increase their desire to get a certain task done by ourselves opposing the doing of the task. How? By ordering them not to do it. Their natural resentment for order taking would have them automatically move in the opposite direction, the direction you really want them to take. More often than not, this method will prove to work quite effectively. This is an example of Strengthening Your Opponent in order to get him to do what you want him to do.

Business Application: In business, the bottom line is always profit. One way of applying the principle of Strengthening Your Opponent to business is to increase the sales of your product by increasing the buying power of your customers. One way of bringing this about is to make sure that each and every customer feels important by linking the success of your product to them on a personal level. For example, instead of just advertising the product as something that will change their lives, you can empower potential buyers by letting them know that they have the power to buy a product that will change their lives. It's the difference between an ad-line that runs "Come in and buy the product that will change your life" and "You have the power to change your life! Come in and experience our product and see for yourself!" The first ad-line is good but doesn't empower the buyer. The second ad-line does what the first does, plus it subtly empowers buyers by requesting that they come in to see for themselves. It empowers them by appealing to their sense of choice. Of course, once the buyer is in the store, the ad has accomplished what you hoped it would and the rest is up to you.

The tiger moving upwind allows the water buffalo the opportunity to enter its prey area without suspicion. This, of course, is good for the tiger and not so good for the unsuspecting water buffalo.

The Lion Rests in the Sun, the Egret Stands by the Lake, That's All

Principle: Just Doing

Martial Action: With his blade drawn and quartered in the middle chamber, my opponent stands boldly before me. He moves to the left, then to the right, and then back to the left again. He is looking for an opening, a weakness in my stance, in my defense, in me, that would facilitate his attack. But I stand in silence, at one with the Great Void, with no plan of defense, no strategy of offense. There is nothing for me to do, nothing that must be done. That is my strength. I have no thoughts of life or death, pain or no pain, victory or defeat. My mind, dissolved in the Great Void of God, is nowhere to be found and so my opponent cannot perceive a single thought. Devoid of thought, there are no tsukis (gaps) for him to enter . . . not even water, with its ability to enter almost everywhere, can find an entrance. Clearly, my opponent's mind is busy at work analyzing, critiquing, pondering his offense—that is his weakness.

He steps forward, I move back; he moves back, I step forward. Suddenly, his sword climbs to the upper chamber and he steps in to strike. I bring my sword to the middle chamber and, thrusting forward, it is finished. That's all. Serene in my movement and mindless in my execution of it, with nothing to do, everything gets done.

Life Application: The application of this single principle alone will change your life for the better in ways that you couldn't presently imagine. You must understand that how you think is how you make your world. Think with impurity and the world becomes impure. Think with purity and the world becomes pure. The thoughts that you have when you are involved in something, a task for example, can take that task and transform it from a relatively simple chore, easy to accomplish, and turn it into the eternally frustrating labors of Sisyphus. It can, of course, do just the opposite and take an enormously difficult task and transform it into something very simple to execute. This is the enormous influence that the lower mind is constantly exerting in our lives every day. Rarely does it allow us to see something as it is, to see a person, object, or event without distortion.

Think back to when you were a child and were given the chore of taking out the trash, doing the dishes, or mowing the grass. What thoughts did you have concerning that task? Do you remember any feelings of resistance to the idea of performing the chore? Did you hem and haw, pass off-colored comments under your breath, or get angry?

329

As an adult, of course, you know how quick and simple those menial tasks really are, but when you were young, well, it was different. In those days, something as simple as taking out the trash, a two-minute endeavor, became for you the labors of Hercules. Oh yes, you took out the trash anyway, but the entire simple process caused you a great amount of aggravation, suffering, and resentment, didn't it? In fact, at the time, you considered such tasks a large infringement of your time and a big interruption in your life.

Certainly, as an adult, you can think back to those days and those feelings with nostalgic amusement, but my question to you is: What has changed? Aren't you even now experiencing much the same thing as you did then? Aren't there tasks that you perform today that are just as repulsive, just as anger inducing, as the minor tasks of your youth? How about things like having to get up early in the morning to go to work, or having to cook or clean everyday? Think about it, what has really changed? Your lower mind is still influencing your life much the same way as it did when you were a child, causing you grief and aggravation when there should be none.

The principle of Just Doing is just that, just doing. That is, miraculously transforming a task, regardless of what it is, into a moving meditation, a selfless act devoid of intention, results, and self-interested thought. Just Doing means that the act that is being done is a pure act, one without any sort of lower mind interference. Just Doing means that the lower mind is quiescent and unable to predicate anything about that act by painting pictures and creating distortions. When one is Just Doing, there simply isn't a thought for or against the performance of that act and no thought of the results. When Just Doing is occurring, revulsion disappears and that act becomes a pure action, an action devoid of self and thoughts of results, leaving you free from any of the negatives that for so long have plagued your life.

In the martial arts, the difference between life and death can often be decided by the appearance or non-appearance of a single thought, any thought. When the lower mind is quiet, then all of one's defense or offense rests solely in the hands of the higher mind. Since the higher mind is incapable of making a mistake, this is exactly where we want our fortunes to rest.

When there is a thought, it is an indication to the martial artist that the lower mind is in charge of our defense or offense and the matter becomes very dicey, often with very dire consequences. When the higher mind is in command, then we are Just Doing. There are no thoughts of time, life, death, easy, hard, pain, injury, or plan. For those well-versed in Just Doing, a fight, regardless of the odds, irrespective of the circumstances, is not any different, not any more frightening or perilous, than reading a newspaper or eating breakfast. Likewise, in life, Just Doing removes all the predicates that may otherwise appear in the lower mind when performing an act. There are no thoughts of easy, difficult, too hot, too cold, too this, or too that. Time ceases to exist and serenity has no choice but to reign supreme.

If you began the day with a period of meditation, then the lower mind would be made quiet and would not be busy painting pictures of your world. When the lower mind is quiet, then the sundry tasks of the day would take on a new and different complexion, one that leaves you immune to the feelings of repulsion, anger, and frustration. The quieter your lower mind is, the freer you are to Just Do.

Business Application: If your job is one for which you have developed a great dislike, if it has become burdensome to you and a great source of personal agony, then clearly, it has become your master. For me to tell you that your misery is all in your mind and has no basis in fact will immediately prompt most of you to take the opposite view by dredging up myriad reasons why those circumstances are not mind-created but are real and substantial in every sense of the word. You will say, for example: "The work is boring, doing the same thing five days a week, fifty weeks a year," or "The work is beneath me, and I resent the fact that my talents aren't appreciated," or, "I'm stuck in a thankless job with no future," or, well, you get the idea. Naturally, these reasons may seem valid to you, but in truth they are really the result of delusions created and sustained by your lower mind. It seems that, over the course of time, the inmates have quietly taken over the asylum and are now running things.

In order to change that—to release yourself from the restrictive bonds forged by the lower mind and gain a lasting, peace-producing control over your working life—you have to put into practice the principle of Just Doing.

You must understand that, wherever you are, you have to be doing something—twenty-four hours a day, three hundred and sixty-five days a year, you are doing something. Even if you are just sitting in a chair, or sleeping, or walking, you are doing something. "Doing" simply cannot be avoided. Of course, if the something that you are doing is pleasant, then you really have no problem, but if that something happens to be unpleasant, then you suffer greatly each and every time you have to repeat that act. Realize that descriptive words used to address unpleasant acts, such as odious, boring, difficult, detestable, despicable, et cetera, are merely labels created by the lower mind that you naively buy into and are not at all real. In fact, they only create a further illusion and insidiously reinforce the concept of unpleasantness. It is a mind-created malevolent cycle that binds you to misery.

To end that self-imposed, beguiling, and abrasive cycle of suffering forever and turn your job into something a great deal more pleasant, you must take the time to quiet your lower mind to the point where all of those arbitrary opinions that you have about your work stop. How? By turning your work itself into the object of your meditation. If your job, for example, requires you to perform the same task eight hours a day, every day, then instead of dividing your time between grumbling and doing that task half-heartedly, focus yourself and concentrate on the physical movements of that task with all of your might, all of your soul. Say to yourself, "This is all I am doing, nothing else," and then just do it. Yes, it will be difficult at first, but in time the process will mature and become something wondrous to experience. This type of concentration will bring you into the present, the here and now. And being in the here and now will keep your mind from wandering into the past or future. Then several things will result. First, you will become more proficient at your job and your work will become more and more flawless. Second, your lower mind will stop painting dark and foreboding pictures and disturbing your peace of mind with its sundry creations. This will translate into your job no longer being a burden to you. Third, you will be vigorously pursuing a course of action that will take you from the mundane to the spiritual. It will evolve you as a person and lead you to greater and greater insights into life and the true nature of existence. The lion rests in the sun, the egret stands by the lake, that's all.

The Crocodile Plays the Host and Waits

Principle: Playing The Host

Martial Action: My attacker, sword drawn high in the upper chamber, tightens and then relaxes his grip. His breathing is uneven and his impatience is evident. I can feel his mind move forward and I withdraw, taking a step to my rear. His body follows and I yield a second time. He advances again and again I withdraw. I have created a pattern in his mind where as I step back, he steps forward, step for step. He is now facing the sun and cannot hope to win. Death is imminent. Once again, I step to my rear, playing host . . . he follows. Then, I lean to my rear as if to take a step, but step forward instead. Out of the pattern that I created, he steps forward as my blade makes contact with him.

Life Application: To Play The Host means to be polite and inviting, to be tolerant and patient. It means that great benefit can be gained by yielding and leading rather than aggressing and opposing. A gracious host is thoughtful and makes no demands of his guests.

Keep a cow constantly confined in the barn and as soon as the barn door is opened, the cow will run away. Keep a cow in an open pasture, one with copious amounts of sunlight, grass, and room to move around, and you will keep that cow near you forever. So it is in life. The more we cling to things, the more we look to control those things and limit their freedoms. Suddenly, the very things that we look to control, the things that we look to keep chained to ourselves, are grimly controlling and keeping us. It is a dark and vicious cycle. When the prisoner is shackled to his jailer, the freedom of both is dissolved and the idea of jailer and prisoner becomes meaningless.

Creating and maintaining peace of mind when the mind itself is chained to objects and the need to control those objects becomes as futile as attempting to keep water in your hand by clenching your hand into a tight fist; the tighter you squeeze, the faster the water escapes your grasp. The best way to hold water is by cupping your hands. So it is in life that one must learn to cup and not to grasp. Playing The Host means just that. It means that the way to keep people and things near you is by detaching from them. It is not the detachment of one who doesn't care about people and things, it is the detachment of one who is simply

334

free from the fetters that are created through unhealthy relationships between oneself, others, and the myriad things of the world. Such detachment will keep you free and unsullied by the people and things around you. Then, even love becomes true and pure. It allows you to give without any thought of receiving, to receive without any thought of debt or dishonor. It will bestow on you a freedom that will draw others to you, and you will gain because of your giving up. This is the way of the host.

Business Application: In business, Playing The Host means to deal with your competition not by opposing their strength, but by yielding to their strength.

In business, Playing The Host can be accomplished, for instance, by extending a cordial invitation to have your competition meet with you in a social setting. It could be lunch, dinner, or even a party. It's really not as novel and strange as it seems. In big business it is done all the time. Dealing with a competitor in a social atmosphere places you in a perfect position to kill several birds with the same stone. First, you will be able to keep yourself informed as to what your competition is doing without reducing yourself to using spies and industrial espionage. Second, you will be placing yourself in a position where you may be able to turn your competition into a useful and trustworthy ally. And third, you can show yourself stalwart, fearless, and simultaneously cordial in the presence of your competition.

In all matters when you Play The Host, you must not be overtly deceitful in your dealings with your guests, for that is not the way of the host. You must truly be the congenial, affable, thoughtful, yielding host. Do that and your guests may very well surprise you by responding positively and following your lead.

The crocodile plays the congenial host, waiting patiently for its prey to enter the water; the rest is a natural consequence of that action.

The Spider Invites, The Scorpion Enters

Principle: Playing The Guest

Martial Action: I walk through the crowded market place, aware that I am being stalked. I sense that my assassins are waiting patiently for the right time and place to initiate their attack. There is no escape for me, it is just a question of where and when. Without hesitation, I opt to play the guest. To this end, I approach my assassins and enter their arena at the time and place of my own choosing. They cannot decline such a cordial and cooperative visitor. The surprise is theirs, the victory is mine.

Life Application: With all of their aspirations and plans, with all of their connivings and intrigues, with all of their benevolence and good intentions, all that can be said is that people are what people are, and they invariably do what people do.

Sometimes people are even-handed and kind and sometimes brazenly cruel and deceitful in their dealings with each other. It is not uncommon for people, for instance, to take advantage of others in order to achieve some sort of victory, some sort of gain for themselves. There are times when even an enemy will suddenly turn friendly in order to further his own interests or perhaps to avenge some past wrong that he thinks you have committed against him. When this happens, you must be on your guard.

When enemies suddenly turn friendly, you must be cautious and understand that they may still be harboring animosities and thoughts of vengeance, regardless of what they tell you. They may greet you with a broad, congenial smile and a polite bow but, in all of that, they may still hand you a cup of poison covered with a surface layer of cream. If you are alert to their deception, then you can use their ruse to your advantage and gain the edge on them before they have time to spring their trap. For example, John Doe believes that some years before you had wronged him in some fashion and he has harbored thoughts of avenging himself ever since. One day, out of the blue, he invites you to a social gathering. He has plans to embarrass you at some point during the night and thus even the score. Suspecting what he is about to do, you can turn the upcoming situation to your advantage and catch him in his own trap. Of course, it would require a certain patience and tolerance on your part, but it can be done. If, for instance, he had planned on airing your dirty linen during the evening, you can place him in the position of not being able to do that by taking advantage of his sudden friendliness and returning that friendliness back to him in front of the other guests. Doing this will build up his ego to the point where he will not be able to say anything negative about you without making himself look very foolish and unstable. No one at the event will ever take what he has to say very seriously if he suddenly tries to embarrass you. It would come off as strange and incongruous with his words and actions. The spider spins a clever trap but never expects a scorpion to enter its web. For such a thing to happen would prove to be most unfortunate for the spider.

Business Application: At a social gathering, the guest always has a great many advantages over the host. The guest knows, for example, that the host must be more cordial and more tolerant than under normal, everyday circumstances. This allows the guest to take certain liberties with the host that otherwise would not be possible. This is so because the host has an obligation not to offend his guests and thereby destroy both the social event and the relationship.

In a business situation, such as being an attendee of a business dinner given by your competition, you as the guest can take certain liberties that the host must cordially respond to. For instance, you have the upper hand when it comes to things like asking questions about his business and directing the course and subject matter of the conversation. Hosts, not wanting to offend or create an atmosphere where guests are not at ease and enjoying themselves, are often forced to yield to almost anything. This is a great advantage to you if you are invited to a party or business luncheon and want to learn more about your host and his life or business, even if it was his original intention to ply you with questions and find out some of your business secrets. Because you are there at his invitation he, not wanting to offend you or create an adversarial situation at that time, will more often than not give you much of the information that you are asking for. So the spider invites all to visit his web, but cannot handle the scorpion.

The Elephant Takes To the Path, the Tiger, Also

Principle: The Path Of Least Resistance

Martial Action: I stand centered in the Great Void and wait in silence as my attacker charges at me like a mad bull in an attempt to tackle me to the ground. Just as he enters my sphere I pivot my body to the right, executing a feminine withdrawing motion with my right hand and a masculine press on his shield with my left. I have created a path within the Great Indigo that he cannot avoid and his original course is changed. As he passes me, I tap his shoulder gently and he crashes to the ground. I created a path of least resistance and his destruction was assured.

Life Application: The mind, like electricity and water, will always take the path of least resistance. In life, to control others is often merely a matter of either placing or removing blocks on their path. In order to establish a relationship with another person, for example, certain factors always exist that can either facilitate or deter that relationship from developing. There are physical factors, of course—factors such as distance and timing. Here, it is just a matter of planning to be at the right place at the right time or seeing to it that the other person is. Assuming that these factors have been taken care of, it now merely becomes a process of removing blocks and creating critical paths.

A block, in this case, can be thought of as anything that will impede the development of a particular relationship. It could, for instance, be anything that the other person might find unsettling about you. For example, it could be a lack of certain character traits that he admires—courage, warmth, a sense of humor—anything at all. These blocks could readily be removed, once you understand what they are, by subtly demonstrating to the other party that you possess them. Of course, it would help to know what the other person is looking for in you prior to your initial meeting. As they say, first impressions are lasting impressions. It is much easier to establish yourself right from the beginning than to reinvent yourself later on.

Naturally, blocks could also be of the physical kind, but these are, with very few exceptions, much more difficult to remove. If you are short and the other person wants someone tall, it's a genuine problem. However, if you are overweight and the other person wants someone thinner, someone in good physical shape, all that is required of you is a good diet and a practical exercise plan. Beards can come and go, hair color can be changed, hair can be cut, makeup can be applied, clothes can be changed, et cetera. It all depends on how far you are willing to go in your effort to remove any blocks that will deter the development of the relationship.

339

Now, to create viable paths in order to facilitate a relationship means to create situations that the other person will find inviting. The more irresistible that situation is, the more the other person will be drawn into it. Of course, it helps to know specifically what the other person finds attractive in a relationship. That I leave to you to find out. In general, however, women are looking for stability and security, a good sense of humor, and demonstrative affection in their partners. Good looks, although important to some woman, are of relatively secondary importance to others. Being handsome is only an initial asset, helping with the initial draw, but without any of the other factors that women are drawn to, your relationship is doomed to failure.

Men, on the other hand, are by nature more visually stimulated than women, and therefore are generally more demanding when it comes to appearance in developing a relationship. This may seem offensive to some women, but this is man's nature and doesn't fall into the category of arbitrary behavior. The fact is that the more attractive a woman is, the more she will draw men to her. Bearing this in mind, a woman should make every effort to make herself as attractive as possible.

After the physical requirements have been met, men are looking for femininity, fidelity, good homemaking ability, and ceaseless moral support. That is, they want a woman, not another drinking buddy. Now, this may seem a little chauvinistic, but a man doesn't want a woman who is contentious and overbearing. An overbearing woman is an affront to everything that is recorded on his higher mind tape, a challenge to the pecking order as dictated to him by his ancient memories. Being contentious and overbearing will only cause strife in a relationship and lead to disaster.

Men want someone they can trust, someone devoted only to them. That's understandable—isn't that what a woman would want in a man? In general, men are not very good housekeepers. Although some men are exceptions to the rule, you will find that men are poor cooks, poor housecleaners, and generally poor all around when it comes to taking care of themselves domestically. Remember, they were brought up with a mother who took care of these things for him. Finally, ceaseless moral support. It is man's nature to provide for his family. This is part of his ancient memory. To provide for his family, he must face the challenges of the tigers of the world in order to succeed. A woman's support is essential in everything that a man attempts to do in order to succeed. Of course, with the changes that have recently taken place in society, a woman also need a man's ceaseless moral support. In short, any woman who demonstrates to a man that she has these traits is creating a path of least resistance to establishing a strong and lasting relationship with a man.

It is important to understand that changing oneself in order to remove blocks and create paths should never be thought of as giving up anything—it is, in truth, doing what may be necessary in order to achieve what you want, a way of getting what you are looking for.

Business Application: The principle of the Path Of Least Resistance is very useful not only in developing personal relationships but also when applied in the business world. Suppose, for example, you had to make that big deal. To succeed, all or as many as possible of the blocks on the path to that success must be removed. Assuming that the time and the place have been arranged by appointment, they are no longer factors. When you meet with the client, you must bear in mind the old maxim "first impressions are lasting impressions." So you must make every effort to present yourself as an already very successful business person. That is, you should have an air of success about you. This immediately affects your client in a positive way by removing the block that either your product is inferior, your company is lacking, or that you are lacking. Those seeking success are drawn immediately to those who they think have already achieved success. This is what makes movie stars, professional athletes, and entertainers so powerful in the world of advertising. Yes, they are well known to the general population, but it is the fact that they are successful themselves that draws people, that compels people to follow their example. If a successful person uses a product, then they will feel compelled to follow suit. This is how the lower mind works. Likewise, the removal of this initial block, the success block, right from the beginning, will compel the client to be much more interested in what you have to offer then if the block were still in place.

The next block to be removed in making that deal is the block of the anticipated hard sell. The fact is that no one enjoys being on the receiving end of the hard sell approach, no one. This approach has been responsible for more deal-breaking than many people imagine. Why? Because the hard sell places the client in a position of having to defend himself against a salesman's aggression. By pushing, you are actually increasing your client's resistance and not breaking through that resistance as many suppose. What you really want to do is not wear him down or wear him out, but to simply weaken any resistance he has to your product by yielding to him. This can be accomplished by carefully controlling your tone of speech, bearing, and friendliness. Your speech should be knowledgeable but not pushy. You should speak plainly to him and not take on the appearance of a carnival barker trying to draw passersby into a sideshow on the midway.

342

Your bearing should be one that displays not only confidence in both yourself and your product, but it should show him, at a glance, how successful your product or service has been.

Your friendliness should come across to your prospective client as a genuine concern for the benefits that client or the client's company will enjoy as a result of buying your product or service. One way of doing that is simply to be yourself. If you try to emulate someone else, you will appear stiff and unnatural. Treat the client like a friend and not a stranger. If you appear genuine to him, he will think of you not in an adversarial role but, on the contrary, he will think of you as actually being on his side. His defenses will be lowered and he will be happily receptive to just about anything that you have to say.

At this point you simply have to create a need in him for your product or service. This can be done, again, by speaking plainly and not giving the client the sense that you are trying to flimflam him into anything. Remember, keep it simple and you will be removing blocks before they are put up. Of course, if the client was the one who approached you, then he is already predisposed to your product or service and it then becomes a question of removing any of the blocks mentioned above in order make the deal.

Finally, back up your product with the support that your company offers their clients. This is the clincher because it will place the client in a position where he believes that he cannot lose. When a prospective client feels that he cannot lose, then the remaining resistance, if any, will disappear and the road toward a successful deal will be cleared of impediments. After all, if you thought that you were in a no-lose situation, what would you do? You would make the deal, of course.

343

Ultimately, it really doesn't make any difference at all what you are selling—products, ideas, services, or yourself. Remove all the blocks, yield, create a no-lose situation for the other party and you are guaranteed to achieve great success in all of your business endeavors.

The elephant takes to the path, the tiger, also; they have no choice, for it is natural for them to do that.

The Sapling Bends In the Wind, the Unyielding Oak Cracks and Falls To the Ground. Which Proves To Be the Stronger?

Principle: Strength Through Relaxation

Martial Action: My opponent, on the verge of attack, stands as tall and inflexible as an oak tree. His mind is as rigid and unyielding as ice; mine, firmly centered in the serenity of the Great Void, is as supple as water. He cannot hope to prevail; his unyielding desire to win, his rigid determination for victory, is the harbinger bringing me the word of his undoing.

His eyes narrow as he positions the blade of his knife in the upper realm of the middle chamber. Intent on my death, he lunges forward. As he reaches the outer boundary of my sphere, I turn to my right and, leading with my right hand, create a path for his mind and body to follow . . . it cannot be avoided.

Relaxed and at one with the ocean of the Great Indigo, I gently lower my stance and flow toward him, my *shuto* (knife hand-strike) penetrating without obstruction. He has become the fallen oak.

Life Application: In the art of Torishimaru Aiki Jutsu, we achieve enormous spiritual strength when the lower mind is made quiescent. The quieting of the lower mind not only relaxes the muscles of the body and allows a great amount of physical strength to flow unimpeded but places the limitless spiritual strength controlled by the higher mind at our disposal.

344

In life, there are many situations that arise that create tension in the lower mind, which affects not only our ability to reason but can affect our physical health, as well. In essence, a tense mind tenses and affects everything that is us and stifles any attempt at a proper and speedy resolution to a situation. Through the consistent employment of proper meditative techniques, all such potential rigidities of mind are removed and all subsequent negative effects of that rigidity on the body are avoided.

When the mind is tense, our energies are dissipated in numerous ways that not only leave us tired and weak but also influence those around us in often negative ways. When our mind tenses over a problem, for example, we are quick to lash out at those closest to us. This only creates further causes of tension which, in turn, drain us all the more. Knowing this, then it follows that the sooner we let go of the cause of the tension, the quicker our energies will return and the faster we will return to normal.

You must understand that the mind and the body are not two different things. What influences one, influences the other. Those suffering from chronic depression, for example, are those who are caught up in the machinations of a mind-body cycle that they cannot break free of. This is so because they cannot resolve the problems that created the original tension in their lower minds in the first place. This is how the mind-body cycle in cases of depression works: When the lower mind fixates on a problem, it spends a great deal of time and energy in order to attempt to resolve it. Most problems that people have are readily resolved and life seems to go on normally. However, it is the nature of the lower mind not to let anything go until it reaches resolution, and when the lower mind is faced with an unresolvable problem, the constant attention that it donates to the solving of that problem utilizes an enormous amount of feminine energy. Often, after a protracted period of time,

345

the energy required by the lower mind to deal with the problem is diminished to the point where it starts diverting feminine energy en route to the body. This loss of energy causes the body to begin to operate at a lower, slower level. When the body reaches the point where it begins to feel the strain of trying to sustain itself, a vicious cycle of vying for energy commences. Since the primary directive for the lower mind is to sustain life, a situation arises where it diverts to the body the feminine energy that it requires in order to function correctly. This leaves the lower mind stilted and thoughts are diffuse and disjointed, not allowing the lower mind to reach resolution of the original problem, and so the cycle continues. The depletion of the feminine energy during this depressive mind-body cycle is enormous and is the reason why so many people suffering from chronic depression are tired all of the time and often reach the point where they confine themselves to bed.

To quickly break out of the depressive mind-body cycle, one has to begin both a regimen of restorative meditation and proper counseling. When a proper regimen of restorative meditation is followed, two things immediately begin to take place. The first is that the lower mind becomes temporarily distracted and, at least for the moment, puts the problem aside. The second is that the lower mind, having the opportunity to rest, allows feminine energy to automatically be restored to the body. The restoration of the feminine energy to the body in turn gives the sufferer the physical strength to become active again. This restored activity, like the meditation, continues to distract the lower mind from the original problem. It is now beginning a cycle of healing.

Of course, the original problem still exists and, if not dealt with, will eventually cause the depressive mind-body cycle to reappear. But this is where outside professional help comes in. When help is given by those who properly understand the nature of both the lower and higher minds, then resolution of the problem comes very quickly. In many cases, it can be resolved in a single session. Through proper counseling, combined with the newly returned feminine energy to acceptable levels, the cycle can be broken forever and life returned to normal.

Business Application: In business nothing ever gets accomplished properly when the lower minds of those involved in that business are tense and inflexible. If, for example, the employer's mind is tense, that tension is felt at every level down the formal chain of command. How can that be healthy for a business, any business? It cannot possibly be. All it does is create a great potential for financial disaster.

Not too long ago, a businessman came to me for help. He told me that he worked day and night for several years to build his business up and now that it was where he wanted it to be, it was suddenly falling apart, and he didn't know why. After a brief discussion, it was easy to understand why his business was suddenly in trouble. It seems that he had become so involved in the business and was so afraid of failure that everything seemed to rustle. That is, even the most benign, inconsequential perturbation in the routine became a major problem for him. There seemed to be no respite for him from his difficulties. This constant barrage of problems caused him to become so tense, so excitable, that he wound up placing excessive amounts of pressure on his employees. This, in turn, tensed his employees to the point where they became prone to making more and more mistakes, which only aggravated him more and further increased his demands on them. This was the beginning of a vicious cycle that placed his business in peril.

Suddenly, there was a rash of requests for vacations and sick days coming from his disgruntled and perplexed

347

employees. He often had to accede to their requests, which further slowed down production. This, of course, not only affected his revenues and his ability to meet his payroll but led to an inability to pay for his raw materials, as well. In short, it had become the worst nightmare of his life. I call this nasty cycle The Success Syndrome. He was caught up in it, and a steady process of disintegration began, culminating in the potential loss of the very thing he was striving so very hard to create and maintain.

Of course, once he understood the nature of the cycle that he was in and once he realized that he, himself—not his employees, clients, suppliers, or anyone else—was its root cause, he was more than ready and willing to make the necessary changes. He was ready to break the cycle and restore both himself and his business to normality.

I counseled him for a week, giving him advice and spiritual exercises. Immediately the disintegration of his business began to reverse itself. He was amazed. Almost immediately he became more relaxed and his strength began to return and he felt better, in fact, he felt absolutely wonderful. In turn, his relaxation, his sudden freedom from pressure, was instantly felt throughout his business' pecking order and caused all of his employees to relax. Being free of the tension that he was causing them, his employees were now better able to concentrate on their work. This translated into increased production, better quality, less absences, less job-related accidents, and so on. Everything had reversed itself. The cycle was broken. Now, this businessman is more successful than ever before and is actually doing less than he was doing to bring that success about. He has learned to bend in the wind and in so doing has grown stronger than he could have imagined.

As common as this man's situation is, it is no wonder why so many businesses are suffering, why so many employers are caught in the insidious cycle that he underwent. The question remains, however, if the tree will not bend as a sapling, will it bend when grown? Of course, men and women are not trees and have the option to bend when needed. It is a question of choice. Yielding is often the best way to survive business as well as life. It is also the way to break vicious cycles of destruction and achieve success. The sapling bends in the wind, the unyielding oak cracks and falls to the ground . . . which proves to be the stronger?

Glossary

Burmese-style Posture: A meditative posture where the calves of the legs rest flat on the floor.

Defensive Loop: A situation created in the attacker that has him responding in an ongoing defensive way.

Feminine Energy (M'retz Na'she): The sustaining life force or energy of the universe.

Feminine Movement: A negative or recessive movement of one object relative to another.

Feminine Vacuum: The emptiness created by spatial relations, which draws the lower mind into it.

Flowing: The unimpaired movement of Ruach or feminine energy (M'retz Na'she).

Frequency Principles: Torishimaru Aiki Jutsu control principles based on the premise that an attacker has what is called a natural operating frequency, or a frequency of vibration, which can be altered so as to distort his sensory input.

Full Lotus: A meditative posture in which the legs are crossed with the right foot placed on the left thigh and the left foot placed on the right thigh.

Half Lotus: A meditative posture where only one leg is placed on the opposite thigh. The other leg is simply folded underneath.

351

Higher Mind: That part of a person that is in contact with the Infinite. It has knowledge of all things, past, present and future, and when accessed and employed is incapable of making a mistake.

Higher Mind Gate: A gate that exists between the higher minds of individuals that, when opened, allows the free exchange of communication between them.

Higher Mind Tape: A part of the higher mind that records all of one's experiences since beginningless time.

Koan: An enigmatic question posed to a student by his master which, once solved, produces a realization experience.

Ki Ai: (Jap.) A mystical shout utilized in some karate styles.

Ku: (Jap.) Impermanence.

Lenient Posture: A simple meditative posture where the legs are crossed in Indian fashion.

Lower Mind: The everyday, ordinary mind that everyone is used to dealing with.

Lower Mind Tape: A part of the lower mind that records all of one's present life experiences.

Major Motion: The motion or movement that the attacker's body is making during his attack.

Makyo: (Jap.) Illusions that sometimes make their appearance during certain stages of meditation.

Mantra: A mystic word or phrase utilized as the object of meditation.

Manifest Universe: The physical universe.

Masculine Movement: A positive or aggressive movement of one object relative to another.

M'retz Na'she: See Feminine Energy.

Mind Path: The course that the lower mind takes or travels both within and without one's body.

352

Minor Motion: The motion or movement that the attacker's weapons (arms, legs, et cetera) are making during his attack.

Natural Operating Frequency: The frequency at which a person or object responds normally to incoming sensory information.

No-Hit: A Torishimaru Aiki Jutsu control principle wherein pulses or columns of feminine energy are projected toward an opponent in such a way as to create an argument or dialogue between the attacker's higher mind and his lower mind.

Oneness With The Earth: An esoteric technique of Torishimaru Aiki Jutsu wherein one becomes immovable against opposing physical forces.

Oneness With The Opponent: An esoteric principle of Torishimaru Aiki Jutsu wherein a practitioner of the art acts in harmony with the attacker.

Path: The route that a strike or weapon takes in order to reach the target.

Pinning: A Torishimaru Aiki Jutsu control technique in which the attacker's mind is drawn downward, resulting in his body becoming immobilized.

Pulsing: A Torishimaru Aiki Jutsu control technique that utilizes short bursts of feminine energy to control the attacker's weapons and/or major motion.

Ruach: Feminine energy, spirit. It is the sustaining force of the universe. It is the foundation of Ki, Chi, and Prana.

Scanning: Esoteric technique of Torishimaru Aiki Jutsu that allows its employer to sense the presence of a subject's shield.

Seiza: A meditative posture. The traditional Japanese kneeling posture.

Siddhis: (Skt.) The mystical powers that develop as a result of one's meditative evolution.

Sheath: The subtle body containing the soul.

Shield: The field of energy surrounding all matter.

Shikan-taza: A Zen meditation. "Just sitting."

Stress Loop: A condition in which a person undergoes a constant, unending series of psychological stresses.

Target: One of a number of internal body structures intended as the object of a strike or kick.

353

Target Replacement: A Torishimaru Aiki Jutsu control technique in which the original target selected by an attacker is replaced by the defender.

Universal Mudra: A special hand posture utilized during meditation.

Zen: A sect of Mahayana Buddhism that stresses the value of meditation and self-reliance.

Index

affirmations, 251

Ain Sof, 209-211, 246

Ain Sof Aur, 209-210, 246

anatomy, 20-22

Ancient Memories, Common, 150, 243

Ancient Memories, Dominant, 150-151

Ancient Memories, Personal, 150, 220, 243-244

Ancient Memories, Recessive, 150-151

Ancient Memories, Sporadic, 150-152

Ancient Memories, 148-152, 172, 194-195, 197, 217, 220, 243-245, 319-320, 327, 340-341

anger, 40-41, 100, 145, 178-184, 187, 234, 257, 279, 281-282, 300-301, 309-311, 314, 330-331

animals, 77, 142, 146, 148, 153, 173-174, 191, 219, 245, 247, 252, 258-259
    communicating with, xvi, 258-259

arbitrary opinions, 145-146, 332

arguments, controlling, 99-100, 187, 321

aura (see magen), 6, 34-41, 77, 80-82, 84, 238

bravery, gender, 199-200

breathing, 40, 74, 77, 79, 81-83, 98, 111, 125-126, 129, 131-132, 148, 156, 222, 228, 248, 265, 287, 293-294, 325, 329, 333

breathing exercise, 156, 228

Burmese style posture, 113-114, 121, 125

business, 22, 38, 47, 51, 61, 141, 154, 159, 225, 240, 263, 268-269, 271-272, 276, 279-281, 285-289, 291, 294-295, 298-299, 301-306, 309-310, 313-314, 316-319, 322-323, 325, 327, 331, 335, 337-338, 341, 343, 347-349

cancer, 255-256

candle concentration technique, 112, 129

clairvoyance, 39, 80, 205

cold, the common, 253-254

Counting the Breaths, 125-126

courage, secondary, 198

da Vinci, 290

Daath Gate, 129

Dark Veil (see Tza'eef A'fel), 229-230

death process, 150, 230-231

defensive loop, 65, 351

déjà vu, 204

355

359

weight training, 25, 27

yielding, 50, 62, 65, 100-101, 131, 192, 258, 299-303, 320-322, 324, 334-335, 342, 349

zafu, 43, 113-114, 129, 131, 155

Zen meditation, 47, 131-133, 137-138, 184, 228, 353-354

☾ REACH FOR THE MOON

Llewellyn publishes hundreds of books on your favorite subjects! To get these exciting books, including the ones on the following pages, check your local bookstore or order them directly from Llewellyn.

ORDER BY PHONE

- Call toll-free within the U.S. and Canada, 1-800-THE MOON
- In Minnesota, call (612) 291-1970
- We accept VISA, MasterCard, and American Express

ORDER BY MAIL

- Send the full price of your order (MN residents add 7% sales tax) in U.S. funds, plus postage & handling to:

  Llewellyn Worldwide
  P.O. Box 64383, Dept. K060-4
  St. Paul, MN 55164–0383, U.S.A.

POSTAGE & HANDLING

(For the U.S., Canada, and Mexico)

- $4.00 for orders $15.00 and under
- $5.00 for orders over $15.00
- No charge for orders over $100.00

We ship UPS in the continental United States. We ship standard mail to P.O. boxes. Orders shipped to Alaska, Hawaii, The Virgin Islands, and Puerto Rico are sent first-class mail. Orders shipped to Canada and Mexico are sent surface mail.

International orders: Airmail—add freight equal to price of each book to the total price of order, plus $5.00 for each non-book item (audio tapes, etc.).

Surface mail—Add $1.00 per item.

Allow 2 weeks for delivery on all orders.
Postage and handling rates subject to change.

DISCOUNTS

We offer a 20% discount to group leaders or agents. You must order a minimum of 5 copies of the same book to get our special quantity price.

FREE CATALOG

Get a free copy of our color catalog, *New Worlds of Mind and Spirit*. Subscribe for just $10.00 in the United States and Canada ($30.00 overseas, airmail). Many bookstores carry *New Worlds*—ask for it!

Visit our web site at www.llewellyn.com for more information.

The Lost Scrolls of King Solomon

Visionary fiction by

Richard Behrens

On a plane bound for Israel, vacationing American history professor Benjamin Stein sits next to an old rabbi. In his hand the rabbi clutches a mysterious black leather cylinder containing the lost scrolls of King Solomon. Written in code and cryptic verse, the scrolls reveal the location of religious artifacts needed to train the coming messiah for his mission here on earth. The rabbi asks Stein to help him in retrieving the holy objects.

Stein doesn't realize that he's about to embark on an action-adventure odyssey of demons, angels, mystical illusions, Satan, and the magical power of an ancient king. Follow this reluctant hero as he discovers arcane secrets of existence, never-before-told mystical techniques, and the messiah's surprising identity.

An appendix to the novel contains step-by-step instructions to the techniques taught in the story so you can enjoy your own hands-on experience of deeper esoteric truths.

1-56718-059-0
6 x 9, 408 pp., appendices, glossary   **$14.95**

Golf: The Winner's Way

Richard Behrens

He can pin a man to the floor without touching him. He can stand on one foot and hold off 22 power lifters. Now, one of the foremost martial arts masters in the world brings the game of golf to exciting new dimensions with his revolutionary concepts for strength, power and accuracy.

"Good golf is all in the mind," according to Master Behrens, and with his simple physical and mental techniques you will enjoy greater accuracy both off the tee and from the fairway, hit more green in regulation, and lower your average number of putts per round. Employ just one principle at a time, and you will happily find that your game improves the first day out. By the time you have incorporated all of the techniques, you will be playing at a level beyond anything you ever imagined.

- Increase your driving distance through the "30-70% Acceleration Principle"
- Create a solid sense of balance that allows you to consistently achieve a proper impact position
- Generate enormous club head speed when you learn to transfer your weight through the swing
- Improve your grip, drive, pitch, chip, bunker play, and trouble shots
- Excel at every hole by "living in the moment"
- Experience the most unique mental power engendering technique in the world, specifically designed for the competing athlete
- Eradicate tension from your game forever

1-56718-061-2
5³⁄₁₆ x 6, 240 pp., illus. $9.95

Inner Passages, Outer Journeys

Wilderness, Healing and the Discovery of Self

David Cumes, M.D.

Whether you scale the sides of mountains or just putter in the garden, wilderness healer Dave Cumes, M.D., shows you how nature can be one of the most powerful and accessible forms of self-healing.

Few are prepared to commit to the rigors of disciplined spiritual practice. It is through nature that we can connect with our higher self most easily. The outer wilderness helps us access the inner wilderness of our psyches. When approached with the right frame of mind, wilderness can facilitate "peak experiences."

This book is for those with an adventurous spirit who may or may not have defined their spiritual path. It addresses the psychospiritual, healing and restorative effects of nature, and describes how to amplify your experience through transformational practices. This book is the first of its kind to combine the spirituality of the last surviving hunter gatherers of Africa with the ancient wisdom of yoga, Kabbala and shamanism.

1-56718-195-3
6 x 9, 192 pp., illus.   **$12.95**

Life Without Limits

10 Easy Steps to Success & Happiness

Robert B. Stone, Ph.D.

How is your life right now? Are there any areas where you still feel—well—quietly desperate? Help has arrived in the form of this playful and conversational self-help guide from Dr. Robert B. Stone. Dr. Stone is assisted by nine wise, but little-known, men and women who over the past one thousand years left behind a valuable legacy for a joyful, desperation-free life.

The key to a life without limitations is provided in ten installments, each discussing simple changes you can make today in the way you do things. Sages from around the world will show you the timeless ways to make astonishing breakthroughs in all areas of your life. You will discover the culprit that acts to block your joy, and you will learn how to dramatically improve your luck . . . use body language to attract others . . . talk yourself into wealth . . . solve any problem no matter where you are . . . and eliminate the fears and phobias that hold you back.

1-56718-698-X
5³⁄₁₆ x 8, 240 pp., softcover $7.95

Celestial 911

Call with Your Right Brain for Answers

Robert B. Stone, Ph.D.

Your mind possess staggering abilities that defy science. Yet most of us live without activating our right brain hemispheres, which is like living with one hand tied behind our backs. Your right brain is essential for healing, for creativity, problem solving and enjoying meaningful personal relationships. Most importantly, your right brain is your connection to the spiritual realm, to where you came from and to your guardian angels. Celestial 911 will teach you how to turn on your right brain hemisphere and contact help from the other side.

A series of 32 Action Plans will help you to open your innate doorway to the invisible world of spirit helpers. Through the simple technique of Controlled Daydreaming, you can begin to manifest your true genius . . . turn up your sexual attraction . . . brighten your financial picture . . . and heal at a distance.

1-56718-697-1
5³⁄₁₆ x 8, 240 pp., softcover   **$7.95**

Chi Gung

Chinese Healing, Energy and Natural Magick

L. V. Carnie

Chi Gung is unlike any other magickal book that you've read. There are no spells, incantations or special outfits. Instead, you will learn more than 80 different exercises that will help you to tap into the magickal power of universal energy. This power, called Chi in Chinese, permeates everything in existence; you can direct the flow of Chi to help you achieve ultimate health as well as any of your dreams and desires.

Chi Gung uses breathing, postures, and increased sensory awareness exercises that follow a particular training program. Ultimately, you can manipulate Chi without focusing on your breathing or moving your muscles in specific patterns. In fact, eventually you can learn how to move and transmit Chi instantly, anywhere, anytime, using only your mind. By learning the art of Chi Gung, you can slow the aging process; alter your metabolism; talk to plants and animals; move objects with your mind; withstand cold, heat and pain; and even read someone's soul.

1-56718-113-9
7 x 10, 256 pp., illus., softcover $17.95